EXECUTIVE

COACHING

Facilitating Excellence in the C-Suite

Meta-Coaching Volume XI

L. Michael Hall, Ph.D.

with Graham Richardson, Master Coach

© 2013 L. Michael Hall, Ph.D. with Graham Richardson, Master Coach

Executive Coaching: Meta-Coaching, Volume XI
Library of Congress, Washington, D.C., Copyright Pending

ISBN

ISBN 978-189000145-2

9 781890 001452

Published by:

NSP —*Neuro-Semantics Publications*
P.O. Box 8
Clifton, CO. 81520-0008 USA
(970) 523-7877

Neuro-Semantics® is the trademark name for the model, patterns, and society of Neuro-Semantics. ISNS stands for the International Society of Neuro-Semantics. For more than 5000 pages of free information, see the web sites:

www.neurosemantics.com
www.meta-coaching.org
www.metacoachingfoundation.org
www.self-actualizing.org
www.nlp-video.com — **www.ns-video.com**

Executive Coaching

Preface

PREFACE

After writing ten books on Coaching, this book focuses exclusively on one kind of coaching— *Executive Coaching*. Why? How is Executive Coaching different enough from the other aspects or forms of coaching? What is so different, unique, and special about Executive Coaching that it requires an entire book within the Meta-Coaching books?

The Uniqueness of Executive Coaching
Obviously, one thing that makes Executive Coaching unique is *its context.* It address as the executive function. It focuses on individuals in executive roles in organizations who have the status, power, and control to lead. It is for those who are commissioned to lead an organization to be productive and profitable as well as sustainable, ethical, and humane. That's a lot!

What's unique also is that the executive role as a role of leadership is today *under lots of pressures*—time pressures, economic pressures, competitive pressures, political pressures, personal pressures, and much more. The executive role is not an easy role. And amplifying the pressures is the challenging of finding colleagues with whom to talk to about the challenges and the pressures. Many executives do not have such colleagues—instead they have people within the organization would use the information against them.

Executives face a lot of personal challenges in how to "have a life" in addition to the immense responsibilities. So many sacrifice their health and well-being; others sacrifice spending time with their children, others get seduced by status, wealth, position, etc. Then there are the developmental challenges—keeping up with the ever-changing markets, personal development, climbing the political ladder within the organization, and sometimes stepping into roles beyond one's competence level, etc.

No wonder Executive Coaching has arisen during the past two decades as a way to enable executives to be more resourceful, mindful, reflective, focused and intentional, and effective, and as a way to transition into a new role or company. In Meta-Coaching we say coaching is for the purpose of engaging in a conversation like none other, and so sometimes Executive Coaching enables an executive to face consequences which, if they don't address them, will derail one's career track.

For many Executive Coaching is like a mini-sabbatical in the middle of the work day or work week that gives the executive some breathing room and a chance to step back to gain perspective. This includes perspective in one's personal life and perspective regarding the trends and directions of the business. Executive Coach Shane Stewart says that it is a chance to get off the dance floor of executive life and up onto the balcony to gain a changed and higher perspective for fresh insights.

Using Meta-Coaching for Executive Coaching
Applying the models of Meta-Coaching to the field of Executive Coaching takes the work in the previous books, *Unleashing Leadership* and *Group and Team Coaching*, to the next level as it addresses the unique challenges of executives. This book addresses those who are stepping into this coaching role to enable them to understand what Executive Coaching is and what it is designed to achieve.

This book also extends the *kinds* of coaching conversations. In doing so, it identifies several conversations that are unique to Executive Coaching. Here also you will find some new coaching skills that are needed to be effective as an Executive Coach.

Finally, unique to this work is the contribution of Graham Richardson, a Master Coach in Sydney Australia. Graham was one of the first four expert coaches that I modeled in 2001 and from which the Meta-Coaching System emerged. Since that time, Graham has supported Meta-Coach Training in Australia, New Zealand, and Europe. As I began modeling the higher levels of expertise in a professional coach, I relied on modeling coaching sessions from Graham for the PCMC (Professional Certified Meta-Coach) and for the MCMC (Master Certified Meta-Coach).

In this book, Graham read through the text and wrote numerous paragraphs throughout as well as offered additional ideas, sometimes challenging mine with important counter-positions. You will also see timely and concise quotes from Graham at the heading of most chapters. So it is a pleasure to present Executive Coaching with Graham Richardson, truly a Master Coach.

PART I:

THE WORLD OF

EXECUTIVE

COACHING

Chapter 1

INTRODUCING

COACHING AND META-COACHING

"Far better it is to dare mighty things, to win glorious triumphs,
even though checkered by failure, than to rank with those poor spirits
who neither enjoy much nor suffer much,
because they live in the gray twilight that knows not victory nor defeat."
Theodore Roosevelt

"Lose your mind and come to your senses."
Fritz Perls

\

Coaching emerged on the scene silently and quietly back in the early 1970s. Today as we look back on that time, most recognize that it was Timothy Gallwey's book, *The Inner Game of Tennis* (1972) that really gave the impetuous to what eventually became the profession of Coaching. The distinctive feature that Gallwey offered was in the shift from the outer game of performance (productivity, profitability, effectiveness, efficiency, etc.) to the inner game of perception (beliefs, self-awareness, principles, etc.). Gallwey noted that something as seemingly simple and obvious as a game of tennis actually involved a whole lot of psychology.

Gallwey discovered that giving directions about how to play the outer game frequently made things worse rather than better. Giving people more and more instructions, even if *what* you say is true and accurate (the rules, laws, insights, understandings, beliefs, etc.), very often had a counter-productive effect. As all of these great ideas and concepts filled the minds of the performers, their game suffered. As they became more and more focused on the rules, they simultaneously were less and less present to the game.

Then came the solution. Gallwey discovered that there was a much better way than telling, giving advice, teaching, informing, and laying down the rules. Filling up a person's head with all of that frequently creates lots of inner noise! And the more noise inside one's head, the more chatter or yelling at oneself, the less the quality of one's performance. Conversely, if he asked awareness questions, performers would come out of that inner world of noise—the quoting of the rules, the understandings, the knowledge, etc. They would then be more available to the outside world and what they needed to do. Years before Gallwey, Fritz Perls recommended a similar strategy in his words that have become foundational in NLP: "Lose your mind and come to your senses."

Gallwey discovered that if he asked the players *awareness questions,* they would stop all of the internal static and noise and begin to see and hear and sense the experience. The awareness questions brought them back to the here-and-now.
> "Which way is the ball turning as it comes toward you?
> Is it spinning clockwise or counter-clockwise?"
> "Is the ball landing one meter or two or three meters on this side of the net?"

For Gallwey, the inner game is the state of one's mind and emotions while performing. With awareness questions and other processes, he discovered that he could *coach* tennis players to move to a whole new level. This discovery also changed other things—it primarily changed the assumption that people need someone to tell them things, teach, and give advice. He discovered that people were a lot more resourceful in being able to function very well. They just needed the chance to perform, get sensory-based feedback, and tap into their resources.

Presto! With this, the field of Coaching was given birth. People didn't need therapy or healing because they were not broken or dysfunctional. They didn't need teaching and advice because they already knew. If they did not need a therapist or a consultant, what did they need? They needed someone who could *facilitate the processes* for deeper communications, meaning-making, empowerment, and unleashing of potentials.

They needed a coach. And in most of the field of Coaching (but not all), this describes what a coach does. A coach facilitates one's internal self-actualizing processes. In Meta-Coaching, this precisely defines what a Meta-Coach does. Accordingly this is how we define coaching:

> *Coaching is the process facilitation of the psychological processes involved in self-communication, understanding, meaning-making, empowering, unleashing potentials, learning, unlearning, change, etc.*

Coaching — The New Helping Profession

In spite of Gallwey's revolutionary discoveries, coaching didn't emerge in the 1970s. Other developments were required before that happened. Among them were the changes that were occurring in companies and organizations during the 1970s and 1980s. These were the decades when companies were first really being *challenged with change*— with the increase of competition from around the world and with the changes that were occurring in people. As standards of living were increasing and international communications were expanding, employees were discovering that they wanted more from their work than merely a job and a paycheck. They want meaning, significance, contribution, colleagues and friends, etc. And in the more progressive industries, people were becoming less and less willing to tolerate the old command-and-control form of management. They wanted a say in things. They wanted to apply their brains and hearts to the products and services that they were creating.

It was during this time that the key business thinkers and theorists were rethinking organizations and suggesting all kinds of new ways to do work. Much of this originated from Douglas McGregor's foundational work in his 1960 book, *The Human Enterprise.* There he applied Abraham Maslow's new psychology about the bright side of human nature to the context of business. McGregor postulated two forms of management and leadership, Theory X and Theory Y.

The old leadership which used Theory X for commanding-and-controlling things assumed that people are lazy, irresponsible, unethical and have to be managed (controlled) by fear and threats. The new leadership operate from Theory Y and assume a very different set of assumptions. They assume that people want to work, to do their best, to take pride in their achievements, to be responsible, to be a part of a winning team, etc. and they are motivated by vision, values, and meaning.

Graham Richardson says that this creates its own challenge. It creates a situation where executives who want to do their best need to remove barriers that thwart the newly kindled passion in managers and employees to make a difference. Yet things like politics, ethical dilemmas, internal and external factors, even cultural issues often (or usually) contradict best work and behavioral practices and as a result create additional frustration for all.

Now McGregor and Maslow were before their time— their ideas too radical for the 1950s and 1960s and even though a few early adapters got on board, most of society was not ready.[1] Yet the new ideas were in their air and as standards of living kept rising, more and more people were becoming ready for *more than just a job*. They wanted a job with meaning, connection, and responsibility. They wanted a job where they could keep learning, take pride in their craft, and enjoy the process. Change was in the air and as the decades passed, the ideas kept bubbling up in the works of the key thinkers of business development: Warren Bennis, Peter Durker, Peter Block, Edwards Deming, etc.

> Situational and functional leadership models
> Downsizing hierarchical organizations
> Empowering employees to tap into human capital (knowledge, creativity, etc.)
> Quality Control as integral to processes

By the 1990s there was so much change and so many new ideas for business that the next change proposed in many organizations was a joke. It was the next "flavor of the month" fad which too would soon pass. Yet that did not happen. The so-called "fad" continued. Year after year, it continued, produced more and more results, and grew up as a profession.

Then there was Meta-Coaching

As the field of Coaching evolved through the 1990s, key NLP developers began applying Neuro-Linguistic Programming (NLP) to Coaching. Robert Dilts, Ian McDermott, and Joseph O'Connor were the first. About the same time, in 2000 I began studying the field of Coaching and thereafter I modeled four expert coaches. From that modeling I developed and launched Meta-Coaching with Michelle Duval.

What I realized from the first was somewhat of a surprise: NLP is ideally fitted for Coaching! Based upon the premises of the new psychology of Maslow and Rogers, Self-Actualization (or Humanistic) Psychology, it started from the assumption that people are not broken, but they work perfectly well. Where there is dysfunction or problems of being ineffective or unproductive, the problem is not with the person. It is a problem of the person's mental maps by which they attempt to navigate the territory of the world. Update that map and enable the person to integrate it into life, and that person's life is transformed.

Then, seeing how the other leaders in NLP had applied NLP to Coaching, I thought that I would take it further. I set out to create a complete coaching system that would be rigorous and systematic. With Michelle Duval, we defined "coaching" and came up with seven distinctive factors. We did this to design the Meta-Coaching System as a systematic approach.

The seven distinctions of coaching define what "coaching" is—its essence and nature. In doing this it distinguishes coaching from the other helping professions. The seven distinctive features of coaching are these:

- *Precise Communication:* A conversation that is dialogue in nature and designed to create clarity and precision.
- *Deep and Reflexive Communication:* A conversation that gets to the thoughts in the back of the mind, the silent thoughts that may even be outside of a person's conscious awareness and that encodes the person's real or deepest beliefs and understandings.
- *Systemic:* A conversation that takes a person's and an organization's whole system into account so that it is holistic, integrated, and whole rather than linear, polarized, and dichotomous.
- *Conscious Change*: A conversation that facilitates a person to identify desired changes and make those changes as a change-embracer. These are changes that the person can integrate so they are sustainable.
- *Measured Execution*: A conversation that allows coach and client to execute the change, implement it into life as life-style. As the change is then embodied and fully integrated, it is measurable.
- *Actualizing Potentials*: A conversation that taps into a person's highest values, visions, meanings, dreams, and make them real

(actual) in life.
• *Process Facilitation*: A conversation that works at the structural or
    process level of experience rather than the content of the client's
    story. It facilitates the client to access his or her resources which
    oneself for self-determination.

Having defined "coaching" as a conversation involving these seven factors,
the challenge then was to identify a consistent set of models that would
inform the coaching and provide direction and guidance in conducting a
true coaching conversation. At the beginning, we had three of the required
models: The NLP Communication Model, the Meta-States Self-Reflexivity
Model, and the Systemic Matrix Model. These were the models for the first
three factors. The next four emerged over the following years and were
invented from the theoretical frameworks and models of NLP and Neuro-
Semantics.

Coaching Factors	**Meta-Coaching Models**
Precision Communication	NLP Communication Model
Deep Reflexive Communication	Meta-States Model
Systemic Conversation	The Matrix Model
Conscious Change	The Axes of Change Model
Measured Execution	The Benchmarking Model
	The Innovation Conversation
Actualizing Potential	Self-Actualization Quadrants
	The Matrix Embedded Hierarchy
	The Meaning-Performance Axes
Process Facilitation	The Facilitation Model

The *coaching factors* (in the box) is how we define Meta-Coaching today.
In the marketplace, there are many different definitions of "coaching" and
more often than not these do not include the factors above. Because of that,
they do not fully define coaching as a distinctive profession.

Our premises about coaching include the following theoretical frames:
• Coaching is for the psychologically healthy and not for those who
    are suffering trauma, personal disordering, great internal pain and

who need therapy
- Coaching is for enabling "normal" (psychologically healthy) people to keep growing and developing.
- Coaching challenges people to balance their lives so that they are "fully functional" as a person in all dimensions of life.
- Coaching is about helping people unleash their potentials that are both known and unknown or unrecognized.
- Coaching is a conversation that inquires about goals and solutions for actualizing one's highest and best rather than focusing on problems.
- Coaching is about change and is for change-embracers, not change resisters, that is, those attracted to change rather than the change-aversive people.

Coaching as a Conversation
You probably noticed that in Meta-Coaching we repeatedly defined coaching in each and every facet as *a conversation.* Now while it is a conversation, it is not a "normal" conversation. It is not a chat and it is not the kind of conversation you'd have at the breakfast table or at dinner. It is a very special conversation. What makes it so special and unique? The answer lies in the following seven factors:
- *Clarity and precision:* Coaching is an unique, intense, focused conversation for clarity and precision. In this way, it is a conversation like none other.
- *Reflective:* Coaching is a deep reflective conversation that gets to the heart of the matter, to the frames and meanings in the back of the mind. These are most often outside-of-conscious awareness and therefore touches the deepest and most vulnerable and most precious core of who you are. This conversation is characterized by the asking of meta-questions as well as framing questions which are almost never asked in normal conversations.
- *Change:* Coaching is a conversation that changes a person, that alters behavior, that evolves beliefs and identity, and that transforms the very direction and intention of life. It is a conversation that activates and empowers one's ability to change and to transform self, environment, behavior, and life.
- *Holistic:* Coaching is a holistic conversation that works systemically with all of you in all of the rich dynamic complexity that makes up a person who is a system living within layers of embedded systems. An effective coaching conversations asks many

system questions to expand a client's perspective.

- *Implementation:* Coaching is a realistic and down-to-earth conversation that aims to actualize, implement, and execute the insights gained and then measure the embodiment of those insights. As the conversation inquires about actualizing, it seeks to measure the intangibles. This means co-creating measures, milestones, and benchmarks to give visibility to the actualization of the dreams.
- *Self-Actualization:* Coaching is a self-actualizing conversation that enables one to unleash every interference and be enabled to *be* fully and completely one's best self—actualizing one's highest meanings and best performances.
- *Facilitative:* Coaching is a facilitative conversation that activates a person to step up to choice point, accept full ownership for one's life, and empower one's sense of response-ability for taking effective action to create the difference in one's world. That's why coaching is not consulting, mentoring, teaching, training, or therapy. It is facilitative as it involves a "ruthless compassion" that believes so much in the person that the coach constantly challenges the client to not sell him or herself short.

Kinds of Coaching Conversations

Given that coaching is a powerful conversation which challenges, changes, unleashes, etc., how many kinds of Coaching Conversations are there? In Meta-Coaching we have identified six basic kinds of conversations—six which are most typical in coaching. Then there are another six in Group and Team Coaching, and then another six that are unique for Executive Coaching—together making a total of 18 kinds of conversations.

1) The Clarity Conversation.

This conversation seeks to understand how and why things are the way that they are. This is designed for clarity and precision. This conversation is an exploration for the purpose of discovering the reality of one's situation, how it operates, the contributing factors, etc., all in an effort to be able to decide what to do. The challenge of this conversation: To face reality on its terms and the willingness to take action on that clarity.

2) The Decision Conversation.

This conversation follows when there is clarity and is designed to lead one to a commitment. Here a person weighs pros and cons of a decision,

---

The Many Different Kinds of Coaching Conversations

1) The Clarity Conversation
2) The Decision / Negotiation Conversation
3) The Planning Conversation   **Core Conversations**
4) The Experiential Conversation
5) Change or Transformation Conversation
6) The Confrontation Conversation

7) The Mediation Conversation
8) The Meta-Conversation
9) The Rounds Conversation   **Group Conversations**
10) Problem-Solving Conversation
11) Collective Learning Conversation
12) Conflict Resolution Conversation

13) The Sounding Board Conversation
14) The Systems Conversation
15) The Paradox Conversation   **Executive Conversations**
16) The Outcome Conversation
17) The Feedback Conversation
18) The Unleashing Potential Conversation

---

identifies the set of values and criteria by which to make a decision, and give weight to each side in order to recognize the "cost" of saying yes or no to the decision. The challenge: To make a decision, to thoroughly think through the decision, and to make a commitment a desired outcome.

3) The Planning Conversation.
This conversation plans a strategy for taking action. From this conversation one may write a business plan, sketch out a decision tree or a checklist of key factors, imagine one or more scenarios of the future, or even mind-map possibilities. The challenge: To create a well-formed plan that is actionable.

4) The Experiential or Resource Conversation.
A conversation based in the clarity and commitment which focuses on

identifying the needed experiences and resources to carry out the plan. This coaching conversation may involve role playing, running of patterns, creating new possibilities, etc. The challenge: To access internal and external resources and apply them in order to carry out the plan, to experience and mobilize the required resources.

5) The Change Conversation.
This conversation facilitates changing things—changing a belief, attitude, habit, lifestyle response, identity, etc. The change here may be at the level of performance, development of person, or transformation of one's direction in life. The challenge: To make a difference by changing from what has been to changing to what can be. To face the risks and possibilities of change.

6) The Confrontation Conversation.
By its very nature, this conversation is challenging inasmuch as it exposes a person's blind-spots and incongruencies. It can be a very fierce conversation as one is invited to face oneself without defense or excuses. The challenge: To face things that may be unpleasant, disturbing, incongruous, or unknown.

7) The Mediation Conversation.
This conversation takes place between two or more persons and is designed to facilitate a conflict resolution between the parties that will be an integrative win/win choice for all. The challenge: To deal with differences between people that has created a conflict; to face and embrace strong emotions and facilitate the parties to work through to a resolution.

8) The Meta-Conversation
This conversation involves stepping back from an experience or a conversation and reflecting upon it from a higher level (meta-level) perspective. Doing this expands perspective and enables the ability to bring additional resources to the conversation. The challenge: To step back from the content or the story and gain perspective, to broaden one's point of view.

9) The Rounds Conversation
This conversation is the most common group coaching conversation and is elicited by simply asking each member of the group to respond to a statement, question, proposal, etc. "Let's start with Roberto and go

clockwise and hear from everyone." The challenge: To have to respond as a group member, to feel that one is put on the spot as one is called upon to be a contributing member of the group.

10) Problem-Solving Conversation
This conversation involves two aspects of the problem solving process. First to clearly define the problem and separate it from symptoms, riddles, and paradoxes as the individuals on a team create a well-formed problem statement. Secondly, brainstorming possible solutions for the problem. The challenge: To stay in a problem-*solving* mode and away from shifting responsibility, blaming, whining, digging into origins, etc.

11) Collective Learning Conversation
This group conversation is designed to facilitate people to think and create together in order to understand something and to build on each person's understandings and questions. For most people and groups, this represents a very high level dialogue where the focus is on learning together. The challenge: To move away from debating and advocating one's position to empathetically listening to other group members and stay open to new discoveries.

12) Conflict Resolution Conversation
This group coaching conversation is designed as a method of addressing a conflict in the group. By facilitating high quality communication skills the group can come to understand each other, the problems the group faces in order to reach its objectives and to resolve the conflict. The challenge: To not fall back on conflicting styles that seek to win at another's loss.

13) The Sounding Board Conversation
This conversation is especially appropriate for Executive Coaching as it provides a space whereby someone in a leadership or management role can talk an issue out-loud in such a way that he or she can hear oneself and reflect upon discoveries. And sometimes to dream out loud, to express desired fantasies of how things could possibly improve without being shut down with judgments. The challenge: To not let the coaching fall into merely a complaining, blaming, or whining session.

14) The Systems Conversation
This conversation involved bringing the various factors, variables, and principles of systems thinking so that the conversation can explore these

aspects of the current system. The design is to find leverage points for change which will let the system evolve. This will have significant impact on a business's culture as an executive learns how to "figure out" the culture and enable it to become a self-actualizing culture. The challenge: To not get overwhelmed by complexity and fall back to simplistic linear thinking.

15) The Paradox Conversation

This conversation addresses a contradiction, issue, or problem that is actually a confusion of levels and hence the issue and its resolution is experienced as a paradox. This means that it cannot be *solved* in the sense of making it "go away." It can only be *resolved* in the sense of being understood and accepted as one sorts out the dichotomies or the levels. The challenge: To avoid treating the paradox as a contradiction that one has to make an either–or choice. To embrace the paradox and discover the confused levels within it.

16) The Outcome Conversation

This conversation is typically the first conversation in coaching and is used to create clarity and precision about what one wants. The template of a well-formed outcome can also be used to identify the client's or an organization's outcome. The challenge: To avoid being reactive rather than proactive in dealing with the challenges of life.

17) The Feedback Conversation

This conversation is designed to provide sensory-based feedback in real time or immediately afterwards so that the client can identify what worked, what did not work, and the degree to which activities succeeded or did not. The challenge: To not react as if feedback is judgment or mind-reading, to facilitate the client to be able to receive the feedback for the purpose of learning and developing.

18) The Unleashing Potential Conversation

This conversation, as a meaningful discussion about one's potentials, focuses on either awakening the sense of potentials, or identifying them, or developing those potentials. The conversation could also focus on enabling the executive to have this conversation with his or her people regarding their place in the organization. The challenge: To not sell oneself or one's organization short by avoiding challenge or stretch goals, to identify, develop, and release the untapped potentials in people and organizations.

Your Executive Coaching Take Aways

To engage in *coaching* and what *executive coaching* you have to know what it *is*. To that end, I have used this chapter to set forth the distinctive features of coaching. This separates coaching from the other helping professions of consulting, training, mentoring, and therapy. This, in part, is what makes coaching in Meta-Coaching a conversations like none other.

•   What will you take away from this chapter that will enable you to be more effective in this domain?
•   What facet of coaching most challenges you?
•   How well acquainted are you at this point with the various kinds of coaching conversations?

End of Chapter Notes:

1. An exception was the computer company that Maslow was invited to as a Visiting Fellow. In 1965 he became a visiting fellow at the Non-Linear Systems, Inc. plant in Del Mar, CA. at the invitation of Andrew Kay, President. The story is told in the book, *Maslow on Management* (1998). Originally this book was titled, *Eupsychian Management.*

Chapter 2

INTRODUCING

EXECUTIVE COACHING

"I listen for their words
because people reveal their inner world by their words and terms."
"When they get upset, there is nothing wrong;
they are ready for a break-through,
if you get out of their way."
Graham Richardson

"Companies cannot evolve unless their executives evolve.
And today this has to happen faster than market place changes.
When an executive evolves it casts a powerful shadow across the organization
as it inspires others on their journeys."
Shane Stewart

Executive Coaching is easy to explain—It is coaching someone in an executive position to be more effective, productive, balanced, self-aware, to be more, to evolve, and unleash his or her potentials. Yet while easy to explain, it is *not* easy to carry out. It's more challenging than it looks. There's lots of reasons for that.

Executive Coaching is challenging, in part, because executives are used to high quality. So when it comes to coaching, they want and expect and demand high quality in the person who facilitates the coaching, the approach, and the results. They do not want amateurs. They do not want to be someone's first attempts at Executive Coaching, and they do not want someone who doesn't know what they are doing. They don't want to be patronized, talked down to, fawned over, or treated with kid gloves.

Executive Coaching is also challenging because the very thing that you, as an Executive Coach, must do is the very thing which the executive does *not* typically or usually receive or experience from others in his or her organization—*challenge. This is especially true for the challenge of confrontation and for the challenge of holding one accountable to agreed upon responsibilities and values.* So let me just jump right into it:

- Are you ready, prepared, and able to do these things?
- How are your confrontation skills?
- How are your skills to speak the truth when your job may very well be on the line?
- Do you have the inner freedom and strength to bring up what may be unpleasant, even disturbing?
- How are your sensory-based feedback skills?
- Are you able to give see-hear empirical descriptions of what you observe in a straight-forward, assertive, and matter-of-fact way?

All of this is absolutely required if you want to be an effective Executive Coach. You must be able to confront with respect, grace, and elegance in order to get to the heart of the matter and hold a "fierce conversation" that doesn't let the executive off the hook. Shane Stewart, a Consultant and Executive Coach in Sydney, Australia notes:

> "Many organizations talk development, but top management doesn't do it. They talk it, but don't embody it. That kills it. Executive Coaches at the top must develop a learning and growing community to be effective."

Defining Executive Coaching

Executive coaching is the process wherein the coach engages someone in an executive position in a fierce conversation to get to the heart of things for the purpose of enabling or grooming the leader to greater effectiveness as well as unleash untapped executive potentials. The long-term purpose of this is to enable and empower the executive to continuously improve his or her skills and develop leadership at ever-increasing levels and/or dimensions.

Actually coaching people in executive positions in organizations or communities is a special privilege and honor. The reason for this may not be what you expect. It's not because of the money or status. That is entirely the wrong motive. It is because, as an Executive Coach, you get to influence the organization at a high leverage point. That is, you get to exercise an influence with the executive and, through him or her, an influence to many, many other people as well. You can influence the culture of an organization and the quality of lives of hundreds, even thousands of people.

As a coach also, you have the unique opportunity in understanding the challenges and opportunities, the pressures and delights, and the beliefs and fears of those who lead and influence the lives of many as they create communities and organizations and the cultures that integrate their premises and visionary solutions.

The Executive Position
Now from the outside, the Executive Position may look like either a completely privileged position of power, pleasure, control, and opportunities. Or it may just as equally look like a position of long hours, immense pressures, intense stresses, and constant criticism. The truth is more modest and radical. It includes both of these and much more. Anyone who has stepped into a higher management level, been promoted to chief executive or in a senior executive role, or has found him or herself in position of being a successful entrepreneur—that person is still fully human with all of the strengths and weaknesses of the human condition. As an Executive Coach, we must never let the glamor of the position blind us to that fact. If it does, then you will lose your ability to be truly effective as an Executive Coach.

The executive's uniqueness involves both success and a position of responsibility. This surfaces human questions about meaning and resourcefulness. People in executive positions are full of the same questions that all people ask:

- What does this work, this job, this project, etc. mean?
- What does it mean about me, about the purpose of my life, and about my skills?
- What resources do I need to keep this up and to handle things effectively?
- How can I be an effective leader and still be a real and authentic human being?
- How can I balance life, work, rest, recreation, hobby, spiritual life, etc.?
- What am I contributing? Does it really count? If so, how can I measure or benchmark it?
- Is this how I truly want to spend my life? What else is there?
- What qualities of life am I missing?
- What about the opportunities for me in my future?
- Who are the next generation leaders? Who am I grooming for leadership in this organization? How am I doing in terms of grooming leaders?
- What kind of a culture am I creating? Is this the kind of culture I want to create? Does it fit in with my larger vision?

A lot of questions! And this is just the beginning. There are many, many more. Another aspect of executives to keep in mind is this: *All executives are not all the same.* There are a great many kinds of people in leadership and in executive roles as there are kinds of people. Unlike the common mis-understanding (myth) at the beginning of the twentieth century which assumed that there was a singular "leadership" personality profile, today we know that leaders come in all kinds of sizes and shapes and with a wide range of personality profiles. There is no one singular personality profile that defines a leader or an executive. It all depends. It depends on the situation, the environment, the task, the requirements of the situation, the skills of the person, and much more.

Then, beyond differences in personality, there is also the differences in what executives want and/or need. It is not an easy question to answer: "What does an executive leader or manager want?" It depends on context and person and company, etc. Now in spite of that, most executives, like most of us want three common human experiences:

    1) They want to be effective and successful at what they are doing.

    2) They want to enjoy those activities and find them as meaningful, significant, and fitting.

3) They want to be acknowledged and rewarded for their contribution.

While this is an over-simplification, by reducing the specific details to these three categories, we have a way to sort out inner and outer goals. It enables us to think in terms of *the inner game of the mind* and *the outer game of expression and performance.* This gives us two very broad categories to work with in coaching, and especially in Executive Coaching—two classes of activities that are inter-related and that systemically influence each other.

Within these two classes of activities are two dimensions of experience and so two broad arenas for coaching. Now we have *two kinds of coaching.* We have two dimensions that we integrate in our coaching. It is not the case that we do one *or* the other. To be effective we have to do both. Doing both enables the coaching to be integrative and whole and when we do that, the coaching to be sustainable rather than flash-in-the pan phenomenon.

The Inner Game of Mind ——	**The Outer Game of Expression**
Understandings	Performance
Beliefs	Skills – Competence
Values	Speaking
Interpretations	Acting
Meaning-making	Relating
Evaluations	Results
Developmental Coaching	Performance Coaching

This is a central theme in Neuro-Semantics. All people, including executives, want to be meaningfully productive as they achieve significant goals that enable them to feel successful in life. In Neuro-Semantics, we map this out on two axes— *the Meaning Axis and the Performance Axis.*

> *Performance* is the outer game of life—what we do, the results we achieve, and the somatic (bodily) states we experience.
>
> *Meaning* is the inner game. This is the game that we play in our mind. This refers to our sense of direction, intention, significance, and meaningfulness. And when you win the inner game, the outer

game becomes a cinch. In coaching executives we focus on the inner game and correlate it to the outer game that the person wants to win. This gives us the key leverage point for change.

Actually, this describes the heart of the domain of coaching. If you ask, "Why is that?" the answer is because coaching is most essentially the life-changing conversation that activates a person's personal powers and potentials for development and transformation in a way that unleashes potentials. It changes a person to become the person he or she is essentially designed to be. It confronts everything that gets in the way and it facilitates finding the pathway to generative and transformative renewal. Today, more than ever before, executives must keep renewing themselves.

Coaching is Post-Therapy
Coaching is *not* therapy and not a cover-up substitute for therapy. Lots of people in the field of Coaching do not seem to know that.[1] Yet if that is not the case, then there is no unique and distinctive "field" of Coaching, just the field of therapy that uses "coaching" as a mild form of therapy—"therapy-light."

For most practitioners in the field of Coaching, coaching is the discipline *after* therapy. It is the discipline *after* people get to "OK" and "up to average," and are ready for actualizing their yet untapped resources. Accordingly, that's why *Executive Coaching is about facilitating the next level of development for the person in the executive role.* It is especially about enabling an executive to face and handle today's challenges and get the results that are required and desired. Often times, Executive Coaching focuses on grooming someone for their next step of professional and personal development. It is about enabling one to begin exploring how to unleash even more potential.

Stepping Back for Perspective
Executive Coaching involves the step-back skill. It is the experience of giving an executive some time in his or her busy schedule to think, to reflect, to register, and to acknowledge whatever is going on in the business, at home, and in one's personal life. For the Neuro-Semantic Meta-Coach, this kind of coaching focuses on enabling an executive's self-reflexive skills. These skills naturally and inevitably arise from the kind of consciousness that we humans have. After all, we have a very special kind of mind or consciousness—self-reflexive consciousness.

Self-reflexiveness means that we can think and feel about our thoughts and feelings and just when we do that, we can step back conceptually to the next level of thoughts and feelings about our first level thinking and feeling. What then complicates this process of reflexivity is that *it never ends.* After you have finished thinking and/or feeling about something, you can do it again. And again. And again. The higher intelligent animals cannot. They stop two or three levels up. But not us. We can always step back another level and it is this reflexive skill that allows us to learn at higher levels and gain more expansive perspectives. It is what facilitates the second loop learning— that is, learning about how we learn. This enables us to flush out our unconscious assumptions.

This self-reflexive consciousness implies several very profound insights and powerful responses.

- With the power of always being able to step back to observe your functioning and processing, you do not ever have to be stuck in your perspective.
- Change or transformation can always be just one step away (i.e., one step up!).
- Whatever you think-and-feel about something sets the frame for that thing. It creates the category or class that you put it in and when you do that, that determines how you interpret things. And if your interpretation creates limitations for you, to change that all you have to do is to change the frame of classification.
- Gaining perspective about the structural functioning of ourselves, our understandings, interpretations, perspectives, personality, functioning, etc. begins by simply stepping back from our experience.
- When you step back, you can then *quality control* the experience. You can ask about the quality of the experience— does it empower, enable, free, expand capacity, etc.? Or does it limit, sabotage, undermine, imprison, etc.?
- By stepping back you can change things quickly and fairly easily in real time and use feedback in the moment to make adjustments. This accelerates learning and development.
- Stepping back enables a team, like an executive team, to do the same thing as a team for the same benefits. Such perspective reduces the stress of conflict, facilitates conflict resolution, and enables the integration of differences.

The Ruthless Compassion Conversation of Coaching

All of this then leads the Executive Coach to hold *fiercely focused conversations* about an executive's beliefs, values, identity, intentions, hopes, and all of the things that in-spirit him or her (that is, inspire). By doing this, the person is enabled to keep him or herself alive, vital, and resilient within the organizational demands and culture. It enables the person to get to the heart of things that creates his or her inner reality— the meanings that they create and give to things.

This fierce conversation can only work if there is sufficient rapport. Any and every conversation must always begin with rapport—with a strong and personal connection with the person in the conversation. In the NLP Communication model, rapport means entering into the person's world. It means matching where the person is physically, verbally (linguistically), and psychologically. This is the foundation that enables coaching to be both challenging and compassionate simultaneously—compassionately challenging, or as Graham Richardson says, ruthlessly compassionate.

To this end, in the field of Neuro-Semantics we have both discovered and created numerous coaching and communication tools for enabling us to hold a fierce conversation whereby we are able to engage an executive in the exploration of meaning for the purpose of unleashing new potentials. Meta-Coaching unifies compassion and a highly focused and fierce conversation, which together defines the nature of Executive Coaching.[2]

Executive Coaching

As already suggested, the field of Coaching is the discipline *after* therapy, *after* people get to OK and "up to average." It is for people who are ready to actualize their untapped resources. That's why coaching generally, and *Executive Coaching specifically, challenges and facilitates next level of development.* The focus in Executive Coaching is therefore on grooming people for the next step of professional and personal development.

As *a step-back skill* Executive Coaching gives the executive a structured time and opportunity within a busy schedule to reflectively consider the vision and mission of the company as well as one's own personal vision and mission. And when done in a sequential way, all of this enables the capacity of the executive's self-reflexive skills.

Defining the Processes within Executive Coaching

Given all of this, we can now pull these together to make explicit many of the fundamental processes in Executive Coaching. The following statements essentially define Executive Coaching. Executive Coaching is—

- A *step back from all of the pressures and stresses* of business to enable one to gain perspective and renew vision and direction as a leader.

- A *reflective time* for thinking and contemplating the mission, strategy, and tactics for better performance and success of the business, and self-actualization of the organization and people, to increase the capacity of managers and leaders.

- A *fiercely focused conversation* that enables one to examine the beliefs, values, identity, intentions, assumptions, hopes, etc. that govern and drive one's experiences and skills.

- A *leveraged dialogue that gets to the heart of things* to give more choice and control to the decision maker. A conversation that addresses meaning-making, framing, handling people, relationships, distinguishing responsibility for and to, etc.

- A *crucible of focus* that empowers more response-ability and accountability in making the things that are most important front and center.

- A *facilitation of the critical success factors* that support leadership, entrepreneurship, resilience, creativity, and productivity.

- *An empowering of an executive* for taking his or her skills and development to the next level, a way to *groom* someone in one's professional and personal development

- A *facilitating the transition* from management to leadership, understanding the difference and enabling the executive to have the courage to unleash his or her potential to real-ize (make actual) one's vision for oneself and for the organization.

Your Executive Coaching Take Aways
What will you take away from this chapter? What are some of the highlights and key points that will enable you to step up to Executive

Coaching? Executive Coaches end coaching sessions with these kinds of questions. The design is to encourage reflection and decision so that what begins in a coaching session does not end there, it moves out into everyday life. Similarly I will end each chapter in the same way— inviting you to reflect on what you have learned and what you will take away to support your development as an Executive Coach.

- Executive Coaching, as with all forms of coaching, centers in the ability to *challenge* people to step up to their potentials and to not sell themselves short. How are your skills at challenging? Are you strong enough within yourself to hold a fierce conversation with someone in an executive role?
- Executive Coaching, as with all forms of coaching, operates from identifying an executive's highest objectives—his or her needs and wants.   When you can do that, you can use the Outcome Conversation to create a coaching contract.
- The temptation will be to stay external in the Outer Game. Yet effective Executive Coaching requires going in—to the Inner Game and engaging the person in that dimension.
- Executive Coaching is not a substitute for therapy and it should not be used as a sneaky way to get an executive some psychotherapy. If that's the case, say so. Be open and forthright about it.
- Executive Coaching essentially involves the meta-move of stepping back to gain a more extensive perspective that then allows a more informed and intelligent response.

End of the Chapter Notes

1. In the field of Coaching, there are many different models and different assumptions about coaching. Meta-Coaching is based on a non-therapeutic model and specifically upon Self-Actualization Psychology which deals with those who are basically psychologically healthy. See *Self-Actualization Psychology* (2008).

2. The idea of the "fierce conversation" came originally from the work of Susan Scott in her books by that title. See Bibliography. The idea of "ruthless compassion" came from Graham Richardson.

3. See the article in the Harvard Business Review, 'The Very Real Dangers of Executive Coaching' (Steven Berglas, HBR 2002). Berglas, a psychologist, warns said that coaching may work initially, but only superficially. His concern with some coaching is that in the long-run it is may exacerbate a person's problems. So his bottom line is that, as an Executive Coach, you will need to be able to recognize when a person's situation and problems requires medical intervention. We would say, to recognize when a person needs therapy and/or is uncoachable.

Chapter 3

LIFE IN THE C-SUITE

EXECUTIVE LEADERSHIP

"The essence of Executive Coaching is helping leaders work through their dilemmas so they can transform their learning directly into results for the organization."

Mary Beth O'Neil (2007, p. xiii)

If you're going to coach executives, it's important that you understand their world—the unique world that they inhabit. The effectiveness of your coaching depends on understanding the social, political, and personal worlds in which they live and move and have their being. Only then will you be able to comprehend the key forces at work which influence the way the executive thinks, feels, values, interprets, and relates.

What is life in the C-suite like? Well, it is very much like life everywhere . . . only amplified in terms of stress, pressure, and public exposure. Life there is full of decisions to make, information to process, people to meet and deal with, conflicts to resolve, meetings to attend, and plans to work on, invent, or re-invent. Life there is also under scrutiny so that one is seldom, if ever, not "on stage."

It is the executive's job to build relationships, connect with people, pull people together, build commitment, communicate and all of this is to lead an organization to higher performance, productivity, and profits. That's a lot! It calls for a focused-approach, a commitment to results, a tough-minded directness to get down to action.

That's the tough side. Yet to be able to get those results requires the so-called "soft" side— the human side of things: respect, hope, connection, empathy, meaning, etc. It requires a lot of intangible items—trust, truth, and transparency.

Political
Life in the C-suite, however, is unlike a lot of other aspects of life for the rest of us in that *it is highly political.* It is more political because it involves more people and more people with different ideas, different positions, different and vested interests. The "authority" to allocate funds and resources gives people in the C-suite increased "power." Consequently it is inevitable that people will curry for that power, jockey to obtain some of it, and "suck up" to get as much favor as possible. They will play political games as in withholding information, "playing their cards" so that they do not reveal their hand, and so on. Of course, one can do this in a healthy and ethical way or in a way that does not meet those criteria. That is, one can play dirty politics.

Today C-suite life is usually highly pressured due to how the organization is driven by profits and short-term thinking. In most places, it is measured and evaluated by the numbers of the quarterly profits and monthly management reports. It is this short-term focus sucks the life out of the executives and the organization. That's because it makes *money* the only bottom-line instead of just one bottom-line among others. Sadly, this is just as true in developing countries as it is in first-world countries. The push for profits and the demand for greater and greater return on investment puts so much pressure on people that those in the C-suite, as well as the rest of the organization, hardly have time to breathe and almost none at all to gain perspective—critical success factors.

No wonder then that Coaching has become a valued resource for executives. If nothing else, it gives a few minutes during the day from time to time to step back, gain perspective, and evaluate the healthiness of oneself and one's organization.

Life in the C-suite is definitely and powerfully *performance driven.* Not only is the question about quarterly profits front and center, but so is growth, expansion, the need for more customers, etc. Because of this, there tends to be almost universally an aversion to bad news because that could mean that things are not growing and profits may not increase. Ironically this focus on performance leads many to "look busy," give an impressive persona of industry and activity, and create tremendous P.R. about oneself and one's company. Yet all of this puts PR above reality. In many places, it is more about image and image-management than it is about actual performance and the development of expertise.

Missing from the C-Suite
Now given the nature and quality of life in the C-suite, there are several things that are typically missing. At the heart of what is commonly missing from the C-suite and from senior management is *meaning and meaningfulness.* That is, work that is personally meaningful that a person can value and feel passionate about. And the first consequence of this is *authenticity*—being real, and living with integrity and congruency. Yet without these things, the quality of communicating and relating suffers. It suffers from the fear of speaking the truth and bringing up unspeakables. All of this gives even more impetus for Executive Coaching and the difference it can make for executives.

What Executive Coaching uniquely introduces is a balance between doing and being. Yes, *doing* is important. Yes, higher performance, greater revenues, growth, expertise, etc.— all of this is central to an organization's success. Yet if that's all there is, then *the soul* of the business and of the people in the business will be frail, even lifeless.

What do Executives Want?
Obviously, everyone in any role of leadership or authority wants to be effective and successful at their job. For this reason, one of the key reasons for Executive Coaching is on executive performance. It is on enabling the leader to get the desires results and create the level of productivity required by the job. So coaches are brought in to facilitate whatever is needed in a leader to help ensure that that leader reaches his or her level of achievement.

Doing what needs to be done and reaching the level of performance required in a professional way means getting that quality of performance in one's body so that it is deeply embedded in neurology and in the one's muscle memory. When it is there, then the performance will be natural, inevitable, and organic. Then the performance will be habitual enough to feel natural and comfortable.

Yet sometimes that is not enough. Sometimes to get the performance, the coaching has to move beyond performance to the personal executive and/or his or her development of leadership. The coaching has to deal with the person in terms of personal, mental, emotional development and not just focus on actions or behaviors. The coaching has to go inside to the Inner Game and deal with beliefs, one's sense of self, emotional and social development, etc. This level of change is developmental coaching.

Coaching the inner game of a person means making mental shifts so that activities are seen as meaningful, significant, and important. As coaching at this level addresses the subject of meaning and meaningfulness, it encourages people to have a life apart from the job. Here is another aspect of executive coaching— coaching for an expanded awareness or consciousness. Why? *Precisely, because the quality of your life depends on the quality of your meanings.*

Characteristics of People at the Executive Levels
What are they like? What can you expect when you meet a senior manager, CEO, CFO, COO, or visionary leader? While people in executive levels involve the full range of personality styles and patterns, there are a few similar patterns for the majority of those who get there. These are generalizations and, of course, it depends on the particular industry, culture, personal history, experiences of a given executive. These characteristics arise due to the nature of business and corporate life in the twenty-first century.

Executives tend to be practical and pragmatic. It's usual for them to think in terms of results, getting things done, and making a difference. Few are interested in abstract theories and historical backgrounds of things. They want to get down to business, identify what needs to be done, and get on with taking care of it.

Executives are driven and intense. This explains a significant aspect of the persons and how they got to where they are. They are full of energy and, more often than not, Type-A personalities who feed off of stress, challenge, and excitement. Because they are purposeful and intentional, they think fast, move fast, and are impatient. When over-done, this can lead to being highly distracted and express many or all of the symptoms of a person in high stress.

Executives are fast responders and time-driven. Time is important to them and so they set and live by their schedules. And if they don't set the schedules themselves, their P.A. (Personal Assistant) does. For them *time* is at a premium. Most live in a fire-ready-aim culture or environment. This also can generate high levels of stress which can then lead to poor decisions, and/or ever-changing things in the company's culture.

Executives are tough-minded and firm. They set goals, objectives, and boundaries and then they hold to them firmly. Most are tough negotiators. They often live behind a persona and may over-identify with their title or status. As a result they may be alien to themselves. Consequently, they may operate from low self-awareness (little intra-psychic awareness) and have numerous blind spots which, by definition, they are unaware of.

Executives will typically default to being either visionary or managerial in their functioning regardless of position. They arrive there as either visionary leaders with strengths in creating meaning, inspiring people for a common purpose, or as managerial leaders whose strength lies in taking action, getting top performance from others, and making things happen. Managerial leaders dominate and so most companies are actually under-led and over-managed. And as Warren Bennis and many others have noted, this is a fatal flaw.[1]

Executives usually have one or two towering strengths and also one or two hidden weaknesses. Most have a towering strength which is their signature presence and style. This is what makes one unique which usually got them to where they are. Typically also within those strengths are hidden weaknesses. When promoted to the next level, they often fail to release some of the unique skills that got them to that place and replace them with a new set of competencies. Further, at the next level, what's a weakness at one level can become a fatal flaw at the next level.[2]

Often strengths and weaknesses are predictive of one another. Someone who is a "people person" as a strength may have challenges in confronting and/or holding someone accountable. Alternatively, someone who "delivers" as a strength may be harsh and weak in people skills. One very senior banking executive was given feedback that he "had a very safe pair of hands and the CEO could absolutely rely on this executive to achieve any business goal assigned to him." However, there would be collateral damage with "blood on the floor" from the impact of how he gets things done. "Woe be to anyone who gets in the way." Another example is the strategic minded executive, who has trouble with execution versus the doer executive who has trouble strategically, that is, beyond the short term.

Executives live in a strongly political environment and are themselves highly political. Most find that they developed political skills and had to become competent in handling differences, positions, and vested interests from various parties to get where they are. Some are very political; some are under-political and so struggle in working with the differing kinds and styles of people.

It's interesting that when we use the word politics in business, it usually carries overtones of negativity as when we label someone as "very political" (e.g., dangerous) or "politically savvy" (e.g., adept, shrewd). Yet whenever people get together, politics are in play. That's because politics is about people relating, managing influence, choices, etc. Politics can be dirty and politics can also be positive and constructive. The difference lies in the style, intention, and psychology behind the political activities.[3]

As a summary of these characteristics Mintzberg (1994) generated a list of his observations about executives and how they go about their job. He says that executives—

- Prefer verbal over numeric information.
- Prefer conversation to reading.
- Gather information on an anecdotal basis.
- Dislike and mistrust general theories and avoid "grand design" type of decisions.
- Prefer to make smaller and incremental decisions.
- Deal with immediates and let an overall strategy emerge.

What do Executives want from Coaching?
Given the characteristics of those in executive positions, what are the key challenges facing executives? What are the problems, issues, and concerns that most engage their attention?

Central to almost everything else is relationships. What the executive focuses on mostly is relating effectively to people in and out of the business, getting along with the board, with stockholders, and the public domain. But that's not all. There are dozens and dozens of facets of relationship that concerns the executive. Here are some of the key ones:

- How to be authentic, transparent, and approachable. How to be a real person and not just a title.
- How do deal effectively with conflict: Conflict resolution processes, confrontations, and addressing "the elephant in the room."
- How to create a balance in Work/Life. How to devote enough time to family while not failing to deal with the pressure to perform, and to succeed. How to strike a balance personally and professionally.
- How to develop as a person, how to develop the qualities of self-management, self-awareness, self-discipline, self-nurturing, etc. How to develop personal openness, growth, and learning. How to be tough and approachable at the same time. How to receive feedback. How to be ambitious and yet humble.
- How to manage stress: How to slow down enough so one can enjoy life, and be reflective about one's life.
- How to make intelligent and humane bottom line decisions: financial goals for the organization.
- How to change, how to keep up with the field and with the trends in one's industry.
- How to fast track high potentials in the business so that they do not feel like frauds when they step into new roles.
- How to get to the truth and tell the truth: How to get the truth from the front line, and how to prevent people from becoming "yes men" who filter the truth and present a watered-down version of reality.
- How to influence people and to develop persuasion skills. How to create loyalty and alliance in people.
- How to frame issues, beliefs, vision, and mission. How to inspire people with stories that are engaging and compelling.
- How to work more effectively with the decision-making process, how to be decisive, how to be tough and yet thoughtful of the people whose lives are affected.
- How to handle the endless meetings and how to make the meetings more effective so that it is not talk without actions.
- How to handle the politics in the organization—the individuals and groups with vested interests and positions. How to know when to compromise, when not to, how to create and use alliances, etc.

How to become politically astute to the positions, interests, and "games."

What are the Executive Coaching Conversations?
If these are the characteristics and the needs of executives coaching, then what kind of Coaching Conversations will Executive Coaching involve?

A Reflective or a Meta-Conversation (chapter 19)
> By stepping-back from the pressures and stresses of everyday business, the executive or leader is able to get a larger perspective of his or her challenges and to renew a sense of vision and direction. A reflective time for reflectively thinking about mission, strategy, and tactics for better performance and success, for detecting patterns, for accelerating learning and creating a learning organization. This requires slowing down, reflecting, discovering and setting one's own compass.

A Confrontational Conversation (chapter 18)
> A fiercely focused conversation that enables one to examine his or her driving beliefs, values, identities, intentions, and hopes for assumptions and consequences.
> A leveraged dialogue that gets to the heart of things to give more choice and control to the decision maker. A conversation to expose blind spots to prevent derailing.
> This calls for openness, vulnerability, reality, and authenticity.

A Self-Actualizing or Unleashing Conversation (chapter 21)
> Empowering executives to advance to the next level of development, a way to groom someone for his or her next step of professional and personal development. This requires vulnerability.
> A facilitation of the critical success skills that support leadership, entrepreneurship, resilience, and creativity.
> A crucible for empowering more response-ability and accountability in making the things that are most important front and center.

A Paradoxical Conversation (chapter 24)
> A conversation that enables one to look at the seemingly insolvable problems and to recognize a paradoxical structure. On the surface they seem like a polarization conflict between two opposites

choices. Yet in reality, there's a confusion of levels that need to be sorted out.

When is Executive Coaching needed?
These are numerous occasions within an organization that call for the value that Executive Coaching can provide. There are also numerous moments in the life of an executive when this kind of intervention is needed.

- *When hiring new people:* When key people are appointed to new roles or hired externally and need to get up to speed as quickly as possible. Today this period is often measured in days, not months.

- *When the organization faces market change:* When an organization is changing whether through downsizing, restructuring, merging, or due to changes in the market.

- *When there are new leaders to groom:* When a person is being groomed by leadership for a promotion.

- *When there is the need for competency development:* When a business wants to retain talent and prevent those who are being promoted to being promoted to a level of incompetence.

- *When a business needs to be rejuvenated:* When the quality of life or of performance lags and needs a fresh rejuvenation of purpose and mission. When the vision and mission itself lacks relevance.

- *When an executive needs to step up to his or her next level of personnel development:* When people are not living up to, or experiencing, their own personal mastery in what they do and so lack the required passion and excitement.

Your Executive Coaching Take Aways
Although there is no singular psychological profile for an executive, there are common characteristics that are typical. Among these are the common characteristics of being practical, pressured, and performance-driven. What are the ideas that you are taking away about executives and life in the C-suite?

What executives actually need is often not what they ask for. Why is that? For one thing, they may not even be aware of what they need. They ask for more efficiency in performance, for more productivity, what they need is more reflection, meaningfulness, passion, personal growth and development, etc. They invite an Executive Coach in to deal with the Outer Game in the business, yet the leverage point of change is in the Inner Game of their mental frames of meaning.[3]

- How familiar are you with the characteristics of the C-Suite?
- What are your best skills for dealing with people who have the typical characteristics of executives?
- If the central need of executives is dealing with the relationships in their lives, what are you best resources for coaching to that need?

End of Chapter Notes

1. Warren Bennis (1985) *Leaders: The Strategies for Taking Charge;* (1989) *Why Leaders Can't Lead;* (2008) *Transparent;* (2009), *On Becoming a Leader;* Tom Peters (1987), *Thriving on Chaos;* Peter Drucker (1999) *Management Challenges for the 21st Century.*
2. See *The Leadership Pipeline* (2001) Ram Charan, Stephen Drotter, and James Noel. Jossey-Bass.
3. The next book in the Meta-Coaching series will be *Political Coaching.*
4. *The Winning the Inner Game* (2007).

Chapter 4

COACHING TO CREATE

SELF-ACTUALIZING EXECUTIVES

"Look after the people, and the results will look after themselves."
Peter Stephenson, *Executive Coaching*

"I believe that questions will naturally emerge and so I let them emerge. That's because they are a way into the person's mind and heart. I listen for their words because people reveal their inner worlds by their words and terms."
Graham Richardson, Master Coach

What happens when a Coach meets an Executive? In Meta-Coaching, we believe that above and beyond all of the listed values and benefits of Executive Coaching, there is a grander and much larger frame—*the frame of self-actualization.* For us this means that our relationship with an executive is not just to facilitate the person being more productive, efficient, balanced, emotionally intelligent, growing, creative, etc. All of these things are good and important. Amazingly, they almost inevitably occur when the executive is self-actualizing.

The reason for this incredible self-organizing process is simple. *Self-actualization itself is the highest human drive.* So when it occurs—people will be growing and developing. A self-actualizing person will be more productive and efficient, will be more socially and relationally aware and competent, and will be more autonomous, responsible, and competent. All this occurs because of the self-actualization drive and how it operates in human personality. Self-actualization means unleashing your highest values and visions and translating them into your best performances. When a person self-actualizes, he or she becomes "the best version of oneself," a fully functioning person" (Carl Rogers), experiencing full humanness (Abraham Maslow), and fully alive/fully human (Sidney Jourard). *It is you at your best.* Who wouldn't want that?

This is the explicit goal that we strive for in Meta-Coaching because Coaching as a field based on how people who are basically psychologically healthy continue to develop. This is based on Self-Actualization Psychology.[1]

It is not based on the older and more traditional psychologies. Those focused on the problem of trauma and hurt and so they fit for people suffering the more unusual struggles—internal distresses from traumatic experiences, personality disorders, neurosis, etc. For executives who internally suffer from an insecure sense of self, low self-esteem, who's ego is so invested in "doing" and "achieving" that without it, the person experiences existential anxiety, angst, and dread—such persons probably need therapeutic intervention and would not be good candidates for coaching.[2] Actually, coaching could do them harm.

While the self-actualization drive is a human drive and within everyone, many are only barely aware of it, if at all. While it is innate, it is not inevitable. It slowly develops over the years of our lives—dependent upon a person first achieving the ability to gratify one's primary drives and needs. That is, the self-actualization drive, as a biological reality, has a biological foundation. For the great majority of people, they hardly give any attention to it. Why? Because their lower needs are unmet. Yet the drive is there— waiting. It is there and waiting to fully emerge when the basic needs are sufficiently gratified.

Self-Actualizing Executives?
"Self-Actualizing Executives—Are there such creatures?" This is the first response that I often hear from people—a statement of skepticism and humor. "And yes Virginia, there are self-actualizing executives." In fact, there are a great many. Today, in fact, there are more and more—men and

women who are visionary enough and insightful enough to know that without a healthy and human work place, the chance of developing a successfully great company is impossible. They not only know and have heard the language of "human capital," of truly empowering people stepping up to leadership and responsibility, unleashing creative potentials —they believe in such and work to create a humanistic culture in their organizations.[3]

Actually, coaching for the self-actualization of executives describes the heart and soul of systemic coaching for the whole person within all of the systems that the person lives and operates.[4] Consequently this leads to a great many aspects of the executive's inner and outer life. The next section (Part II: Executive Challenges) details many of the aspects regarding how *Self-Actualization Coaching* impacts in the life of an executive. These challenges minimally include the following:

- Psychological and emotional well-being
- Direction – vision and mission
- Accurate and timely Feedback
- Change and transformation
- Leadership that's inspiring, competent, and authentic
- Politics and political skills
- Culture — cultural change and development
- Derailment and blind spots

As an executive self-actualizes, the executive integrates the "hard" and "soft" sides of business. Then as a leader or manager, the person is able to simultaneously be effective both with people and in terms of business acumen. In fact, the old polarity disappears between these two aspects of an effective business person and the new synthesis gives one an unique synergy.

Coaching the Self-Actualizing Executive
How often does an executive ask to be coached for his or her "self-actualization?" Okay, not that often. At least not in those words. Perhaps we should ask, How often does the leader want to step up to his or her leadership? Or perhaps, How often does an executive want to unleash more potentials to take his or her company to the next level? Or, How often does an executive ask to create more work–life balance, more ability to handle conflict, more understanding of her board, more ability to control his competitive drive, etc.?

All of these questions are invitations to be coached on various aspects of self-actualization. Each question implies the presence of the self-actualization drive and indicates an area for actualizing a person's higher development. In this, you as an Executive Coach have to attune your ears to hear a person's desire to develop and to move up to yet another level of development. If you don't hear this, you'll not be able to effectively facilitate the executive's self-actualizing.

Self-actualization takes many forms. For one thing, a person may seek self-actualization in just one area, a few areas, or even in several areas. That enables a person to actualize just one aspect of—business acumen without self-actualizing one's self as a person. Because of this always notice if your executive client is wanting to self-actualize *as a person* or only in a singular aspect of life.

Regarding this, you can expect that most clients will start with an aspect of life. Their goal will be to unleash their potential in leading, managing, negotiating, etc. Yet along the way to doing that, they will discover that in order to actualize their fullest potentials in that area, they will have to *be* more. This realization will then open them up to actualizing their very self.

When you coach people for actualizing their highest and best, people will normally simply talk about improving something, learning, growing, getting better, or eliminating some interference or block. They will talk about wanting to know more, understand more, feel more, relate more authentically, do more, have more, give more, be more, etc. Now while there is a language of self-actualization, most people have not learned that language and so will *not* code their requests in that language.

Self-actualization can occur in a thousand ways because it is about unleashing more and more of one's potentials and become increasingly more fully human. And doing this at work— doing this in the context of business and within the culture of a corporation transforms work to be more human and humane. This reduces the old dichotomous statement, "It's not personal, it's business" which has often been used as an excuse to take actions that are hurtful, even cruel, to people. It has consequently led to the creation of a workplace environment that did not support people. It has created hostile environments and/or those lacking heart or soul. The culture that results is cruelly competitive, politically negative, solely oriented toward money, status, and position, etc.

Coaching the Self-Actualizing Executive
To Self-Actualize the Company
As individual leaders and managers self-actualize to become truly effective leaders, they have the unique opportunity to lead their companies to become self-actualizing companies. I wrote extensively about this in *Unleashing Leadership* (2009). This means organizing for self-actualization. It means creating a culture that fits the values and criteria of self-actualization, which is what we mean by "a coaching culture."

Self-actualizing leaders within a self-actualizing company synergize short-term thinking and planning with long-term thinking and planning. What results from this is the ability to see immediate needs, the numbers needed this quarter, etc. in terms of the long-term vision and mission of the company. Consequently this reduces the temptation to sacrifice the long-term vision for the short-term benefit of money and success.

A distinguishing feature of self-actualizing leaders in a self-actualizing company is that they create three bottom-lines for their company. These are summarized as profit, people, and purpose:

- *1) Profit* is obvious because if the enterprise is not commercially viable and profitable, it simply will not survive.

- *2) People,* as in *developing and growing people,* is becoming increasingly more obvious these days. That's because as businesses change, they are increasingly dependent upon *human capital—* intellectual capital, relational capital, and social capital. Companies will only be able to survive if they can attract and keep good people. The "battle for talent" has arisen in organizations precisely because of this. And the concern about retention and engagement similarly reflects a growing awareness of the crucial role of developing people.

- 3) Finally, *purpose or passion* because with rising standards of living, the self-actualization drive kicks and we ask, "Is this all there is?" As we think about meaning and meaningfulness in our lives, we think about leaving a legacy. We think about improving the world, about making an impact on the world, and leaving it better than the world we received. These concerns give evidence of the self-actualizing drive.

Systemic Self-Actualization

When we speak about *actualizing* a person's potentials or an organization's potentials, the actualizing by definition will be systemic. It will involve the whole of life and so will be holistic in all of the rich layers as it considers systems within systems. While it is true that a person could actualize one aspect of life (career, relationships, health, passion, etc.) and not other important aspects— it is usually not healthy or ecological to do so. Doing that creates an out-of-balance life which will almost inevitably be non-self-actualizing and therefore unsustainable. Senior executives are prone to this yet in the long-run it undermines them.[4]

This principle similarly holds true for an organization. For any company to truly become the very best organization that it can become, it must create a self-actualization culture that will affect every aspect of the company's life. For half a century or more, business experts, theorists, researchers and experimenters have been identifying more and more factors that will create organizational success, corporate excellence, and move companies to good and then from good to great.[5]

During these decades these factors have sometimes turned a company around and enabled all the people within to become highly successful and even a "great" company. Yet oftentimes a single given success factor was not enough and it did not have a systemic influence. Consequently, it might have made things somewhat better or it could have had a negative reaction and actually made things worse. What was missing was a larger frame that could hold that factor or even several factors in place. What was missing was a Self-Actualization Culture— a coaching culture.

Your Executive Coaching Take Aways

In coaching and in Executive Coaching, *the highest frame of all is the self-actualization frame.* This frame holds all of the most cutting-edge ideas about personal and organizational development. So when you, as an Executive Coach, focus on the self-actualizing drive in people, in the executive and in the people he or she leads, you are working to facilitate a revolutionary change and the creation of a self-actualization culture.

- Given that, what are you taking away that will enable you to see, recognize, and work within the Self-Actualization frame?
- What do you need to learn about self-actualization or about coaching?

- What skills do you need to develop?
- How and when will you engage in that skill development?

End of Chapter Notes
1. See *Self-Actualization Psychology* (2008).
2. See Appendix A.
3. See *Unleashing Leadership* (2009) for companies and the leaders self-actualizing enough to create them. Also see *Hidden Value* (2000) by Charles A. O'Reilly and Jeffrey Pfeffer.
4. See *Systemic Coaching* (2012) for an entire work on systems thinking and coaching.
5. See *Good to Great* by Jim Collins.

PART II:

EXECUTIVE

CHALLENGES

Chapter 5

EXECUTIVE CHALLENGES

*"How can you call yourself a leader in this new world
if you do not have coaching skills?
How can you lead by example?"*
Sir John Whitmore

"Coaching is the development tool of the 21st century.
If you cannot coach, you cannot lead."
John Welsh

The executive position is a position of tremendous challenge. People who step up into executive positions are those who find stepping up to take on a challenge exciting. *Challenge* lies at the heart and soul of being an executive just as it also lies at the heart of Executive Coaching. Executives are challenged in many ways and for many things: for unlocking opportunities, seeing the possible, and making real the potential.

If you think that stepping up to any executive role is a walk in the park, a position of ease, a place beyond challenges—think again. Everyone in an executive role is challenged to be highly productive, to make the business profitable, to get the organization aligned to a singular vision, to resolve conflicts, to groom the next generation leaders, to deal with changes in the marketplace, to deal with all of the politics in the organization, to develop an effective culture, to avoid being derailed, to create and lead great teams, to handle feedback, and to do all of that while maintaining a healthy work–life balance. Talk about a whole series of challenges!

No wonder Executive Coaching centers in enabling, empowering, and equipping executives to handle all of these, and many more, challenges. As an Executive Coach, these are among the key pressures that executives face and which Executive Coaching inherently addresses. There are challenges around teams and partnerships, about sponsoring people, looking for high potentials, getting critical talent into the organization, addressing under-performance and lack of engagement, and much, much more.

Blakely and Day, (2012) in *Challenging Coaching* speaking about the importance of challenge and change in an organization write this:

> "Its [challenge] absence in a business environment leads to complacency, indulgence, apathy, and disinterest. When the stakes are high, a lack of challenge causes people to 'play small' in an environment that is forever demanding that they step up." (p. 18)

If challenge lies at the essence of Executive Coaching, then here is a set of challenging questions for you:

- How are you at challenging?
- How are you at challenging men and women at the highest levels of an organization, who may not have anyone in the organization to challenge them?
- Do you have both the courage to do so as well as the skills to carry it off effectively?
- What beliefs, understandings, or decisions do you need so that you can be completely comfortable with challenging?
- What skills do you need to develop or refine to become highly competent in challenging in the right way?
- Can you challenge compassionately? Can you do it while nurturing, caring, and making the conversation safe?

What is a Challenge?

The simplest challenge that you can present as a coach will be your *testing questions*. In testing questions, your yes/no question tests the person in order get a decision or commitment from your client.

> "Are you sure?" "That's really the most important thing for this session?" "You can do that?" "Definitely?"

The next level of challenge brings up critical facets of life and again gets a commitment from the client. Within these challenges is the ability to hold a person accountable.

> "So you are now at the place where balancing work/life is no longer optional for you?" [That's right.] "And you are ready to do whatever it takes to create that balance?" [Yes] "And you won't pull back or make some excuse if the work pressures at work get too strong?"

Coaching Challenge

If anything is central to the very essence of coaching itself—it is *challenge.* After all, challenge is one of the most fundamental aspects of coaching, if not the most important. Unlike therapy which is about healing, peace, homeostasis, and equilibrium, coaching is about the disequilibrium. You disturb the peace when you challenge a client to stretch forward and take on new challenges.

This contrast between two of the helping professions (coaching and psychotherapy) highlights a critical difference in the populations which accord to each profession. Those who need therapy come from a state of hurt, trauma, internal torment, defensively stuck, etc. They desperately need change and, just as desperately as they need change, they equally resist the changes that they need to make. What they lack is the inner security to face the very changes they so desperately need. Coaching clients live in a very different world. They do not *need* the changes they seek as much as they *want* them, desire them, and seek them. They are change-embracers, not change resisters.

As people living at a much higher level of "need," what they *need* is to actualize themselves, to be their very best self, and to give back. They need to contribute and make a difference in the world. So the reason for seeking after and *needing* knowledge, meaning, purpose, music, beauty, mathematics, etc. is to first express themselves and their gifts. Second, it is to offer that expression as a gift to others. That's why they want change. They look for it, plan for it, and embrace it as that which adds variety and excitement to life. Such change makes them come alive.

So unlike psychotherapists whose expertise lies in the fact that they have developed their skills to patiently listen to a traumatic story, to be present with that story of distress, to comfort, nurture, to communicate safety, etc., the coach's expertise lies in the opposite direction. The coach's expertise is that of challenging, stretching, pushing a client out of a comfort zone, disturbing the peace, and creating an optimal level of disequilibrium. The coach does that through challenge and, at times, even confrontation.

The point of all this is that *coaching is,* by its very nature, *challenging.* So if a person does not want to be challenged, then don't ask for coaching. Select coaching and you will be challenged. And if the coach is skilled—you will be profoundly challenged! You will be challenged about your beliefs, assumptions, understandings, skills, frames, decisions, identity, and so on. Challenge is what you sign up for when you sign up for coaching.

> "The basic difference between an ordinary man and a warrior is that a warrior takes everything as a challenge, while an ordinary man takes everything as a blessing or a curse."
> Carlos Casteneda

Now, if coaching is challenge, then why in the world would people intentionally and consciously choose coaching? From the perspective of therapy it seems strange. Actually, it is much worse than that—it sounds weird, unreasonable, and undesired! Yet from the perspective of Self-Actualization Psychology, the reason is simple:

> Challenge enables people, who are living mostly from the higher need of self-actualization, to actualize their highest and best potentials. Challenge awakens people to new possibilities.

They are safe and secure enough to now *want* to stir things up, create some discomfort, and recreate their world with a new direction and orientation. It takes a lot of security to *want* that and to be ready for that. Yet that's the case of psychologically healthy people who have learned to cope with their basic needs. After effectively coping with the survival, safety, social, and self needs comes the skill of mastering the higher needs by developing the ability to trust oneself in understanding and meeting the needs. It's been said that therapy makes a person comfortable to one's space whereas coaching opens doors so a person can move out into new spaces.

This is the nature of the drives that exist in the higher realm of self-actualization. Unlike the lower needs which are *driven by deficiency,* the higher needs are *driven by abundance.* The nature of these two realms are best seen in the personality and motivational pattern of each produce.

    1) Lower needs: The more, the less motivation pattern.

2) Higher needs: The more, the more motivation pattern.

In *the more, the less* pattern, the more that a person gratifies a particular lower need, the less drive that need creates. It creates less and less motivation. Then when gratification satisfies the need, it goes away. Need satisfaction reduces the intensity of the need. Maslow noted that it can even result in post-gratification forgetting, that is, one forgets afterwards how driving the need was before it was gratified.

Conversely, in *the more, the more* pattern, the more that you gratify a higher need, the more that need grows. And the more it drives you. As a result, your motivation

> Challenge is what you sign up for when you sign up for coaching.

grows. The more you learn, the more you are capable of learning and the more you want to learn. The more beauty you create, the more your capacity for creating beauty develops, and the more beauty you want to create. The more music you can create, the more music you want to create and the more you are capable of creating. This is true for all of the *being-values* of self-actualization: justice, equality, order, contribution, meaning-making, etc. This "the more, the more" pattern describes all of the higher drives. This explains why self-actualizing people want, hunger for, and get excited when they are challenged.

The Challenge of Executive Coaching
Given that coaching is challenging, you can anticipate that challenge is precisely what lies at the heart of Executive Coaching. No wonder a person in an executive role must be ready for challenge and have sufficient ego-strength to face the challenges of the coaching. This calls in question the so-called "coaching" that is actually a form of psychotherapy but which is being promoted as "coaching." In many places, what is called coaching is not actually coaching, it is therapy in the guise of coaching.[1]

This is true for many people who come into coaching from the field of Mental Health who are highly skilled as therapists. Yet they have not been prepared by rigorous training for challenging clients. That's outside of their professional development. So when they attempt to step into the coaching role, they are just too nice, too caring, and too much like a doting parent. That's why it's important to check a coach out, how the coach views coaching, and the coaching skills that the coach brings to his or her work. "Will you challenge me? What's your style of challenging?" True coaching is inherently challenging.

Challenge is the heart and soul of Executive Coaching because executives live in a world of constant and unending challenge. Therefore they ask for coaching to be empowered to handle the challenges. This is also true because coaching itself is a profession of challenge. That's why coaching as a discipline differs from therapy and why all of the leading theorists in the field of coaching separate coaching from therapy.

Checking for Ego-Strength

If you are going to challenge someone, make sure that the person can handle the challenge. The ability to do so is what we mean by the term "ego-strength." *Ego-strength* is the strength of your mind-body-emotion to *face* whatever *is,* for what it *is,* without caving in and without experiencing a stress fight/flight response. It is the ability to cope with, and then master, the challenges in your life. Ego-strength paradoxically grows out of a solid sense of self, self-esteem, self-worth and dignity, and confidence in your skills. It takes a lot of self-development to have robust ego-strength.

Developmentally, all of us were born without any ego (sene of self, "I," or "me") and so without any ego-strength in handling life's challenges. Yet with the development of the self, the development of a solid sense of self, ego-strength develops as we move through the world —learning, developing resources, becoming more skilled in coping with our needs and the demands of the outside world. Ego-strength develops as we learn to effectively cope with self, relationships, and work.[2]

If you plan to be an Executive Coach, you will want to plan to develop your skills of challenging. You'll need them. Without them, you'll find yourself unable to effectively cope in this context. So *how are your challenging skills*?

- How are you with stirring things up, bringing up things that could very well disturb, upset, and evoke strong emotions?
- How are your skills in being able to create the "space" where you and your client can enter into a conflictual and/or challenging subject and sit with it without the need to flee, defend oneself against it, etc.?
- Are you able to challenge with compassion? Are you able to challenge with a respectful voice and a gracious style?

When it comes to the art of challenging, *the key is challenging when you are in a compassionate state.* It is challenging when you have full control over your voice, tone, tempo, etc. The problem is that most of us wrack up the courage to challenge only when we are in a state that doesn't support this. It is common that we don't challenge until we are angry, disgusted, or fed up, etc. But, of course, when we challenge while in one of those states, the way the challenge comes across creates another problem. The person then focuses on how we are challenging, rather than the challenge itself.

Those in executive roles face a great many challenges. In the next chapters we will be covering the following executive challenges: emotional well-being, change, direction, work—life balance, politics within the organization, leadership, culture, derailment, feedback. These challenges are the key areas of Executive Coaching. These are the challenges that bring most executives to coaching. Within them also are processes that will enable you to challenge with respect and grace.

"But Do I Have to Challenge?"
Asking about your skills of challenge inevitably evokes your beliefs and understandings about challenge.
- Do you like challenge? Do you like challenging?
- What do you believe about challenge?
- What are the values and benefits of providing challenges to people.
- What are your personal challenges to challenging?

If you don't have lots of exciting answers to these questions, then take some time to create a list of values about challenge. Use these questions to explore the higher levels of your mind about challenge. Then you can set frames that will enable you to develop a true inner joy in challenging. As you do, note any place of limitation so that you can begin to expand that area for yourself. What many coaches discover is that there are fears that they may hurt someone's feelings or that they will be disliked or rejected.

***Caveat:* What if the Executive Doesn't Want Challenge?**
Let's look at the other side of this equation. Namely, some executives simply are not interested in challenge. They have enough challenge without asking for more. They are more interested in survival or maintaining the status quo. Graham says that this is where ruthless compassion empowers a coach. While we need to respect the client's world-view, at the same time we need to be able to create the container (a crucible space)[3] that makes it

safe to explore how much challenge a person can or wants to experience. At that point you can then help them navigate their options. Challenge and compassion go hand-in-hand in giving the Executive Coach the skill of dealing with this ambiguity in the service of the executive.

Another aspect of the ambiguity here lies in the interests of the employer, who often pays for the coaching. While the coach is not responsible for the outcomes (the client is), the coach is responsible for effectively facilitating the outcome. Sometimes the outcome is initially planned by the executive or employer so the client may not have chosen the particular outcome that he or she is being told to deal with. Sometimes the objective may change one or more times in the duration of the program. In these cases, talk about it. "What's your attitude now about the reason and prescribed objective of the coaching?" How the Executive Coach handles this will critically affect the success of the coaching for both the executive and the company.

Your Executive Coaching Take Aways

If you take anything away from this chapter, be sure to take away the importance of challenge. It is what you do as an Executive Coach; it is what Executive Coaching is about, it is what an executive needs from coaching. Be sure also to check out your own understandings and beliefs about challenge so you can make whatever adjustments that you need in order to develop your Executive Coaching skills of challenging.

You may also want to explore ways of informing people about your style of challenging. This will prepare you to be able to articulate how you will frame challenge as one of the values you provide as a coach and one of the characteristics of high quality coaching.

- What are your best beliefs about challenge that put you in a state of curiosity, excitement, and joy?
- Do you have any beliefs, memories, understandings, etc. about challenge that limit you or evoke an unresourceful state? List these so that you can then be coached to address them.

End of Chapter Notes

1. See Appendix A for more about this.
2. You can strengthen your own or someone else's ego-strength. In Neuro-Semantics we have a pattern "Strengthening Ego-Strength." It is in the *Coaching Mastery* training manual and is presented in the third module of Meta-Coaching.
3. See the book, *The Crucible and the Fires of Change* (2010).

Chapter 6

THE CHALLENGE OF

EXECUTIVE WELL-BEING

"There is plenty of evidence to show that there is a strong correlation between emotional intelligence in the leaders, executives, and managers within a company, and the delivery of superior business results."
Peter Stephenson, *Executive Coaching*

"When they get upset, there is nothing wrong,
they are ready for breakthrough, if you stay out of their way."
Graham Richardson

Is life in the C-suite compatible with emotional well-being? Can a person, male or female, succeed as an executive *and* stay alive to relationships, emotions, passion, learning, caring, and all of the other so-called "soft" facets of life? Or do the demands and stresses on executives inevitably undermine and threaten one's emotional well-being? How can an executive deal with all of the stresses, demands for results, conflicts, etc. and keep a healthy balance between work and life, work and play, and stay emotionally alive and vibrant?

With these questions, this chapter addresses what is perhaps the most important and the driving question of Executive Coaching—*the question of one's mental and emotional health as an executive.* In fact, historically the most often asked question that launched Executive Coaching in the first place was this question about the executive's work–life balance.

> "Can I have a life, a real life with my family and friends, and succeed in an executive role?"
>
> "Can I do this job and maintain a healthy lifestyle and mindset?"

Emotional Well-Being

As we explore this challenge, let's begin by asking, "What is emotional well-being? What do we mean by emotional well-being?" Our working definition is that emotional well-being is being emotionally healthy, well, whole, vibrant, energetic, and intelligent. Therefore this means experiencing the following:

- An optimal balance between work and the rest of life.
- A continuing and rejuvenating passion about work and life.
- Healthy relationships with people at work: caring, compassionate, empathetic, encouraging, etc.
- Healthy relationships with people at home: love, compassionate, empathetic, encouraging, etc.
- A solid sense of self that's not dependent upon work, success, results, etc.
- A sense of interest, passion, and fascination outside of work.

A healthy and whole leadership in an organization requires individuals who are themselves healthy and whole. This is the ideal. Yet the demands and challenges of anyone in an executive role puts stress on one's individual health and family life. It comes with the job— long hours, big decisions, conflicts, political positions and interests, ongoing meetings, last minute decisions, constant calls, emails, and text messages, etc.

As an Executive Coach, start with the person. "Is the person psychologically healthy? Is the person healthy and whole mentally, emotionally, behaviorally, linguistically, and relationally?" If not, begin the coaching here. The exception to this is when the lack of health is a matter of trauma and a function of personality distorting. In that case, the executive needs therapy, not coaching. Start here by making this the subject of your initial inquiry. This will establish the premise that being psychologically healthy and whole is the foundation of taking on the challenges of an executive's life. After all, coaching itself is holistic in that it deals with the whole person. So, "How is the person coping with the basic needs of life?"

A great tool that will help you with this is the Self-Actualization Assessment Scale.[1] It is now online and you can use it with executives to determine if they are "getting by" or are living in the red zone (deficiency in need satisfaction) or in the green zone (thriving).

At the essence of psychological health is the person's ability to *create rich and robust meaning.* This applies to creating meanings for work, others, and for one's self. Regarding creating meaning, there are numerous levels of meaning-making, yet the most important skill is the flexibility to recognize the meanings already created and the ability to suspend what does not help and invent meanings that do.[2]

- Is she or he living meaningfully?
- What is the person's vision and mission in life?
- What really matters in life?
- How is the person's sense of self?
- Is his or her value a *being*-value so that the person's worth is non-contingent. As long as a person has an ego-invested sense of self his or her worth is contingent on his or her success.

Living a life full of meaning so that it is richly meaningful is what we often refer to by the term "spiritual." A person's life is *spiritual* to the extent that *one's life is about fulfilling significant meanings* and not just about money and fame. It is spiritual if you live by virtues and values, and not merely if it only serves your purposes without consideration of others. It is spiritual if your life is being inspired by values, goals, and meaning above and beyond you. Then you are living for something bigger than yourself.

A special facet of meaningfulness which supports an inspirational or spiritual life is making the distinction between who you *are* and what you *do*. Then you can consider what you do as distinct from your being. Separating your being and doing enables you to own and glory in being a human being above and beyond your achievements and activities.

- Are you in a healthy connection with yourself?
- Does your *being* lead to and determine your *doing*?

All of this affects the personal challenge of being real. Are you for real? If you lack authenticity, it will be hard, if not impossible, for people to believe you, trust you, or want to follow you. In the place of authenticity, many leaders attempt to use the PR of their states, position, money, etc., yet that can just as easily create a sense of arrogance and actually undermine trust.

A meaningful life is the foundation of an authentic life. It is a life in which you are true to yourself and to your highest values. It is a life in which you live those values (e.g., integrity).

Emotional Intelligence

While it is common to consider those in the executive roles as those people who are typically of high IQ, the same confidence does not hold for EQ. The truth is that, as Daniel Goleman noted in his books, leadership is, by definition, emotional as it involves being involved and emotionally engaged with people. It is resonant

> Separating your being and doing enables you to own and glory in being a human being above and beyond your achievements and activities.

leadership; it is primal leadership. Goleman also indicated that *leadership is resonant leadership* inasmuch as it involves a healthy emotional connection and engagement with the people and so the leader's influence in leading and connecting at an emotional level.[3]

At the practical, everyday level, this means caring about people, understanding them, and communicating empathy to them. About all of this, Dotlich (1997) notes that emotional intelligence is actually more important for creativity than high intelligence. People who are merely intelligent, and not necessarily empathic or creative, often do not have the ability to build on other's ideas. They are unable to synergize with others or their empathy is limited only to certain individuals. Typically this means it is only limited to those of the same background or education level. All of this inhibits creativity.

A Passionate about Work and Life

In terms of meaning, inspiration, and authenticity Alan Downs in *The Fearless Leader* (2000) and in *Secrets of an Executive Coach* (2002) argues that *passion* is the key to true success in life. Listing such great executives of our time such as Jack Welch (General Electric), Bill Gates (Microsoft), Warren Buffet (Berkshire Hathaway), Richard Branson (Virgin Atlantic), and Lew Platt (Hewlett-Packard) he writes:

> "What each of these outrageously successful executives share is that they exploit their talent and are *deeply in love with what they do.*

When their talents were not valuable to an organization, they didn't try to change their talents, they changed the situation so that their talents were fully utilized." (Italics added)

He then asks an incredibly important question about one aspect that often challenges execution:

"Why don't passionate people get burned out? They are doing what they love. Their love of their work sustains them. When it feels like your work is dominating your life, all you want to do is to escape." (2000, p. 4, 125)

"Being a successful executive is more than being brilliant, savvy, tenacious, and forceful. Truly successful executives are *passionate* about their work. They *feel* strongly about what they do, and their inspiration is contagious. They are energized by their work. Unless an executive's inner flame or inspiration and passion is lit, he will never reach his potential." (2002, p. 4)

According to Alan Downs, this is the cornerstone of Executive Coaching. He argues that the successful executive is both "emotionally and mentally fully engaged in his work." Given that, as an Executive Coach, your challenge will be to focus on *facilitating executives to rediscover their emotional engagement in the work they do.* Your commission will be, that as a coach, to become a detective of the corporate life, to peel away all its facades and games to help executives find the delicate balance of fulfilling their own inner desires while succeeding on the job.

This reminds me of the famous quotation by George Bernard Shaw about passion.

"I want to be thoroughly used up when I die, for the harder I work the more I live. I rejoice in life for its own sake. Life is no 'brief candle' for me. It is a sort of splendid torch which I have got hold of for the moment, and I want to make it burn as brightly as possible before handling it on to future generations."

If passion is this important for executives, then maintaining and developing the torch of their inspiration will be at the center of your Executive Coaching. In this, it has long been known that an executive who is inspired will outperform an executive who isn't and will do so every time. So executive well-being begins with being emotionally engaged with work and people.

> "When an executive is in trouble, it is almost always has something to do with how he feels about his job and/or his life. You will help him clarify those feelings and create a plan whereby he can begin to feel better about what he is doing. Your end goal is to have an executive who feels inspired and motivated." (23)

> "To understand this crisis, we must understand the essence of passion and its centrality in a fulfilled life. Passion is an idiosyncratic experience of what really excites you and turns you on. What's more, passion is organizing and flowing, changing with the seasons of your life. Passion is a journey, a life stream, and a consist discovery." (177)

Are you emotionally engaged with your people? How much? How much passion do you feel? The crisis of passion is typically one of the most painful experiences in an executive's lifetime and destructive. Why is this crisis so destructive? It's because of the loss of meaning. Now nothing that the executive has worked for means very much to him or her. With this loss of vision—there is a loss of inspiration and passion. It is as if one has "sold his soul" and abandoned the vision which generated the original passion.

It is interesting that the word "passion" is related to and sounds like the word passive— something you wait and receive for and something done to you. Yet passion is not passive. Passion is what you choose, develop, and cultivate. That's why the more you give yourself to your passion to experience it, the more you follow your passion, the more of it you will have available.[4]

Passion in Two Dimensions
In a recent blog on passion, Graham described two kinds of passions and challenged the myth that passion has to be the *hot* kind.

> "There are two kinds of passion—the attractor and the repeller. It is noticeable that passion can appear as hot, overpowering, and dangerous and when it is like that—many people tend to avoid it. It can also appear as inspirational, engaging, and infectious so that people want to participate in it and promote it. Some people are negatively impacted when they feel they are being put under pressure to be passionate. Or they may have seen the repeller at work and so framed it that they do not want to emulate this. In these cases, the coach needs to find a reframe that helps the executive to disconnect these external registers and to create a very personal and positive meaning around contribution to others and themselves.

Susan Cane, in her book *Quiet,* explores this empathizing with the more introverted who, by the way, represent the more successful executives historically, unlike Jack Welch, Branson, et. al. who are loud and somewhat egotistical. These folk are often not notorious because they do not seek the limelight and, in fact, actively avoid the limelight, (e.g., Martin Luther King, Jr., Gandhi, Mother Teresa). These individuals were introverted, and not necessarily seen as passionate, yet they were. They had a deeper and more profound passion. This corresponds with Jim Collins' *Good to Great* Level 5 Leaders—a combination of "fierce professional will balanced with humility."

Optimally Balancing Work and Life

Well-being for anyone, including executives, includes a healthy balance in life about what you do, who you relate to, what you do for fun, the contribution you make, the children you raise, etc. It means balancing the pressures with your ability to *have a life.* It means balancing the *doing* and *being* facets of life.

The way most people look at things, there's a gigantic gulf between working and play. Work is what you do during the week, then comes the weekend when, hopefully, you can get to play, or relax, or have some fun. They perceive work as something you *have* to do and contrast that to play which is what you *get* to do and *choose* to do. This dichotomous thinking creates an unnecessary and unhelpful difference. None other than Confucius said:

"Choose work you love and you will never have to work a day in your life."

That corresponds to my personal sense of things. In *Inside-Out Wealth* (2010) I address this dichotomy and tell the story of being in Moscow one time when I was presenting that training when someone there asked me about how much time I work every day to create my own success. I commented that I have not "worked" a day in my life for over twenty years. "Work?" No. I have just been doing what I love doing. My sense is, "I can't believe that I get paid for doing this!" Similarly, in the book *Everyone's A Coach* (1995), Don Shula wrote,

"I think it's fabulous that I get paid for doing what I love to do." (p. 68)

In writing that Don Shula then quoted Joe Greene, Defensive Line Coach for the Dolphins:

"I think it's fabulous that I get paid for doing what I love. To me the enjoyment of coaching is not a perk; it's an essential ingredient of winning."

Finally, to add to all of these voices that have integrated work and play, it was author James Michener who wrote:
> "The master in the art of living makes little distinction between his work and his play, his labor and his leisure, his mind and his body, his information and his recreation, his love and his religion. He hardly knows which is which. He simply pursues his vision of excellence at whatever he does, leaving others to decide whether he is working or playing. To him he's always doing both."

Executive Emotional Intelligence
What comprises emotional intelligence in a person or in an executive? Using Daniel Goleman's formulation who argued that executive leadership is made or broken by a person's ability to handle their own emotions as well as the emotions of their colleagues and followers, there are four components:[5]

- *1) Emotional awareness.* Emotional intelligence begins with your knowledge and understanding of your emotions. It is to know and to be aware of the state that are you in.
- *2) Emotional monitoring.* This refers to the ability to observe and monitor your emotions and to be able to motivate yourself.
- *3) Emotional management.* This refers to your ability to control and regulate your emotions.
- *4) Emotional connection or relationship.* This refers to using your emotions to connect: experiencing empathy for others, connecting, communicating effectively, and resolving conflicts.

Executive Emotional Awareness
Every leader has to ultimately lead emotions—the emotions of those following and every person who does that has to use his or her own emotions in leading. For Goleman, when you are able to make the emotions fit, match, and touch people, you become a *resonant* leader. Your emotions then resonate with others. When you don't connect with the emotions of people, you are a *dissonant* leader.

Obviously, as an executive leader, if you cannot manage your emotions very well or if you have little or no awareness of your emotions, you undermine your leadership. Effective leadership builds up a foundation of self-awareness because it plays a crucial role in being able to convey empathy to others and that enables you to direct the emotional tone of a group or organization.

Because executive leadership is supposed to bring out the best in others, a leader needs E.Q. in order to facilitate *emotional aliveness and vitality* in the vision and mission of the company. This enables people to be more open to dream and to hope. Being emotionally alive lets one be transparent to self and to others, and to use one's authentic openness to others. When an executive is emotionally closed, he or she will waste energy in defense maneuvers and cut off creativity.

Executive Emotional Monitoring

If an executive leader wants to actualize the creative potentials in followers, then the executive has to spend time listening, seeking to understand, validating, being patient, persistent, empathetic, etc. Ah, yes, these are the so-called *soft* skills. Then, when people feel that their ideas, beliefs, joys, struggles, aims, and aspirations are understood, they are much more likely to follow.

All of this will test a person. It will test one's patience, persistence, resilience, etc. This explains why the soft skills are really not soft; they are *tough*— challenging and robust. That's why Executive Coaching often addresses these aspects of leadership enabling the executive to develop this aspect of emotional intelligence. One litmus test you can use for this involves asking such questions as: Do people feel understood? What are the emotions and needs of people in this company? What are their perspectives, understandings, beliefs, and frames?

Graham described an executive that he worked with who was telling himself a story about his perception of other people's incompetence. He would then experience negative emotions from that story (i.e., anger, disdain, frustration) and that would lead him to react in a dysfunctional way by attacking the persons. In the coaching, I invited him to change the story to one of compassion by telling himself that they were doing their best and needed to be understood. He did and his states changed to those of curiosity, listening, and supporting. The effect this had was that his people became less fearful of his reactions, they felt understood, and he realized that perhaps they weren't so incompetent after all. It dawned on him that they were frozen into states of confusion by his own behavior. He texted me, "I used the story – emotion – behavior technique in a conflict situation with a peer ... and, what do you know? It worked!" This was a great example of an executive managing his emotional intelligence for his state of mind and changed his behavior. The positive outcome that resulted surprised him.

Executive Emotional Management

Goleman writes, "Ultimately the most meaningful act of responsibility that leaders can do is to control their own state of mind." (p. 47). So at the heart of coaching emotional management are the following:

- *Accepting emotions as felt meanings and exploring them.* Emotions are simply the difference between map and territory—what you think, expect, believe, and what you experience in the real world.
- *Take care of your body since your emotions are functions of your body as well as your mind.* How well are you taking care of yourself? How is your sleeping, eating, exercising, health, illness, etc.?
- *Listen to your emotions as information signals.* Emotions involve motion as indicated by the word's original and construction [e(x)-motion]. That is, emotions are designed to *move* you. Not only do they make you feel more alive, they move you to take action if you choose to act on them.
- *Quality control your emotions to check that they serve the ecology of your life situation.* Merely feeling an emotion does not mean or demand that you act on them. We have many ways to distort and even pervert our emotions so they need to be checked out before acted on.
- *Learn how to qualify your emotions by meta-stating them with higher level qualities.* Because we can create and experience a feeling about a feeling such as joyful learning or fearful anger, when you bring an emotional state to an emotional state, you texture the first state by the second. In coaching, Executive Coaches use this process (of meta-stating) to create highly refined and qualified emotional states.[6]

Executive Emotional Connection

Your empathy and integrity invites trust. Before people will be willing to follow an executive's vision or act on the company's initiatives, they must trust the leader. Yet trust is a quality that cannot be demanded; it must be earned. How is it earned? The executive earns it by *being trust-worthy*—worthy of trust because the executive does what he or she says.

"All relationships are built on trust; if you don't have trust, you don't have much of a relationship." (Goleman, 2002, p. 162)

To bring out the best in others requires a high degree of empathy. *Empathy* is the *sine qua non* of all social effectiveness in life. Empathetic people are superb at recognizing and meeting the needs of clients, customers, and subordinates. They seem approachable because they actually want to hear what people have to say. They care. They listen carefully, picking up on what people are truly concerned about, and they respond.

Your Executive Coaching Take Aways

If the health of a company, group, or organization is related to the health and well-being of the executive leaders who are leading, then one role for Executive Coaching is facilitating the health and well-being of the leaders. This includes mental and emotional well-being, balance in life, the ability to relax, enjoy oneself, connect to others, live with passion, and have a life apart from work.

•	How prepared are you to coach for personal well-being? What about emotional well-being, personal vitality, passion, etc. do you need to learn more about?

•	Given that personal well-being is a function of the meaningfulness of life, what processes do you use to explore this aspect?

•	How do you sell the importance of life/work balance to executives?

End of Chapter Notes

1. You can see and use the Self-Actualization Assessment Scale by going to the Neuro-Semantic website and clicking: http://www.neurosemantics.com/assessment-scale-form. To learn how to use this scale, write and ask for the "Self-Actualization Scale."

2. Meaning-making is the subject of the third book in the Meta-Coaching series, *Unleashed!* (2007). It is also the theme of *Winning the Inner Game* (2007) and of the book, *Neuro-Semantics* (2012).

3. Daniel Goleman (2002) *Primal Leadership: Realizing the Power of Emotional Intelligence.* (1995) *Emotional Intelligence.*

4. See *Inside-Out Wealth* (2010) for a process for creating, developing, and expanding a new passion for something.

5. NLP has from 1975 been about E.Q. although it has seldom been presented about this. Yet Denis Bridoux has authored a basic NLP book under the title, *Step Sevens to Emotional Intelligence.*

6. About meta-stating, see *Meta-Stating* (2007), *Secrets of Personal Mastery* (1997), or even *Winning the Inner Game* (2007). The process of meta-stating is that of bringing one mind-body-emotion state and applying it to the other. If you bring joy to learning, you can then create a more rich and complex state—joyful learning.

Chapter 7

THE CHALLENGE OF

VISION

"Go confidently in the direction of your dreams,
live the life you've imagined."
Henry David Thoreau

"Ours is a world where people don't know what they want
and are willing to go through hell to get it."
Don Marquis

As an Executive Coach, you know the importance and the power of vision. A person with a vision is a powerful person precisely because he or she lives life on purpose. Such a person is intentional. Similar to Australia's Crocodile Hunter, Steven Erwin. who passionately explained why he loved working with animals.

"This is my purpose!" he said in his uniquely passionate way raising his voice and gesturing with his hands. "This is my job, my mission — the reason I was put on this planet was to save wildlife!"

It is this power of intentionality that enlivens an executive so that he is not just "a suit," but a man or a woman with "fire in the belly." If passion then is one of the central aspects of personal success and of corporate success (chapter 6 an aspect of well-being and emotional intelligence), then in

Executive Coaching you will frequently focus on coaching executive leaders about their vision for the organization or business that they are leading. This should be no surprise since, after all, vision and direction lie at the very heart of visionary leadership.

> "Your time is limited, so don't waste it living someone else's life. Don't be trapped by dogma -- which is living with the results of other people's thinking. Don't let the noise of others' opinions drown out your own inner voice. And most important, have the courage to follow your heart and intuition."
> Steve Jobs

Nor is this a single concern that you can deal with and then move on. Vision is an ongoing concern. That's because vision, like everything else a leader does, is also subject to change. After all, markets change, industries go into decline, new industries arise, new opportunities arise, and with all of these changes, a company's vision or a leader's vision may also have to be adjusted and redirected. All of this requires that constant attention if we are to keep vision fresh and vital.

Now while this is true, the context of Executive Coaching is not always that drastic. Sometimes a vision does not need to be re-designed or transformed, sometimes it simply needs to be renewed or rejuvenated. As we can get used to anything, we can also get used to a vision so that it loses its punch for us. We can forget how it once moved us passionately. Or the language by which we express a vision can become so familiar and habituated, that it no longer creates excitement or vitality within an organization.

There's another dulling factor. An executive can get caught up in the everyday activities and demands of the business, that he or she can lose track of the vision. This typically happens when urgent things, and lots of them, shout so loudly about the everyday details of running a company that the vision seems to become a whisper. Or it can be viewed as a luxury that one doesn't have time to indulge in. It can eventually become a faint whisper that one can hardly even hear. That's when the urgent trumps the important. Then in the midst of all of the activities a person can forget his or her *why*. Those leading can lose the motivating meaningfulness of a vision that once thrilled them to such an extent and it got them out of bed every morning with a sense of vitality. Frequently, this is what Executive Coaching focuses on— renewing and refreshing the vision and restoring a sense of excitement.

What are the challenges of vision for those in executive roles?
  1) Finding Your Vision
  2) Keeping the Vision Alive
  3) Rediscovering the Vision when Lost
  4) Inventing a Vision
  5) Balancing the Vision
  6) Communicating the Vision
  7) Living the Vision

1) Finding the Vision

The vision questions are exceedingly easy to ask and profoundly difficult to answer. So after asking what seems like easy and obvious questions, as an Executive Coach you have to wait— patiently wait for the question to begin to refresh the vision:

• Where are you going? Why there? What is there that's so important?
• How are you leading there?
• Are you doing what you love?
• Are you following your passion?

As you coach the executive, focus on becoming a connoisseur of his or her profession so that you are constantly asking vision experiencing questions that will reactivate the vision or enable the construction of a new vision.

• What is your real love?
• What frees you to feel most alive?
• What lifts up your spirits and gives you a peak-experience sense?

Actually, everyone and every organization has a vision. Often, however, it is not at a conscious level and it may even be at odds with the espoused vision. When this is so, most people feel it as a cultural disconnect. In getting alignment to the vision across the entire organization—people need direction from leadership. They do not need directive or authoritarian leadership, but they need authoritative leadership for vision and purpose. Connecting the vision to the delivery of results so it is not just "blue sky" hoping and wishing. It can be measured, communicated, and celebrated.

2) Keeping the Vision Alive

Ludwig Wittgenstein wrote:
  "If we take eternity to mean not infinite duration, but timelessness, then eternal life belongs to those who live in the present."

The work of refreshing the vision for any of us is the work of identifying the meanings and enriching those meanings until we reach a point of meaningfulness. This often describes the very heart of what you as an Executive Coach will do with a client. Alan Downs, in *The Fearless Executive* (2000) asks a question that I think flushes out the difficulty with this. "Why don't passionate people get burned out?" He answers, "They are doing what they love."

Love is the answer. It is their love of their work and their excitement about their vision that sustains them. They are passionate about something that they find especially meaningful and, for this reason, they do not burn out, not even when they put in long hours of hard work. Without love and passion, when work alone dominates one's life, then eventually all a person will want to do is to escape.

For the person who has an exciting vision, *the journey itself is the reward.* What others would consider "work," or long hours, is for the self-actualizing executive the fun of doing what one loves. It is just play. It is an expression of one's passion. Then passion will keep one working day after day, pushing through failure and hardship—all in service of a grand idea. This is *being*-motivation and is driven by the *being*-needs and values.

What if an executive doesn't have a passion? Then find one or create one. If a person doesn't have a passion for the work, he or she would be better off doing something else. That's because passion is the source of your executive creativity. Following passion requires that one act to make the vision real.

3) Rediscovering the Vision when Lost

Executive Coaching works to the extent that the coaching conversation enables the executive to re-experience the vision, values, and the meaningfulness which originally excited him or her. Such a vision will arise first from the coaching dialogue. For the executive, it will be discovered in the dialogue. But there must be more. There must be the transference from mind-to-body so that the person *feels* the rich meaningfulness of the vision and acts on it.

In Meta-Coaching one of the ways we do this is by facilitating the Mind-to-Muscle pattern. This pattern describes the natural neurological process whereby we take something that we have in mind as an understanding, a concept, or a principle, something that we *intellectually know is true* and transfer it into our neurology so that we *feel it as true.* We do this transference linguistically or more accurately, neuro-linguistically.[1]

What we have discovered is that to say something in different formats (as an understanding, belief, decision, etc.) requires different degrees of physical and neurological involvement. Saying, "I *know* that X is true" engages less of your neurology than saying, "I *believe* X is true," or "X is true for me." Doing so expresses the difference between a concept or principle and a belief. Then saying, "I *will* from this day forward do Z because I believe X" engages even more neurology. Try it and notice what happens within you. Take a simple statement that you know in your mind which you don't feel in your body.

"I know that regular exercise increases energy and vitality."
"I know that spending time inspiring people with the vision wins minds and hearts."

We call this pattern *The Mind-to-Muscle Pattern* and use it to commission the body to feel our ideas. While there are more patterns that accomplish this conceptual-to-embodiment transference, all such patterns involve this Mind-to-Muscle process. In Meta-Coaching we use this process to activate and mobilize one's physical resources.

Responsibly embrace your vision. Typically, people lose their vision by being overwhelmed by circumstances. Then they draw a disabling conclusion, "I'm not in control of my vision." The sabotaging element within this, which Executive Coaches are alert to, is failing to take full responsibility for oneself. Alan Downs says, "Never allow your client to become a victim." At each and every point when a client begins to talk or act as if a victim of circumstances, your role as the coach is to hold the executive accountable to his or her responsibilities. Do that by evoking fresh courage so the person will step up to the challenge or crisis and take effective action.

When does a person's vision need to be rediscovered? Whenever a person's vision has become blunted, bland, or has lost its fire. That's when it needs to be rediscovered and refreshed.

4) Inventing a Vision

If you don't know and don't seem to be able to *find* your passion, then *create* it. What would you like to become passionate about? What talents, skills, interests, likes, etc. would you like to develop a passion for? If you don't know where to start, begin with your abilities, interests, and opportunities. What activities could you fall in love with or become absorbed in? What happens if you think about your work as "an expression of your love?"[2]

Once you have an area, identify the skills that you will need to develop. Do you know anyone who is successful in this area? If so, then identify some skillful people in this area and interview them. Then decide on how much time you are willing to devote to learning this area and developing the required skills.

Inventing a new passion requires rich meanings. So identify the beliefs, understandings, meanings, and decisions that will create more interest and passion for you. Are you willing to put in the time and effort to becoming interested and then passionate? What high intention would support you in this? What level of commitment are you willing to invest and what beliefs would support your commitment?

5) Balancing the Vision

Sometimes the problem with vision is not that it is too small or too dull, the problem is that it is too big. It surges forth like a tsunami. When this happens a person can become so blinded by a vision that one loses track of the other values in life. When this occurs, an executive can lose perspective and will need to balance the vision so that it fits into life more ecologically. Otherwise, a vision too dominating and too all-consuming can lead one to ruin health, relationships, finances, etc. Then it is not ecological.

Not only can this happen, it is actually not all that uncommon. When a vision becomes one's love, and one does not burn-out by it, the opposite happens. One becomes more and more energized by it. Then a new challenge arises. The challenge is *how to manage the "fire in the belly"* so it doesn't consume one. This becomes the focus of Executive Coaching when an executive comes to realize that "apart from this, I have no life!" Sometimes it arises, not because of the executive's awareness, but because a spouse or child rudely brings it to the person's attention.

6) Communicating the Vision

The next challenge is figuring out how to express the vision in a way that others will catch the vision and feel its excitement. Leaders who can do this will go far; those who cannot have their days numbered. Nor is it an easy task to artfully and persuasively articulate a vision so that people find it exciting, compelling, and memorable.

* What is the vision like?
* How does the vision fulfill the higher *being*-values (the self-actualization needs).
* How will this vision change the world or at least our lives?

Some people have the opposite challenge. For them, communicating a vision that delights and thrills is sometimes difficult to articulate because it's hard to even imagine how anyone else can *not* see what they see or feel what they feel. For this executive, it seems and feels so real, so compelling, so obvious, that to try to communicate it seems superfluous and unnecessary. Yet it is necessary. What are the words, the metaphors, the stories, the language that will excite and incite?

7) Living the Vision

Executives need to be exemplars of what they are leading. That is obvious. As an exemplar leader, *living the vision* means demonstrating it in action—in one's very way of being in the world. For other executives, this is the challenge and problem. Instead of being caught up in the vision, an executive may be caught up in everything else—all of the urgent demands of meetings, and budgets, and decisions, and everything, but the vision. This, of course, is a major cause of both burn-out and dull-out.

Living the vision requires finding everyday procedures and rituals that manifest the vision. This may involve inventing a whole new set of processes for "how we do things around here."

This is when the vision becomes embedded in the culture so that it is "the way we do things around here." The most powerful visions are those which are not apparently the vision of the leader, but become the vision of the culture. When that happens, then everyone is touched, moved, and inspired by the vision and then it is their own and not the sole property of the leader.

Coaching to the Vision

Executive Coaching, like coaching itself, inescapably deals with vision and so coaching to vision is the bread and butter of what an Executive Coach does. In Meta-Coaching we use the Well-Formed Outcome format as our way to do this. The 18-questions of the pattern (which you'll discover and learn about in chapter 17 *The Outcome Conversation*) formats a vision or desired outcome in a structure that facilitates the actualizing process.

Similarly, the first axis in *The Axes of Change Model* and conversation is the motivation axis with the polar opposites of challenge ans awakening (you'll read about this in chapter 9, *The Challenge of Change*).[3] As a coach, you play the twin-roles of challenger and awakener and when you are awakening, you are coaching to the vision.

Your Executive Coaching Take Aways

Coaching inevitably is about vision and enabling clients to find or create a vision that will endow life with their rich meaning and vitality. Effective coaching requires the ability to elicit and develop the visions of clients.

- To what extent do you feel competently skilled to awaken a strong sense of vision in your executive clients?
- Are there any beliefs, understandings, or frames that hold you back from this?
- How do you best evoke an inspirational vision?

End of Chapter Notes

1. See Appendix B: *The Mind-to-Muscle Pattern.* Also the book *Achieving Peak Performance* (2005) focuses on the processes of implementation.

2. You can also use the SWOT analysis questions to create a new passion as you explore your Strengths, Weaknesses, Opportunities, and Threats.

3. *The Axes of Change Model* is fully described in Volume I of the Meta-Coaching series, *Coaching Change.*

Chapter 8

THE CHALLENGE OF

FEEDBACK

"I see everything a client offers me as a contribution,
even criticism is a contribution.
Everything adds value in some way."

"Beware of over-playing to your strengths.
That can get you out of balanced and create negative consequences."
Graham Richardson

If an executive is going to grow and develop, that executive will need feedback, and lots of it. The person in the executive position may not want it, may not use it, may not like it, and may not want you to give it— but nevertheless *they need it*! Our weaknesses require it, our blind spots require it, and our next-level skills require it. That's because what got an executive here may not that person any further. The best way for anyone to grow and develop, and especially someone in an executive position, is to get high quality feedback and put it to good use.

When it comes to coaching, it is not far from the truth to say, "Coaching is all about feedback." Feedback is not only important to the process, it is its core. It's important for what is unique about coaching because in the coaching relationship feedback is, to a great extent, what the client is "buying." This is especially so in Executive Coaching.

I say especially in Executive Coaching because in the context of senior managers and executives in organizations one of the occupational hazards built into many corporate cultures is that colleagues and others

> "The hallmark of a great organization is how quickly bad news travels upward."
> Jay Forrester

do *not* share information. In fact, they hold back bad news. Instead of sending bad news upward as quickly as possible, those in organizations tend to insulate those above them from the bad news. The result of this is the presence of the *"Yes man" culture* where the closest advisors of executives rubber stamps what they communicate so they hear what they want to hear, rather than the reality of the situation. In this way organizations are structured to be unable to speak and hear the truth. What's real has little chance of being brought into the light of day. The culture that develops from this is one highly fearful of being candid and forthright.

Many executives hire Executive Coaches precisely and exclusively for this purpose—to receive feedback from someone who will give them the truth of the situation and the truth regarding how they come across. Executive Coaches are hired so that executives can obtain clean, sensory-based feedback that's not biased by internal politics, friendships, vested interests, etc.

Why is this? What is so crucial about the need for feedback? Mostly, learning. Ideally, it would be best if all of us considered the events and experiences of life as not truly over until we have learned from them. So after an event, the ideal is to review it for the purpose of learning from it and adjusting ourselves.

> "What have I learned?" "What lessons will I take away from this experience that will make me a better leader next time?"

This is the heart of what we seek to accomplish in Executive Coaching. We coach to inspire executives in developing a fascination about what they can learn from their experiences: what did not work, why it did not work, to what degree it did not work, and what could I have done that would have made it work?

As an Executive Coach, there are numerous challenges in responding to feedback. What are the challenges of feedback for executives?

1) Giving actual "feedback" rather than judgment or advice.
2) Giving real-time feedback during the session.
3) Recognizing the levels of feedback
4) The courage to Give Feedback

1) Giving Actual Feedback

This is the first problem and it is a significant one. Many executives, so used to working with consultants and business experts, are used to, and want, advice and recommendations. For them, the idea of a coach calling forth resources and answers from out of them by facilitating their own discovery and learning is a new and strange experience. How many Executive Coaches have heard their clients impatiently demand, "Just tell me what you think! What's your expert advice?"

The problem with most of what goes under the term "feedback" is that it is not actually feedback at all. It is a form of judgment. What is called feedback is actually advice or opinion. A person introduces his or her evaluation and personal opinion calling it "feedback." This is also true when the person gives praise and compliments. These too are evaluations, not sensory-based feedback. The one factor that makes feedback so unique, special, and of high value is that it is sensory-based.

The other problem that most executives face relates to how to get truthful feedback. That's because the higher up one's position and status in an organization, the less likely that the executive is actually getting the truth. That's because with status and position comes power, the power to reward and the power to punish. No wonder people do not want to be the "bearer of bad news." They do not want to be a whistle-blower so they keep their mouths shut. If they are forced to give feedback, they tell the person what they suppose they want to hear or water down any "negative" information. Consequently one of the diseases that executives experience in their roles is that of the disease of being shut out from honest feedback. Additionally, they shut people out from giving feedback.

It was in the face of this kind of thing that the old fable of the Emperor's New Clothes arose. None of his politically shrewd advisers would dare tell him the truth. It took the innocent eye of an observer (a child) to blurt out the truth, "The Emperor has no clothes, he's naked!" Executive Coaches are frequently brought in to provide this kind of brave innocent eye communication.[1]

One of the best ways to groom a leader is to use on-the-job experiences to stretch the person and to give sensory-based feedback about the

> "In a time of drastic change, it is the learners who inherit the future. The learned find themselves equipped to live in a world that no longer exists."
> Eric Offer

experience. Yet giving feedback alone is not sufficient, the person needs time to reflect on it and learn from it and bring it up again. A person will probably also need to learn how to reflect and how to learn from feedback. There's an important reason for this. That's because if a person reacts in a defensive way, nothing will be learned. *Yet feedback is for learning.* It is to accelerate learning so that one can develop learning agility for being able to more quickly and efficiently adapt to a situation.

A complicating factor is that there may very well be some functional incompetence in an executive. A person may have been promoted beyond his or her competence and so actually not understand how the business works or the actual business model in the business or how to handle specific situations. In such cases, an executive may isolate himself from the operations, the information, the processes, and leave it to others to learn. Or she may delegate the activities to avoid facing her own incompetence or letting anyone else know about it. Or an executive may simply not be interested in learning how an enterprise executes its products and services. In that case, if the person does not have a good relationship to feedback— this becomes the focus of the coaching. When coached for receiving feedback, this may become a powerful leverage point for transformation.

Obviously, to more effectively receive and learn from feedback, most executives will need to develop their capacity for listening to people. Used to telling and directing, listening is often an under-developed competency in a great many executives and senior managers. It may be under-developed, yet it is critical for learning to understand the perspectives of others in the company.

Here are some skill development questions to consider in learning how to receive feedback:
- What do you think of feedback from others?
- How often, if ever, do you ask for feedback?
- If you became aware that you are always receiving feedback from

the system, simply by the responses or lack of responses you are
receiving, how do you describe the feedback you are receiving?
- What skills do you exercise when receiving feedback from others?
- How are you developing yourself for your current job?
- What skills are you learning and what skills are you planing to learn
for your future development?
- Where are your learning shortcomings?
- Are you working at the right level?
- Are your people working at the right level?

Distinctions of High Quality Feedback

High quality feedback has certain features. In Meta-Coaching we emphasis
that following as essential for this level of competency.

1) Rapport-based: Establish respectful rapport. High quality feedback
operates from rapport; it requires connecting with the person who will
receive it. At the center of rapport is matching a person's physiology,
gestures, energy, and then moving to match a client's beliefs, language,
understandings, values, etc.

2) Outcome Relevant: Identify the outcome of the feedback. High quality
feedback functions to give information relative to the client's outcome and
objective. This is what makes the feedback relevant.

*3) Tentative: Offer feedback tentatively while seeking the person's
validation or dis-validation.* Tentative means that we do not give it in an
absolute way, but with an awareness of our fallibility and the relativity of
situation and context and all of the other factors that may influence the
experience. After presenting feedback tentatively, ask the person about his
or her thoughts about it.

4) Timely: Make the feedback timely. The feedback needs to be given in a
timely manner, when the action or experience is fresh and, best of all, in
real-time during the coaching conversation.

*5) Person— Style Distinction: Elicit your client to separate feedback and
from the style of the feedback.* High quality feedback is offered in a way so
that a person has no confusion that his or her actions *are* personal. It's

about the behavior or the response. The person is more than, and different from, that response. A way to support this is by using neutral words, words that are not semantically loaded.

> "We must be the change we wish to see in the world.
> Gandhi

6) *Helpful and Supportive: Invite the client to reframe feedback as acceptable and valued.* Ask, "How is feedback valuable to you? How will you use it to improve your actions and responses?"

7) *Sensory Specific: Give sensory specific behavioral feedback.* High quality feedback is sensory-based, a person can see, hear, and sense what you are referring to without mind-reading or hallucinating. Sensory-based feedback differs from evaluative in that it is presented in empirical language. It is offered in language that can be seen, heard, and felt. It is this language that you can immediately represent on the inner screen of your mind. Words that cannot be representationally tracked are more abstract terms and therefore evaluations.

2) Giving real-time Feedback during a Session
The very best time for feedback is in real-time when you are with a client. When you are with your client and you are watching and observing, you can call attention to the moment-by-moment experiences that are occurring. You can also do this when working with a team or board.

Zoom in on patterns of both effectiveness and ineffectiveness in what you give feedback about. These patterns could be communication patterns, relational patterns, listening patterns, etc. And what if you miss something? Here is the wonderful thing about patterns—behaviors within a pattern will repeat. After all, they are patterns! If you miss a moment to reflect back a behavior, no worry, if it is a pattern, it will occur again. A pattern is a consistent response that a person or a group has learned and habituated so now it is automatic and regular.

As an Executive Coach, simply focus on being real and honest with your client, and when the pattern emerges again, note it and comment on it at that moment. That's the prime time for giving feedback and what will make the feedback so timely.

Typically, the life of modern executives is typically so busy, so packed with meetings and activities, and so packed with information overload that there is virtually no time for reflection. There's hardly any time available to examine what the organization is doing, has done, and is about to do. There's hardly any time for the coaching itself. There's little precious time to reflect on trends, values, criteria, etc. So when the person is late, when he or she cancels unexpectedly, when the executive leaves the session early, these are wonderful opportunities for giving feedback on the executive's handling of time. Call for a meta-moment to slow things down and bring to the person's attention [Meta-moments are described in chapter 20, *The Meta Conversation.*]

Of course, to do that you'll need to set it up ahead of time as you preframe that the best feedback is in *real time*. This will prepare the executive for the challenge of just-in-time feedback.

> "I will be interrupting you from time to time especially when I may detect a pattern that might be sabotaging your best efforts."

3) Levels of Feedback

Once you refine your discernment skills so that you are able to identify feedback from evaluation and make the distinctions necessary in your linguistics to actually give feedback, another issue rises. Feedback can occur at numerous levels. Blakey and Day (2012) identify three levels of feedback that leads to three levels of accountability. Give feedback to hold your executive client accountable at each level.

1) Feedback at the individual level.
Feedback at this level will hold the client accountable for the personal sphere of taking action and following through. As you note the behavioral goals that your client has set for executive professional development, then give feedback when she comes through and does that well as well as when she misses a moment.

Other aspects of feedback occur within the levels of every individual's system. You can give feedback for external behavior, at the level of linguistics and language patterns, at the level of relational interactions, at the level of thinking patterns and cognitive distortions, etc.

2) Feedback at the contract level.
Feedback at this level relates to the coaching contract that you negotiated

with your client to deal with behaviors, time issues, following through on activities, etc. Feedback at this level involves reminding the person of the details of the contract that he or she could have, in all good conscience and intention, promised and then forgot.

3) Feedback at the team and organizational level.
Feedback at the organizational level relate to the wider system within which the executive operates and relates to colleagues, stockholders, customers, suppliers, staff, etc. This will be feedback to the executive about the effect of actions, communications, and decisions on the rest of the system.

4) The Courage to Give Feedback
How much courage does it take to give someone in a position of authority and who has lots of power in that role? For many coaches, this creates an accountability dilemma inasmuch as it evokes lots of different fears and apprehensions.
- What if you offend your client?
- What if you are too bold and brash and the client fires you?
- What if you find yourself unskilled in holding the executive accountable to his or her own promises, or values, or beliefs?
- What if you cave in and end up acting as a fawning acolyte?

Without the courage to give feedback, the coaching will inevitability easily degenerate into small talk about shallow and superficial things. It will be just a nice chat. It will not a meaningful and challenging exploration of next steps of development. A sign that this is happening is when the coaching becomes predictable, boring, and safe. In that case, the coaching session will seem to be without energy, focus, or direction.

To develop courage, begin by realizing the importance of feedback and its crucial role in coaching.
- "This is what coaching is about."
- "I've been hired to feed real-time and empirical feedback."
- "To withhold feedback out of fear or timidity, or intimation is to cheat the executive of valuable information."

A way to set up the context for the courage to give feedback is by preframing it. Preframe that you will give feedback. Then question how the executive wants you to give that feedback.

How would you best like for me to offer feedback?
What is your typical way of responding to bad news?

How can I support you to enhance the quality of your responding to feedback?

Your Executive Take-Away
Feedback is as critical to give as it is challenging and difficult. Effective feedback that makes a difference is easy to describe. It is immediate, sensory-based (empirical), grounded, relevant, given caringly with rapport, tentative, and actionable. Giving this quality of feedback, however, is an art and requires time and effort to develop.

Yet though feedback can accelerate an executive's learning for development, high quality feedback is one of the most commonly missing elements in the C-suites. More common is a culture of cover-up and political dancing to tell those in a higher status what we think they want to hear rather than the truth. This is where courage and backbone will serve an Executive Coach very well.

- How skilled are you today in giving clean, sensory-based feedback?
- What are you doing to refine your feedback skills?
- Are there any beliefs or understandings that you need to reframe in order to more effectively give feedback?
- Where is your courage level in giving feedback to a person in a power or executive position?

Notes at the end of the Chapter
1. The idea of an "innocent eye" comes from Self-Actualization Psychology. This is the unbiased, unprejudiced perception that is able to see cleanly and descriptively. See the training or training manual, *Unleashing Vitality.* www.self-actualizing.org.

Chapter 9

THE CHALLENGE OF

CHANGE

As an Executive Coach, it is your role
to be a courageous champion of change.
L. Michael Hall

"Being an effective learner is vital if you want to be an effective leader."
Ian McDermott (*The NLP Coach*)

"I believe in the importance of openness to change,
openness to being shaped, and being held accountable.
Coaching is not about being a guru.
Because there are always new challenges coaching can change us."
Graham Richardson

L eaders are ultimately change agents. So are Executive Coaches. If both the executive and the coach are change agents, what's the difference? The difference is that Executive Coaches enable and facilitate the changes that executive leaders need to make, both within themselves and as part of their skill set, as they facilitate change in their companies and organizations. We can think of the leaders as the primary change agents and Executive Coaches as the meta-change agents— change agents for change agents.

Change Facts and Factors
Now given that an Executive Coach is a change agent to a change agent (someone in an executive role), both will need have a good understanding about change. On the personal level they need to be completely open when it comes to change and ideally they need to be easy to work within the terms of the changes they want and/or need to make. Right!? Well, not always and perhaps not even usually. Leaders, as it is the case with all of us, can get used to and comfortable with the status quo so that they become slow to change if not resistant.

Yet executives are, by their job, ultimately change agents within their organizations. This is true of visionary leaders to see the future and the importance of making changes to stay up with changing markets and trends. It is equally true of managerial leaders who are responsible for integrating the changes so that the organizational system can take advantage of the changes. Together, executive leaders, both visionary and managerial, work as the leadership team within an organization to facilitate and integrate change into the company, organization, or association.

Now as either a leader *leading* change (visionary leader) or a leader *integrating* change (senior manager), when there's no need for change, then there's no need for leadership. If things are going along just fine and there's no need to change anything, then there's also no need for visionary leadership, or very little need. Leaders are needed when things are changing, when new challenges, problems, and situations are arising and when the speed of change itself is changing. Otherwise we only need management of the current processes to keep things progressing.

Of course, where there is change, there is risk. There are decisions to make, there are plans to make, there are resources to access and allocate, etc. Risk, as part and parcel of change, reveals that in every change you can expect both gains and loses. Every effective decision for change requires that you weigh each and compare them against the criteria used to evaluate what is a loss and what is a gain. Even within positive change there's inevitably the loss of some values.

This obviously leads to the Decision Conversation—a coaching conversation designed to enable one to thoroughly think through a decision so that it's a smart and timely decision. That occurs when the pros and cons of the change are thoroughly understood and when the advantages and disadvantages are weighed up against a person's prioritized values.[1]

LEVELS OF LEARNING AND CHANGE
Robert Dilts

IV: Change^4	New Matrix	Revolutionary Change
III: Change^3	New Identity	Evolutionary Change
II: Change^2	New Behaviors	Discontinuous Change
I: Change^1	Expanded Behaviors	Incremental Change
0: Change^0	Habitual Behaviors	Same Behaviors

Change in people and organizations is necessarily systemic. Therefore those leading change have to consider the ramifications of change. That's because even a small change can have extensive systemic influence as it can influence all kinds of things throughout an organization. As a leader of change, it's important to know that every system is designed for homeostasis. That explains why we experience this healthy homoeostatic mechanism as "resistance." What we call resistance is simply the system keeping itself stable.

Frequently at the beginning of an executive coaching assignment, the executive will be nervous, even anxious, about the process. As the coach, you may be asked, "Do I have to change myself and is that even possible or desirable?" People harbor such concerns. Obviously, coaching is about change, it implies change, and for some, change can be quite frightening. This is especially true if a person is not certain regarding the outcome. "Will this be okay?" "Will I still be myself at my core?"

Graham Richardson says that as an Executive Coach, we need to be in awe of anyone who has the courage and vulnerability to put him or herself up for this kind of challenge! He notes also that this can provide you a gateway to building rapport with compassion which can then open the way to challenge and enabling the self-actualizing process.

The Levels of Change

Not all change occurs on the same level. There are, in fact, several levels of change. That's because change occurs on various levels. What are these levels?

- At the first level are *Behaviors.* This behavioral change is handled

---

LEVELS OF CHANGE / LEARNING
Gregory Bateson

Level IV:	**Change^4 — New Directions** Revolutionary Change: Change of Direction
Level III:	**Change^3 — New Person;** Evolutionary Change: Change of Self or Identity
Level II:	**Change^2 — New Behaviors** Change to new class of Behaviors, Skills, Strategies
Level I:	**Change^1 — Expanded Behaviors** Change to new Flexibility
Level O:	**Change^0 — Programmed Responses or Habits** No change of response; same responses continually produced.

---

by Performance Coaching. We begin by changing something external and explicit—behaviors, sets of actions, and quality of performance.

- At the next level up are the *mental and emotional states or frames.* Here we change what is internal and personal. This is handled by Developmental Coaching which focuses on changing beliefs, values, identity, understandings, intentions, permissions, memories, imaginations, etc. At this level of change we are focusing on changing who we are.

- *Assumptions* are at the next level. Transformational Coaching handles this level of change, which is the highest level. Change at this level involves changing paradigms and assumptions about life and human nature. Changing paradigms transforms one's model of the world, one's premises about life, and one's direction.

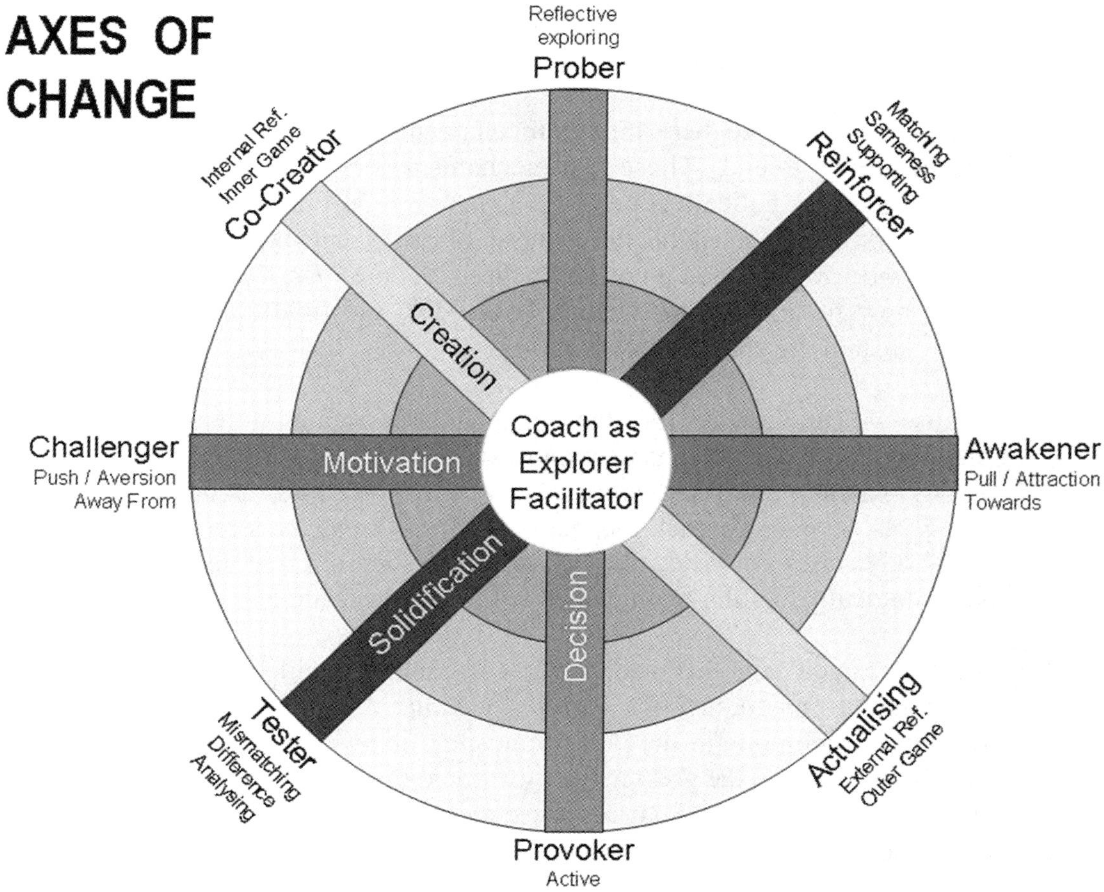
AXES OF CHANGE
Reflective exploring
Prober
Matching Sameness Supporting
Reinforcer
Internal Ref. Inner Game
Co-Creator
Creation
Coach as Explorer Facilitator
Challenger
Push / Aversion Away From
Motivation
Awakener
Pull / Attraction Towards
Solidification
Decision
Tester
Mismatching Difference Analysing
Actualising
External Ref. Outer Game
Provoker
Active

The Dimensions of Change

We can also distinguish change in terms of two dimensions— remedial and generative. In *remedial change* something needs a remedy because something isn't right. Something needs fixing. In *generative change* we generate new possibilities for moving to the next level of development. Of these two dimensions of charge, the first is the change of therapy. The second is the change of coaching.

The Mechanisms of Change

In Meta-Coaching we use *The Axes of Change* as a model whereby individuals and organizations go through the process of generative change.[2]

The model answers the question: How does a psychologically healthy person or group change so that the change generates new choices, opportunities, competencies, etc.?

For *generative* change there are four mechanisms that facilitate the process from beginning to end. These four mechanisms first operate a sequential way and then systemically.

> First, there must be the arousal of sufficient energy to change (*motivation*), then a commitment to change (*decision*), the know-how for making the change (*creation*), and finally the ability to sustain the change (*integration*).

Because we can view each of these mechanisms on a continuum, we are able to perceive each mechanism and axis in terms of its polar opposites. That is, as a continuum *each mechanism has within it integrated opposites.* This gives richness to each mechanism. So as these axes relate to four mind-body states polarities, they govern the processes that describe how psychologically healthy people change through learning and coaching.

Once I realized that the mechanisms of change could be treated as a continuum, I constructed *The Axes of Change Model* using four meta-programs which contain the polar opposites. Now a meta-program is a perceptual filter and the great majority of them involve opposite filters like optimistic/ pessimistic.[3] So using these meta-programs I was able to more fully describe and utilize the key factors involved in change:

> *Motivation:* Energy to move toward a desired change or away from an aversive problem. This gives the push and pull energy of motivation for making a change.
> *Decision:* Commitment to the change based on value clarification, a clear understanding of the cost, and a decisive choice that commits one to that choice and course of action.
> *Creation:* Invention of a strategy or blueprint for how to carry out the change and the first steps of implementation.
> *Integration:* Incorporation of the change into one's lifestyle by reinforcing what works and testing/ refining what doesn't work as well as desired. This then enables the change to last as one's embodied way of operating.

The Axes of Change Model
Using these four meta-program continua you, as a change agent, can handle

the polarities that are inevitably present in these four mechanisms of change. This makes the model richer as it utilizes the different possible filters that people bring to the subject of change.

1) The Motivation Direction Meta-Program: Toward / Away From.
•   What are you motivated to move toward and what do you move away from?
•   What propels you away from pain so you feel aversion?
•   What have you had enough of and are ready to change?
•   What propels you toward an exciting vision of the future?
•   What attracts you as a value and a pleasure that awakens you to new possibilities?

Generative change begins with motivation because without motivation, there will not be sufficient energy for change. As a meta-program, the polar opposite aspects of motivation come into play—*the away from aversions and the toward attractions.* This axis integrates these two energies and creates a synergy of pain and pleasure—a propulsion system. Here leaders tap into both desire and disgust.[4]

2) The Response Meta-Program: Reflective, Inactive, Active.
•   How do you respond when faced with information or a request?
•   What is your first action when you get a great inspirational idea— to immediately act on it or to think about it?
•   Are you primarily reflective in your style or active?
•   Do you sometimes oscillate between thinking something through to have a well-formed plan to just acting and seeing what happens?

In working with getting a decision or commitment, we use the Response Meta-Program. This one answers the question, "How do you respond when you feel motivated to move toward a goal or away from a problem? This axis relates to how a person comes to a decision. It enables a leader to work with the understanding and readiness of people to make a commitment. The response style moves between reflection and action—thinking through the pros and cons of the decision and then of making a decisive commitment for the change.

These first two axes prepares and readies a person for change. Neither motivation alone or decision alone or even both together creates the change, it simply prepares a person for the change. Now there is the energy to change and the decision to change. The next axes moves from readiness for change to the actual creation and implementation of the change.

3) The Frame of Reference Meta-Program: Internal / External.
- When it is time to create change, where do you put your attention?
- Do you focus on mentally inventing your plan, strategy, or vision or do you think in terms of when, where, with whom, and how you will do that?
- Is your focus of attention inwardly on your internal processing or outwardly on your external references?
- Do you put your attention on the Inner Game or on the Outer Game?

This third mechanism of change is that of *creation*. Here you actually construct the change and you do so either inwardly or outwardly. The polar opposites here govern the inner and outer games because you are either referencing one or the other. Which do you prefer? Ideally, you first spend time on the inner game getting your plan and strategy worked out and then you go to the outer game. In this way, you first do the mental planning and strategizing and then you take action to do, to execute the plan, and to actualize the implementation.

4) The Relationship Meta-Program: Sameness / Difference.
- When a change begins to occur because you are actually *doing* something to make it real, where does your attention go—the what you are doing that fits the plan or to the things that do not fit?
- Do you focus on what is similar to your design or to what's different from that design?
- Do you pay attention and care about sameness or difference?
- Are you able to match even the first smallest approximations of what you want or do you discount it and mis-match it as different from what you want?

The fourth mechanism of change is *integration*. This enables the change to last thereby making it sustainable. This mechanism begins after you have taken the first actions of change. At that point, do you look for what's working, for what is even to the smallest degree of what you want? Or do you look for what's wrong, what's not working, what does not fit with the plan? A focus on what is the same as the plan leads enables you to reinforce what's working. And whatever you reinforce, grows.

A focus on what is not the same, what is different from the plan leads to discounting what's working, and not validating it. That will cause it to not grow. One first matches for sameness and then, when the change is strong enough, for testing. Then one focus on differences. This mis-matching will then test and refine the change to make it better.

Leading Change

Without question, leading change is challenging. Even for an experienced leader, leading change in an organization always brings its special tensions and stresses. After all, as the leader you have to address the multi-faceted nature of the change. In Executive Coaching, addressing this brings up a whole multitude of questions, skills, beliefs, and understandings about the person who will be making decisions about change.

- What does the executive believe about change?
- What does the executive believe about leading change?
- What does the executive believe about risk?
- What does the executive believe about decision-making?
- What does the executive believe about execution (implementation)?
- What does the executive believe about reinforcement?
- What does the executive believe about testing and kaizen?

The Challenge of Change Itself

What are these challenges that change introduces and how do you, as an Executive Coach address these challenges? To answer this, we will explore the following three challenges:

1) The Challenges of Change itself
2) The Challenge of Executive Change
3) The Challenge of Organizational Change

Whether you are coaching an executive to make a personal change or to become more empowered and skilled in leading organizational change, there are similar challenges in both.

The first challenge is that of safety. People and organizations have to feel safe to change. Where there is not safety, people feel threatened and/or endangered, and so respond defensively with fight or flight responses. Enabling safety therefore becomes one of your first tasks as an Executive Coach. A fundamental way to do this is to facilitate the listing of the pros and cons of the change decision. As people realize the value of the change and the cost of not-changing, it will facilitate a greater sense of confidence to change.

Safety is further developed by identifying and accessing resources. The more resourceful a person is, the more secure, the easier the change. When this is for an individual, we call personal security *self-efficacy.* When it relates to a group, we call the sense of security by other names—group stability or cohesion. Next comes the risk management of creating contingency plans in anticipation of what could go wrong.

The second challenge is resistance. People resist when they feel insecure and not safe. They also *resist* if they don't understand. They resist when they feel that the change is being imposed upon them without their input. In these cases the resistance indicates a lack of rapport. There's not enough connection between the ones leading the change and those who are being asked to change or who are impacted by the change.

People also resist when there is a sense of loss. In fact, people will often love change and will seek variety and stimulation. But, if they sense loss, or are suspicious that loss will be involved, then they would typically prefer to stay where they are, even if where they are is not ideal. They will choose "the devil they know over the devil they do not."

Then there is the challenge of follow-through. "Will the change last? Will the person or persons continue so that the change will become permanent? Or will it be a flash-in-the-pan phenomenon? Follow-through involves persistence and resilience. It refers to the ability to implement a change, receive feedback to see what works well and what does not, and to made adaptive changes so that the change develops and evolves.

Very often there will be a lot of cynicism around change. This could result from change fatigue. Once people go through many iterations of change, especially when every new wave of change promises a better way of doing things. When done too often, or too quickly, this can create the mind-set of "This too will pass." Then they learn to wait it out until the next great new idea comes around disrupting things all over again.

The other impediment occurs when, after the change, comes a change-back. This happens when an executive gets a new coach or goes on a course and comes back "a changed man." Yet without follow-through and ongoing attention to a change, this too will pass and will not last. Just sit back and watch—the shiny new MBA immersion will wear off. Then as things will go back to where were, cynicism deepens, and people will quote the old fatalistic proverb: "A tiger doesn't change its stripes."

Then there is the factor of the sheer volume and magnitude of change. Companies take on massive change initiatives and very often with several changes in parallel. This inevitably causes overwhelm. Some of these changes are what is very pleasantly known as "cutting heads" in order to stream-line or cut costs. Yet nearly everybody knows that what this really means— more pressure and stress. People are now expected to do more with less. Sometimes this is seen as the definition of leadership—inspiring people to align to a vision, turn out the expected results, and do it more efficiently. In such cases, "the vision" is usually hot air. The real vision (the hidden one) is to increase the profits for the shareholders.

The Challenge of Executive Change
These four mechanisms of generative change can create all kinds of challenges for any executive who is contemplating change. As such, it raises numerous questions for you as an Executive Coach:
•   Is she motivated enough to change?
•   Has he made a decision to change?
•   Is she committed to the change?
•   Has he created the change or is he in the process of creating it?
•   Has she integrated the change so she now walks a new talk?

The Challenge of Organizational Change
How does a leader lead his or her organization through change? The process is about the same as what occurs when you use the four axes of the Axes of Change. Yet there is a difference. So in Neuro-Semantics we add one more axis and changed the order to generate a model for leading a change initiative with a group of organizations. This gives us *The Axes of Leadership Change.*[5]

As an overview, to lead an organization to transform its culture (create a transformational cultural change), five change mechanisms are involved:

Motivation —   The energy that moves people to change and to want to evolve.

Meaning   —   The significance and understanding of what to change to, the vision of the transformation. This corresponds to *Creation,* the third mechanism in the

		Axes of Change.
Commitment	—	The buy-in and decision to make the change so that there is an absolute engagement. *(Decision)*
Solutions	—	The creative solutions that embody the change that solves well-defined problems.
Kaizen	—	The continuous improvement of the new solution that actualizes the change and fully integrates it into the organization. *(Integration)*

When we pull all five of the axes together, we have two stages (or loops) for change in an organization. The first stage is designed as the meaningful leadership stage. The second one is the organizational leadership stage.

Loop I: Meaningful Leadership. The energy of leading that influences and motivates a vision of a new direction, a new world. Here the executive leader leads with ideas, values, and visions that sets the direction. The executive leader plays the following roles in leading the group's motivation and meaning.

Motivation	1. Challenger
	2. Awakener
Meaning	3. Framer
	4. Empowerer

Loop II: Organizational Leadership. Once there is meaning and motivation for the change, the executive leader then facilitates change by structuring the change in order to give form to the vision. This involves managing the plans and strategies for creating a lasting change in the group which will carry out the vision. The executive leader creates the atmosphere, the culture and the form. He or she handles obstacles, creates ongoing renewal and relevance.

Commitment	5. Collaborator
	6. Enroller
Solution	7. Problem-Definer
	8. Problem-Solver
Kaizen	9. Cheerleader
	10. Refiner

There are lots of *activities* in actually leading minds and hearts in the process of change. As an Executive Coach you facilitate the leaders to get buy-in and commitment via the vision. Then comes the hard work of creating— inventing actual solutions to be implemented. That is followed-up by the continuous improvement (kaizen) so that the executive actually leads people in these activities. All of this obviously involves leaders who are active, dynamic, holistic, and healthy.

Leadership is not only dynamic in that it is an active doing, it is also multi-faceted. There are many dimensions and arenas of leadership and no single person can play every role of leadership. A *leadership team* is needed to share these functions and collaborate in leading the change initiative. (Chapter 20, Collaborative Leadership).

Your Executive Coaching Take Aways

Because coaching is essentially about change as a coach you are first and foremost *a change agent*. As an Executive Coach you work to facilitate generative change at the personal and corporate level with an executive. Given this, as an Executive Coach, you need to be highly informed about how change works and skillfully competent as a change agent at many levels—individual, team, organization, and organizational culture.

Among the models for working with change, *The Axes of Change Model* is uniquely a model for generative change rather than remedial change. It involves four mechanisms that allow you to know where the person is in the process of change and the change roles that are required to effectively facilitate the change. For organizational change, *The Axes of Leadership Model* gives five mechanisms and ten roles for an executive in facilitating change in a company.

- Where are you on a scale of thoroughly understanding how change works?
- What are the skills that you currently have for facilitating change and what are the next set of skills that you will be developing?
- How well do you understand the Axes of Change Model?

End of Chapter Notes:

1. The second axis in the Axes of Change model is Decision which occurs between the poles of reflection and action.
2. See the book: *Coaching Change, Meta-Coaching Volume I* (2004) for a full description of the Axes of Change.
3. Meta-Programs are perceptual filters like glasses and so color perception. See *Figuring Out People* (2005).
4. See *Propulsion Systems in NLP* (2003) that details several propulsion systems.
5. See *Change Leadership,* Chapter 13 of *Unleashing Leadership.* (2009).

Chapter 10

THE CHALLENGE OF

LEADERSHIP

"Why do I do Executive Coaching? Because I have great leaders to launch into the world."

Graham Richardson

"Leading others is a very complex human endeavor. Leaders need confidence and self-esteem if they are to provide consistent direction and withstand scrutiny and criticism. On the other hand, excessive confidence has been shown to be a significant problem in isolating leaders from needed feedback and learning. Finding a balance between confident decisiveness and open humility is a key challenge for leaders."

Michael Frisch, et. al (*Becoming an Exceptional Executive Coach,* p. 154)

"As important as the skills are, lack of skills is not what derails most leaders; skills are too easy to learn. If you want to predict people's ultimate success as leaders, evaluate not their skills, but their *leadership character."*

Mark Miller (*The Heart of Leadership,* p. 1)

Here's *another challenge for those in executive roles—Leadership.* It's challenging because while leadership seeks to get people to do what we want them to do, leadership involves winning far more than just behavioral compliance. *To be truly effective as a leader one has to win the minds and hearts of people.* Then those following will *see the value* of complying and *want to be a part* of an initiative or an organization and will *apply* their minds and hearts to the shared experience. This task is not one that's easy to accomplish. Not at all. It requires a lot on the behalf of the leader. And this is where Executive Coaching comes in.

The new demands upon executives for leadership explains one of the great drivers behind the emergence of Executive Coaching as a distinct field. Men and women are finding themselves in leadership roles or being asked to step up to leadership roles and not sure how to prepare themselves for the challenge.

In his book on *Leadership,* Rudi Guiliani described how he prepared to become the mayor of New York City. He asked himself and others, "What does a major need to know to be effective?" He then set out to find experts in those areas. When he found them, he hired them to come and present their expert knowledge to him and his staff. He said that this was his "Mayor School"— a key facet of his education to becoming the effective mayor that he did.

> *To be truly effective as a leader one has to win the minds and hearts of people.*

Similarly we could ask, "What does a leader need to know to be effective?" "What skills does a leader need to be competent at?" What are the challenges of leadership for executives? Here is my list for this chapter.[1]

> 1) The Challenge of Understanding People
> 2) The Challenge of Developing People
> 3) The Challenge of Bringing out the Best in People
> 4) The Challenge of Winning the Hearts of your People
> 5) The Challenge of Grooming Leaders
> 6) The Challenge of Flexible Adaptability
> 7) The Challenge of Character— *being* the Leader
> 8) The Challenge of turning a group into a High Performance Team

1) The Challenge of Understanding People

What does leadership require? It requires having a basic understanding of human nature in terms of what drives people, how they function, and how they change. Leaders don't need a degree in psychology, especially in the older psychologies which address how people become hurt and traumatized. Yet they do need a basic understanding of adult developmental psychology about how basically healthy people think, interpret, cope, develop, learn, get along with others, create alliances, etc. They need to have a basic model for how people develop their skills and become contributing members of an organization or community.

Yet understanding people is no simple task. People are complex. They are multi-dimensional and multifacetic which means they have so many aspects which can be in conflict that often they will not even understand themselves. This is where the NLP model offers constructive insight. In this communication model, there are numerous premises that facilitate understanding humans. These premises about human functioning were discovered in modeling several professional change agents who were especially effective in understanding and leading others.

Here are premises about human beings and human nature that NLP started with, premises inherited from the Human Potential Movement:
- Each person differs due to and according to the different maps they have constructed about the world.
- Each person operates from his or her own personal map.
- Each person's behavior makes sense. It makes sense to them according to the internal mental maps that the person is operating from.
- Every person's mental maps or models of the world *filter* and *color* things. Each of us hear according to how we filter things.
- Behind all behavior is some positive intention. It may be *behind* it several levels up, yet people do what they do for positive reasons for themselves.
- The meaning of your communication is the response you get whether you intended or wanted to get that response. Therefore you never know what you *communicated,* only what you said, not what the other person heard.

These premises set the stage for active listening (seeking to understand), patience, looking for the best in people, and developing accurate empathy.

2) The Challenge of Developing People
A leader could be excellent as an individual contributor, but lack the required skills for managing and leading others. To move up to the next level requires knowing how to develop talent, set objectives, coach for the unleashing of new potentials, select effective team members, handle conflict, delegate, and so on. In this, leadership is about enabling others to be successful. And that involves emotionally engaging people and teams— energizing and inspiring them, providing resources, guidance, and

standards. As one leads in this way, it creates role clarity for everyone and the opportunity to collaborate for a higher purpose.

These things help people to develop. It enables development at all levels—mental development, emotional development, linguistic and interpersonal development. This is what Jim Collins described in *Good to Great* and his five levels of leadership.

3) The Challenge of Bringing out the Best in People

Once a leader understands people well enough to connect with them and facilitate their development, a leader needs to develop his or her own personal leadership skills—those of leading, coaching, and facilitating skills to bring out the best in people. This goes far beyond mere knowledge about the psychology of people. It requires a person to be able to connect with people, to empathize with their model of the world, to seek to understand, to create trust and rapport, to communicate effectively, to inspire, to enable, and to empower.

These are no longer just skills for the helping professions. These are essential skills for leaders who know that the old command-and-control authoritarian way will not work with people today. These are skills for leaders who actually win the minds and hearts of people. The challenge does not end when a leader develops and employee these skills. It continues afterwards. That's because if they are not sustained, things can easily go back to an unhealthy work environment.

Whereas once upon a time being a leader was primarily a matter of status, position, and power. This is no longer true. A title or a status today does not make a person a leader. Today, effective and real leadership begins with the competence to lead. Without knowledge, understanding, and developed skills a person will be incapable of leading. Leadership now begins with being able to function in a particular role and that requires having the competence to effectively function in that situation. Graham Richardson writes:

> "If you do not have these skills, what are you? You are a manager in the industrial mold, wielding power as mechanical instrument, and not necessarily connecting with the human element."

Today leaders who seek to bring out the best in people focus on the untapped potential in their people. They work at leading by discovering the processes for how to tap into human capital and they do this to make their intellectual, emotional, personal, social capital available. The first step in doing this is to prize the internal human capital—to appreciate and value it. Richard Branson describes this in his typically unique style in *Like a Virgin* (2012):

> "What if CEO stood for 'chief enabling officer?' What if that CEO's primary role were to nurture a breed of intrapreneurs who would grow into tomorrow's entrepreneurs?" (p. 114)

4) The Challenge of Winning Hearts

The challenge of leadership today is winning and touching the hearts of people. People will no longer follow leaders because they *have to*. Those days are gone. Today people follow leaders because they *want to*. Leaders today lead by influencing—that is, by communicating, modeling, being exemplars, inspiring, inviting, requesting, dialoguing, etc. And doing all of that requires lots of

> "The first responsibility of a leader is to define reality. The last is to say thank you. In between, the leader is a servant."
> Max DePress
> *Leadership is an Art*

competencies along with a big dose of patience, persistence, belief, commitment, and resilience.

Today the most effective leadership is situational and functional. Long before the 1960s when Situational and Function Leadership models arose, Abraham Maslow had discovered and articulated that kind of leadership. His work with the Blackfoot Indians of Alberta Canada led him to discover that *real leadership is situational*—it depends on the situation, the context and what is needed in that context. And as it depended upon what was needed, he discovered another fact about real leadership: *Leadership is functional*. The person who is best at a task, a skill, is the best person to go first—to lead out. From this arose the idea of home-grown leaders. And this is where Walt Mahler comes in.

Because people will no longer blindly follow leaders, it is not positional authority. The command-and-control type of authority is no longer an effective style in most organizations.[2] Today, it is personal authority. It is the kind of leadership that informs people because they want to know why they should do what they do. They also want to know, "What's in it for me?"

5) The Challenge of Grooming Leaders

What is the purpose of leadership? Here is a shock for some leaders— the purpose of a leader is *not* to create followers. The purpose of a leader is rather to *create other leaders*. Leadership is to identify and develop the leaders who will carry on the vision. That's why succession plans and development plans for the next generation leaders is so critical for long-term successful leadership in organizations. In other words, the task of grooming leaders. An effective and true leader will constantly be on the look for talented people who have, or could have, the attitude and character required for stepping up to leadership. That person will be mentoring, coaching, encouraging, acknowledging, commissioning, to create the next generation leaders, etc.

For this purpose effective leaders rely on collaboration and inspiration rather than authority or commands. For this purpose also leaders design trainings

> The purpose of a leader is to create other leaders.

and coaching processes within their organizations to facilitate the new and upcoming leaders. They create, as it were, their own "university of leadership."

6) The Challenge of Flexible Adaptability

For years and years, Walt Mahler worked quietly within General Electric as a consultant. Only after many years of quiet steady work did his ideas and understanding about homegrown leadership become evident. What eventually drew attention to his ideas were the results that began to appear.

What were those results? It was the ability of General Electric, as an organization, to create so many great leaders and CEOs. The co-authors Ram Charan, Stephen Drotter, and James Noe describe this in their book, *The Leadership Pipeline*. As they became interested in the consulting work of Walt Mahler at General Electric, they noted, that GE had became "a virtual CEO factory." By the time Jack Welch was selected as CEO, there were a great many highly qualified people to chose from that those not chosen went on to other leading fortune 500 companies as CEOs, and became exceptionally successful there.

How could a single company produce so many great leaders who each went on to be highly successful and effective CEOs in other corporations? The answer is that GE, with Mahler's consulting, had created a "leadership pipeline" in the company. This "pipeline" was designed in such a way that GE would "grow" leaders from within—leaders who would understand the organization and be able to continue to evolve the culture.

The leadership pipeline enabled Mahler to lay the foundation for modern succession planning approaches as well as how to develop leaders and this

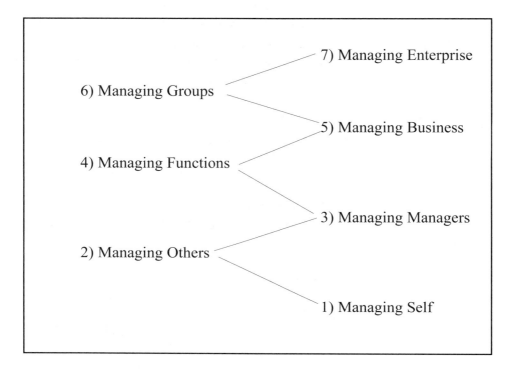

model was not only used by GE, but also in Citigroup, and numerous other companies. So no wonder this model provides so many of the secrets behind GE's success in developing leaders.

The Leadership Pipeline

Now central to success is the challenge of leaders at every level to adapt to the required changes when they move up in the organization. That is, with each move up the pipeline lots of things have to change. Lots of things have to change *inside* the leaders. They have to change their values, their focus, their time allotment, and their skills. They have to adopt new ones and they also have to let go of their previous values, focus, time allotment, and skills. If they don't, they clog up the pipeline. Then they will micro-

---

The Leadership Pipeline

Begin reading at the bottom with the first level—Managing Self—and move up the scale.

7) Managing Enterprise – Enterprise Manager
> Long-term vision, culture development, align all people, develop social organization, handle local politics, etc.

6) Managing Groups — Group Manager
> Integrating groups of companies, strategy, and culture so all of the companies work to a single vision and purpose.

5) Managing Business — Business Manager
> Strategy of the whole, thinking time for reflection and analysis, integrate all of the functions.

4) Managing Functions — Functional Manager
> Integrate the functions of an organization, learn about the other functions, understand how it all fits together and interacts effectively.

3) Managing Managers — Manage Manager
> Pure management, building team, empowering people to function more effectively, focusing on transferring skill to the whole team.

2) Managing Others — Manage Others
> Give directions, delegate, enable, coach, makes time available, approachable. Shift from focus on self to a focus on helping others, enjoying watching them develop.

1) Managing Yourself — Manage Self
> Self-direction, competence, achievement, know-how, set to act and carry through. Being a great individual contributor: a skilled craft person.

---

manage using the skills of their previous level thereby making themselves ineffective at the next higher level.

Central to grooming of leadership is the realization that *all leadership is not the same.* How a person leads at each level differs, and sometimes differs quite significantly. There are six passages in this model and each of these passages represents a change in organization position. Each one requires that a person acquires *a new way of managing and leading.* And to do that, one has to leave the old ways behind in the following areas:

- *Skill requirements:* New capabilities for new responsibilities.
- *Time applications:* New time frames for use of time.
- *Work values and activities:* New important activities for the focus of one's efforts.
- *Focus on attention:* Attending to interests that corresponds to see new values.

7) The Challenge of Character— *Being* the Leader

Today the leaders who succeed with people, who are deemed trustworthy to follow are leaders of integrity, competence, and authenticity. Today people scrutinize their leaders more than ever. They demand much more of their leaders as they will simply not tolerate incongruence, incompetence, and inauthenticity. Today executives who want to be leaders have to *be* the leader that people will follow. So just as Ghanda said: "Be the change you want to lead," so today, a leader must "*be* the leader that you present yourself to be."

For people to trust you, you must be trustworthy. That is, you must be competent, consistent, and congruent. This means doing what you say, carrying out what you promise, and following through on your word. To do otherwise is to sow the seeds of cynicism and distrust. Leadership capacity is therefore now dependent on your character.

This gives us a new definition of charisma. Originally we thought of charisma as someone who was the life and soul of the party. Friendly, jovial, optimistic, attractive. Someone slapping backs and lavishly praising. We now know that real charisma involves trust and authenticity. Yet mostly in business, it is the combination of "fierce professional will with humility." This is Jim Collins' description of the highest leadership level —"Level 5 Leadership."

8) The Challenge of Turning a Group into a High Performance Team

How does an executive leader transform individuals, especially strong personalities who have a lifetime of reinforcement for their individuality, into a collaborative team? This is an incredible challenge and the one addressed in the previous volume, *Group and Team Coaching* (2013).

Coaching Executives for Leadership

Coaching for leadership is a challenge. It's a challenge due to of all of the myths and misbeliefs about leadership. This first challenge requires that we push through the misconceptions and enable the executive to be crystal clear about the kind and quality of leadership which he or she wants. Because great leaders are also great followers, the challenge is to help a leader to follow when appropriate. Great leaders know how to receive, how to learn, and how to be a great team player. They know the limits of their competence and as a situational and functional leader, they know when and how to step back to allow others a part. And to do so gracefully.

Your Executive Coaching Take Aways

The new leadership of the 21st century is a very different kind of leadership from all the previous centuries. This explains why Executive Coaching has become its own unique field. Executives need help in adapting to the new leadership which is required. The old command-and-control leadership is no longer effective and with every passing year becomes less and less effective.

Today executive leadership is about *people*—understanding them, developing them, bringing out their best, winning their hearts, grooming them for leadership, flexibly adapting, and developing the personal character to *be* the leader that they can be.

- Given that leadership is a challenge, and also a highly misunderstood concept that suffers from lots of myths, what is your current definition of leadership?
- How well do you feel that you can challenge and coach the leadership skills of an executive? What's your next step for development in this area?
- How well do you understand the Leadership pipeline and the impact it has on coaching executives?

End of the Chapter Notes

1. See *Unleashing Leadership: Self-Actualizing Leaders and Companies* (2009) which describes in detail the process for developing, grooming, and unleashing leadership.

2. Command-and-control is still effective in one area: crisis or emergency. When there is absolutely no time for reflection or discussion, when life and death is on the line and someone needs to give a command, then this type of leadership has its place.

Chapter 11

THE CHALLENGE OF

POLITICS

"Because *politics* is part of 'the way we do things around here,'
and which is what is expected of one to get things done, to thrive and survive,
it is a manifestation of the *culture*. They go together.
You change one, you change them both."
Graham Richardson

It's never takes long in Executive Coaching before the subject of politics comes up. And it's no wonder. That's because the very nature of organizational life involves *politics*—political interests, political consequences, and political competition. Given this, the challenge for any and every executive is the challenge of how to deal with the political nature of organizational life. This is an inescapable reality. Wherever human beings come together to work or play together, there will be *politics*. That is, there will be the question of:

> *How* do we get along with each other? How do we make decisions? How do we allocate resources? How do we appoint people to certain positions? How do we invest certain roles with the power to fulfil needed responsibilities?

Politics is ultimately all about relationships— about relating, getting along, making agreements, figuring out roles and positions, identifying positions and views, communicating, negotiating, etc. It is about how we organize ourselves to work together and make decisions. It is about how we structure the allocation of resources and power.[1]

If politics is about relationships, and about getting along, then there is no escape from politics. The only question before us is whether the politics is negative or positive. Are the politics at play humanizing and respectful or dehumanizing and disrespectful? Do we like the way we "play politics" by using various communication and relational patterns or do we hate the way we "play politics?" What politics have we inherited in our organizations? What politics do we want to change so that we can have a truly human enterprise?

For an Executive Coach, there are numerous coaching challenges in this area. Among these I'll mention the following challenges:
        1) Accepting and understanding the role of politics.
        2) Dealing with dirty politics
        3) Creating positive politics

1) Accepting and Understanding the Role of Politics

As we all know all too well, the terms *politics* and *political* have been besoiled and dirtied to such an extent that we now use these words almost exclusively to indicate something negative. We even use them as insults. To say about someone, "He's very political" is typically taken as a criticism and not a complement. Hardly ever is it viewed as a strength. "Oh, it's the same old politics as usual." This is usually understood as meaning that people are doing under-handed things, keeping secrets, bribing to get a favor, not being open or straight-forward, secretly positioning oneself with others to create a coalition against an issue or another group so that they get their way to the disadvantage of others.

When it comes to politics within an organization, or within a department, what we call politics are the factors that determine how an organization is governed. When we pull apart the term "politics," we get "polis" which refers to a "city." The term *politics* originated to indicate the process of how to run or manage a city. It describes how we govern, manage, or handle a community or group. So "politics" means we are dealing with communicating, establishing roles, making decisions about things, dealing with differences, talking about different positions we have on things, confronting each other about choices, the use of power, leadership, coordinating activities, cooperating with each other, hierarchal relationships, vested interests, coalitions of people wanting something in common, etc.

If all of that says anything, it says that *we cannot **not** have politics.* We do not have the choice of being apolitical however much we try. The only question is the kind and quality of politics that we create. Will our politics be healthy and

> "These are the hard times in which a genius would wish to live. . . . Great necessities call out great virtues."
> John Quincy Adams

positive? Will it serve the greater good? Will it operate to create a good society— one of equal access to everybody? Or will our politics be self-serving, competitive as if we are each other's worst enemies, will we try to win our point of view or our position by besmirching the other person's point of view and position, and if the success of one person is at the expense of another?

If we are inescapably political due to our social nature, where do our politics come from? Here's a surprise. See if you can detect it. They originate from our beliefs and assumptions about human nature.

Our beliefs about ourselves and others informs us about people and so determines the nature and quality of our politics. If we believe that human nature is bad, evil, flawed, and that people can be graded in terms of their value, then our politics will reflect valuing some people and groups over others and treating some as superior and others as inferior. We will then set up the rules of law to keep people in their place, control people through fear and punishment, and prevent open and free discourse.

Conversely, if we believe that we are all equal as human beings, that we are all equally valuable as persons and able to contribute to the larger good, then our politics will encourage a deep democracy and a respect for the basic human powers or rights: freedom of speech, freedom to assemble, freedom to pursue your gifts and potentials, etc. This will encourage freedom and movement in the economic educational, and vocational areas so that these things fall to a person's choice, not to his birth status, skin color, race, etc. We will then want people to be well-educated and as well-informed as possible— knowing that the higher quality of information will facilitate better decisions as a community.

In organizational politics, the choices will be between Theory X and Theory Y of management and leadership. In the first (Theory X) the politics will be that of command-and-control and authoritarianism. In the second (Theory Y) the politics will be that of equality, democracy, and openness.

What is the surprise in this? *Your politics is a function of your psychology.* As you think and believe about people, groups, human nature, human needs, development, growth, communication, etc., so you create your politics. So you create the quality (or lack of it) of your politics.

*   What is the political game in the organization?
*   What are the rules of this game?
*   How is power acquired in this game?
*   Who is jockeying for position, power, or influence?
*   What roles are symmetrical and which are complementary?
*   What are the formal roles and lines of structure?
*   What are the informal processes at work where the real power lies?

2) Dealing with dirty politics

Then there are the "dirty" politics. These are the ways of relating to each other that undermines relationships, that interferes with communication, that sabotages another's interests and preferences, that uses unethical and immoral means to accomplish one's purposes, etc. This is what we mean when we talk about "politics as usual" and it typically involves such behaviors as:

*   Power *over* others, not *with* them.
*   Keeping secrets; keeping information away from others.
*   Coalitions that compete for the resources and justifies almost any means to the desired end.
*   Threats implied and directed to create away-from pressure.
*   Covering one's backside so as to reduce personal accountability.
*   Accusing and blaming others for your own faults and failures.
*   "Looking good" (image management) to curry favor for promotion, higher pay, or to avoid losing one's status or even one's job.
*   Joining cliques who protect each other or who actively disadvantage other individuals or cliques, while looking for power over others, or avoid others having power over them.
*   Jockeying for power positions by withholding information.

These are some of the indicators that dirty politics are in play. And there are more. So what are indications that there are dirty politics going on in a business or organization?

- *Silo mentality:* Operating as if we are completely independent of each other and in competition.
- *Competition:* Us against them. Internal competition so that the company is fighting against itself! And while, on the surface, this sounds utterly ridiculous and self-destructive, it is extremely common.
- *Secrets and secrecy.* The fear of being open and honest and the sabotage of every effort to put things out in the open.
- *Vested interests* and hidden agendas. This is driven by failing to speak up in an open and candid way. What speaking occurs is often to the wrong people in the wrong contexts.
- *Lack of accountability* for resources and commitments. No one is held accountable for failure to follow-through.
- *Unending blaming and accusation* for complaints and problems.

Politics become "dirty" when the ways we interact with each other and govern our interactions are oppressive and dehumanizing. They are "dirty" when people feel that they are in a double-bind ("Damned if they do and damned if they don't.") and when people feel unappreciated and without any power to influence the system. It is "dirty" when the communications are careful, poised to create certain impressions, and blocked from being open and above-board.

To deal with such dirty politics requires courage to challenge the system. It requires people to speak up to change the culture, to confront unethical behavior when it occurs, and to be a whistle-blower against corruption when necessary. It requires the ability to plant the seeds of ideas about a healthy and more positive politics, and then to coach and mentor people individually to make this new kind of political culture real.

3) Creating Positive Politics

Since politics is simply the process by which we relate, interact, make decisions, use power, etc. then politics as such is not the problem. So what is the actual problem? *The problem is how we think about politics.* It is our frames and beliefs that create our interpretations about politics. These interpretations then lead us to engage in the problematic political behaviors.

We can now run a quality control check list of our group political behaviors.

- Is it in service of others or of our vision?
- Is it used exclusively for self-service?
- Are we collaborative in our style?
- Is it respectful for others and for differences?
- Does it empower ourselves and others?
- Is it in the best interests of the organization, your sphere of influence, and of yourself?

The process whereby we create positive politics is essentially the same process that we use when we create a self-actualizing or coaching culture in an organization. A first step in beginning to create positive politics is to create a map of the current politics. Then we will be able to identify and recognize how our current politics is working. By doing this we can answer the questions:

- How are the key people related to each other and to the various groups in the organization?
- How do we think about change or a new initiative?
- How do we govern ourselves? What are the processes that we use?
- What are our policies and practices for making decisions and sharing power, etc.?
- What are the agendas that people have within our organization?
- What do they really want?
- What are the assumptions about human nature, control and power, competition and collaboration that the leaders and the people in our company hold?
- What do we as a community believe about information, truth, truth-speaking?
- If I tell the truth, will I be penalized? Will I lose my job?
- With regard to the board of directors, how are decisions made?
- How do those in charge allocate resources?
- How does this company recognize and honor those who contribute and make a positive difference?
- Do we have a culture whereby we can make our thinking style and assumptions known and transparent to each other so that it is open for examination?
- What would have to change so that could occur?

Your Executive Coaching Take Aways

Politics are with us and always will be. That's because politics simply describes how we govern our house—our city, our community or organization. The question about politics is not whether we have a choice of being political or not, but the kind and quality of our politics. The challenge is for us to coach so that executives will move from negative politics to positive politics and to create a whole new kind of corporate culture.

When you coach an executive, you'll want to stay alert to the fact that you are inevitably dealing with someone who lives in a highly politicized environment. Knowing that, coach him or her to be effective in exposing dirty politics and creating positive politics. Make this the heart of your coaching. Are you prepared for that?

- What are your first thoughts and impressions about "politics?"
- What do you need to change about your ideas and beliefs about politics so that when political issues come up, you are prepared and in a good state to address them?
- Do you know the difference between negative and positive politics?
- How well informed and skilled are you in facilitating an executive through the political landscape of his or her company?

End of Chapter Notes
1. The next book planned in the series of Meta-Coaching books is one on *Political Coaching.*

Chapter 12

THE CHALLENGE OF

CREATING CULTURE

"Culture and leadership are two sides of the same coin,
and neither can really be understood by itself."
Edgar Schein (1985)

"If one wants to understand a system,
one should try to change it."
Kurt Lewin (1952)

In organizations, who is in charge of the company's culture—cultural quality and cultural change? Whose job description includes "to create a positive culture in this organization and to guard against anything that would sabotage the vision and mission that creates our culture?"

I hope that the answer is obvious—*the leaders.* In particular, the executive leaders and the senior managers. If there is anyone who is in charge of creating culture within an organization, it falls to those who occupy the executive roles. After all, who else could be? Leaders are the ones who have the most influence and ability to create the culture of the business, do they not?
•   Yet do most executives see it this way?
•   Do they feel responsible for the culture of their company?

- Or do they also feel a victim of the culture that they inherited?
- To what extent do those in the executive roles look upon this as their job?
- What do leaders need so that they see culture development as part of their job description and able to fulfill it?

Now at the head of those responsible for creating the culture is the executive leaders. This is why Executive Coaching frequently focuses culture and cultural change. Edgar Schein writes, "One cannot separate the process of leadership from the process of building culture" (p. 171). The development of culture provides stability, meaning, and identity for both the individuals and the organization.

Here then is a challenge—and it is a big one—in Executive Coaching. The importance of this arises from a single fact. *A company is only as strong and vital as its culture.* In fact, a company's culture is its distinctiveness—its branding. That, of course, makes culture crucially important. This, of course, raises many questions for leaders:
- What exactly is culture and how do leaders create it?
- What are the processes by which culture arises among people?
- What is a self-actualization culture?
- What is the relationship of Executive Coaching and culture?

Part of the reason this is critical is because if the leaders get the culture right, then most of the other aspects of organizational effectiveness is made right. When a company has the right culture, they will experience employee engagement, customer service, a strong brand, productivity, profitably, increasing market value, etc. To address this, let's focus on the challenges of culture and cultural change within the context of Executive Coaching.
   1) Understanding the current culture
   2) Encountering a sick or toxic culture
   3) Changing the culture
   4) Executive Coaching for a cultural change

1) Understanding the Current Culture
Before focusing on understanding the current culture, let's begin by getting clear on what we mean by "culture." What is it, where is it, and how does it work?

Regarding where is it—culture is everywhere!
Wherever a group exists, culture exists. It
exists as our way of interacting. That's
because we inevitably and inescapably
develop ways of interacting, communicating,
and getting along when we are with others.

> *A company is only as strong and vital as its culture.*

Literally, a *culture* results due to how we have *cultivated* our minds,
emotions, speech, and actions. It's "how we do things around here." Edgar
Schein (1985) describes cultures as "solutions to past problems."

> "The major external adaptation and internal integration problems that
> every group must deal with and attempts to show that culture can best be
> thought of as the stable solutions to those problems. Culture becomes
> abstracted into a set of basic underlying assumptions." (1985, p. xiii)

> "Culture and leadership, when one examines them closely, are two sides
> of the same coin, and neither can really be understood by itself. The only
> thing of real importance that leaders do is to create and manage culture
> and that the unique talent of leadership is their ability to work with
> culture." (p. 2)

The culture of an organization arises from the habituated solutions to
problems and is why a culture is simply "the way we do things around
here." For that reason, it soon comes to be taken for granted and assumed.
And when taken for granted, we no longer notice it. In fact, we become
unconscious of it. As culture becomes unconscious, it then operates to
constrain what people within the organization are able to do and/or not do.
It constrains by means of the built-in assumptions (or frames) that are taken
for granted. The invisible "culture" of an organization operates as a set of
implicit and silent assumptions.

As an Executive Coach, you will undoubtedly frequently inquire about the
company's culture, where it is today and where the leaders are wanting to
take it. To access the current culture of a business or organization, consider
where things are using the following factors as a checklist:

1) *Safety.* People feel safe and secure and therefore don't need to
be defensive, reactive, closed, fearful, etc.
2) *Respect.* People feel respected and honored by their presence
and the contribution they make. Are they treated as persons and not
interchangeable parts in a machine? Therefore there's no need to
personalize or take a defensive stance.
3) *Openness.* People are generally open to new ideas, to

communicating bad news, to being transparent, and to sharing all relevant information. Is communication open and transparent so that people know what's going on and have a voice in it?

4) *Empowerment.* People have a sense of being in control of themselves and their jobs. Do they feel that they play a significant role in the organization? They feel that their voice counts and that they are listened to by management and others.

5) *Learning.* The organization is itself a learning organization and therefore open and responsive to the environment. Is the company organized for harvesting and using the learnings that people on the front line and up the management levels to the senior managers?

6) *Creativity and innovation.* As the organization is a learning community, do each of the wild and crazy ideas from all parts of the organization get a hearing? Do the people new to the company and who are still not paradigm-blind get to input their ideas?

2) Encountering an Irrelevant Culture

Cultures can and do become irrelevant. Sometimes they change quickly, but most of the time they change slowly and almost imperceptibly. A culture, as an expression of a human community, can outlive its usefulness as the world moves on. They change as markets, values, beliefs, etc. grow and develop so that what once was normal and acceptable, becomes dysfunctional and unacceptable. All one has to do is recall how women were once treated, or minorities, or how children were once treated or punished to understand the slow yet inevitable change that occurs within every culture. When cultures change, they usually simply grow old and become redundant—unuseful and irrelevant. Then they lose their power to win the allegiance or loyalty of people.

Cultures can and do simply become irrelevant. That happened to the culture of Knighthood in mediaeval Europe. Within that culture to be a Knight you had to be a lord of a castle, ride a horse, fight in hand-to-hand battle, lead a group of 50 men, etc. Do that, show courage and bravery and you could be knighted. Those were the prerequisites. All of that is now gone. Why did that happen and how? It became irrelevant. The irrelevance began as lords eventually wanted to be knighted without having to be a fit soldier or engage in fighting. So as those requirements were eventually dropped, the meaning of Knighthood changed. It began to mean less and less. It offered less and less challenge. Eventually fat, lazy, but rich men could *buy* Knighthood! And with that change, so the culture of

Knighthood changed. Today it is all but a memory of a culture from long, long ago.

3) Encountering a Sick Culture
Beyond the challenge of becoming irrelevant, cultures can, and do, also become sick, and even toxic. They can become so toxic, in fact, that they cease to be human or humane. In a company dominated by a spirit of bureaucracy, the bureaucratic rules can become so important that they become more important than the people they were meant to serve.

This is no new problem. It has been around for millennia. In the first century, Jesus of Nazareth challenged the leaders and culture of his day when he provoked them by breaking some of their rules about the Sabbath. "Man was not made for the Sabbath; but the Sabbath was made for man." What then results? Sometimes people are sacrificed for the sake of the rules. In cultures of authority or power, those in control often push authority or power at the expense of human compassion and well-being.

A culture is sick to the extent that it does not allow the full development and growth of the persons within that culture. So to the extent that the culture prevents people from fulfilling their basic (lower) human needs and their higher human needs (the higher or self-actualization needs), to that extent the culture is not healthy. Every culture that denies or constrains healthy human functioning is doomed to fail. It's just a matter of time.

3) Changing the Culture
For an executive and an Executive Coach, the question is, "Does the culture of the organization support the human spirit?" In the book *Coaching with Spirit* (2002), Teri-E Belf quoted the following that speaks to the kind of culture that organizations need:
> "An organization that is built on the basis of a coaching mindset is able to capture the human spirit— and it is this ingredient that aligns personal and organization goals and results in high performance." Bianco-Mathis, Nabors, and Roman (2002)

When it comes to changing a culture, we have to ask, What kind of a culture do you want as a leader? How much do you already have that as part of your culture? What needs to change? For Executive Coaches the answer is easy—we want a coaching culture. We want a self-actualization culture. What will such a culture be like? What will be the qualities and characteristics of such a culture?

It will be a Learning Culture. It will involve people who have learned to think on their own, to ask questions, to invite others to think aloud with the leader, in the pursuit of solving the problems that we face. Given the speed of business today, learning is more critical than ever. In fact, coaching has entered the business world to enhance the learning in organizations and to improve the transfer of that learning from the training room back to the business. Coaching enables learners to take charge of their own learning and to create continuous learning— even learning on the run to keep up with things as the world and the markets as they keep changing. Learning how to keep evolving roles, procedures, and processes to be relevant and productive.

It will be an open and transparence culture. It will be open to change and development. It will empower people to act autonomously within a value framework of collaboration. This is about being open and above-board with information and decision making within an organization. The opposite is a closed culture full of secrets where people treat information as power and use information as a tactic of control.

Ricci and Wiese in *The Collaborative Imperative* write that when you're open and transparent you will be transparent about the answers to three questions regarding the decision making processes within the organization:
      1) Who made the decision,
      2) Who is accountable for the outcomes of the decision, and
      3) Is the accountability real? (p. 49)

It will be a culture of respect and care. It will be a culture that gets rid of the old mantra, "It's not personal, it's business." We will then realize that *what we do in business is personal.* It cannot be otherwise. The culture will highlight care and respect because to work in an environment without care or respect is to work in an environment that does not promote or protect that which is human and humane in us. Yet within a culture of respect, people will treat the company as "a good place to work." They will have one or more friends there, and will care about the people they work with.

It will be a high performance culture. To have this kind of a culture we need a strong sense of responsibility and ownership. This is what we mean by the term "agency." Every individual in the organization will see and feel oneself as an active agent. This experience will create "can-do" attitude — a strong bias for action. People will then naturally take the initiative to get things done. This is the culture which will make it easy for people to take pride in their work and accomplishments. That, in turn, will increase engagement, productivity, passion, higher performance, and joy.

It will be a culture of engagement. This will stand in contradistinction to a culture of dis-engagement where people merely comply without putting their mind or heart into their work. It will be a culture where the leaders win the minds and hearts of people so that they are fully aboard with the vision and mission of the company.

What cause people to become engaged? The meaning, purpose, and reason for being is clear and compelling. If it is not, if it doesn't reward work well done, then the organization is flying blind

It will be a culture of fun and enjoyment. Leadership will find ways to elicit fun in employees and managers so that people enjoy the work environment and the comradrie that they experience at work. George Zimmer, CEO Men's Wearhouse fully believes in this and has written:
> "The goal of business is that we can have fun, and we are dead serious about it; it's even in our corporate bylaws." (Quoted by Dave Logan, *Tribal Leadership,* p. 117)

It will be a culture that combines short term and long term perspective. This will create a culture that doesn't cut short processes that cannot be achieved in a quarter but which takes longer to be effective. Today, short-term thinking about the profits of this quarter are creating all sorts of problems in organizations from higher stress levels, mistakes, reactivity, negative emotions, and lower productivity.
> "To survive, CEOs must learn to value short-term and long-term results, develop the skill to balance both, and invest time required to achieve this balance." (*Leadership Pipeline,* p. 117)

All of these are facets of a Self-Actualization Culture. In *Unleashing Leadership* (2010) I devoted chapter twelve to this subject. In defining the culture of a self-actualizing company I listed twelve features that would indicate such a culture:[1]
> *1. Financial Intelligence and Stability:* People make enough to live

and meet their basic requirements.

2. Safety: People fulfil their need for stability via their work, knowing their world and feeling sufficiently safe in their career.

3. Personal Development: People feel that they are learning, growing, developing, relating, etc.

4. Meaning and Meaningfulness: People see and feel the significance of their work so that they find it inspiring.

5. Empowerment and Responsibility: People feel a sense of control and power in what they do, and not a victim of a system that is unresponsive to them.

6. Respect: People feel recognized, acknowledged, and appreciated by their leaders and colleagues within their company.

7. Social Connections: People feel connected to others so that they think of their company as a "great place to work."

8. Synergy: People feel that what they do cooperates and collaborates with others so that together they are creating something more than the sum of the parts.

9. Creative Engagement: People feel that they are using some of their best knowledge and skills at work and so are engaged in a creative enterprise.

10. Openness and Learning: People feel that there is an openness in the company and people so that together the organization is a learning organization.

11 Peak Experiences: People regularly have those moments of joy and ecstasy that make life feel special and worthwhile.

12. Peak Performance: People see that what they are doing together is of high quality and from time to time a world-class or a peak performance.

Within a self-actualizing company the culture that develops is one that grows out of the vision of self-actualization and fully embodies the premises of self-actualization. Specific elements of a self-actualizing culture have been described by hundreds of forward thinking business leaders and consultants. These elements are typically the very qualities and values recommended for business success and organizational development. As a result, in terms of content, very little of this is brand new. What is new is the background structure of the psychological frame that generates this new culture—self-actualization. That is, nearly all of the ideas, models, processes, and technologies in the fields of organizational development and business consulting are actually simply *pieces of the self-*

actualization puzzle. It is the model of Self-Actualization itself that is the framework for the puzzle.

Warren Bennis beautifully described the purpose of a self-actualizing company in the following words without ever using that word.

> "Since the release and full use of the individual's potential is the organization's true task, all organizations must provide for the growth and development of their members and find ways of offering them opportunities for such growth and development. This is the one true mission of all organizations and the principal challenge to today's organizations." (2009, p. 184)

Executive Coaching for a Cultural Change

What do we have to do to become a self-actualizing company? How do we achieve a culture that characterizes this high level of development? Four essential aspects of creating this cultural change involve the leadership, the level of engagement in people, the design of the new organization, and the creation of the new culture.

1) Establish a Collaborative Leadership Team.

It takes leaders. It takes visionary leaders and managerial leaders working together to facilitate a culture change that is deep and pervasive. A single individual cannot do it alone, it takes a team to achieve this. It takes a team that's made up of both visionary executive leaders, disciplined managerial leaders and employees who see and care about this vision. Richard Branson (2012) writes:

> "One of my key lessons over the years has been to surround myself with great management teams who complement me and ensure that we have the all-round skills to make our businesses succeed." (p. 19)

2) Lead people up the levels of engagement.

A self-actualizing culture is co-created and results in a high level of engagement. To do this, leaders have to address resistance to engagement. They cannot allow the attitude or actions of dis-engagement to continue or to spread. When it spreads, it spreads like a virus. Such has to be confronted and defused as soon as it arises. Then there has to be designed structures and processes so that *compliance* is made easy and natural.

To lead people up the levels of engagement, leaders have to communicate clearly, precisely, and with inspiration to win the minds and gain *agreement.* Invite communication from people at all levels so that they feel heard and feel that their contributions are considered.

In the process, one also has to be an exemplar leader that is "the change." This will win the hearts for *allegiance.* Leaders at the top also need to empower people, that is, share power to create co-leadership as you gain *full engagement.*[2]

3) Design the Organization for the Self-Actualization Culture.
While we have to have policies about rules and procedures, we need flexible and humane rules. The rituals for "the way we do things around here" need to be designed so they enable the desired culture to develop and thrive. This requires us to build in regular and constant feedback and benchmarks whether weekly or bi-weekly. This will enable us to constantly monitor the system so we can quickly adjust it.

To create culture change we need to design things so that every stakeholder in the company (i.e., customer, employee, investors, leaders, etc.) is able to "Seek the Peak." Chip Conley in his book, *Peak: How Great Companies Get their Mojo from Maslow* describes how to create a pyramid so each group within an organization can seek their self-actualization peak. He did that by building a hierarchy of needs for the customer, the employee, and the investor. Doing this allows you to understand where people are in meeting their needs. Then the executive leaders can intelligently help them to meet those needs.

4) Establish a Self-Actualizing or Coaching Culture.
Finally to create a self-actualizing culture, we have to be clear as to what that entails and what it will look like. Here are twelve such characteristics that I listed in the training manual for Unleashing Self-Actualizing leaders and companies.

> 1) *Inspirational:* Vision of possibilities and potentials.
> 2) *Transparency:* open, responsive, intense, direct, and constant communications: clarity, precise.
> 3) *Learning:* continuous improvement, feedback, risk taking, training, coaching, etc.
> 4) *Empowerment:* equipping, training, and coaching people to own and develop their inherent powers of responding.
> 5) *Collegial:* respect, democratic attitude, leaders are personally involved, look for information from people, collaborative.
> 6) *Responsible:* Empowered, self-managing groups, quality integral

to processes, proactive, disciplined, accountability, etc.

7) *Results-oriented:* productive, customer-focused, clear value proposition for customers.

8) *Self-Managing:* formation of teams in a department which manages itself.

9) *Enjoyment:* Humor, laughter, joy. Excitement and inspiration in importance and significance of the work.

10) *Congruence:* Credibility by doing what one says, walking the talk, being dependable.

11) *Flexibility:* Adaptable, responsive to market, etc.

12) *Accountability:* held to give account for one's tasks and responses.

Your Executive Take Aways

Anyone who coaches within organizations and companies will be in some way and to some degree *coaching to the culture* of that company. This becomes true with a vengeance for the Executive Coach. There's a reason for this. The reason is because if there's anyone in charge and responsible for the culture of a company, it is the leaders (both executive and managerial leaders).

A culture is not a mystical or mysterious thing, it is simply "the way we do things around here." A culture is literally "cultivated" (or created) by how we cultivate the minds and hearts and activities of the people who live and work in the organization. As you become clear about the culture that you want to facilitate— how will this affect your coaching?

• As a change agent and Executive Coach, how prepared are you for enabling executives to discover, detect, face, and deal with the cultures that are in their companies?

• If the quality of the culture goes to the leaders who created it or tolerate it, are you ready for challenging them regarding this?

• How will you integrate such challenge into your style of coaching?

• What do you currently know and understand about a coaching or self-actualization culture and what do you need to learn?

End of the Chapter Notes:

1. In Neuro-Semantics we have developed a training for leaders and managers based on the book, *Unleashing Leadership*. It is the fourth training in the *Seeking the Peak trainings*. See www.self-actualizing.org

2. For more about engagement, see Chapter 8 of *Unleashing Leadership*.

Chapter 13

THE CHALLENGE OF

EXECUTIVE DERAILMENT

"Development is the ultimate perk.
It can't be taken back once given, and it leads to other benefits."
The Leadership Pipeline, p. 163

"Coaching is not about you . . . it's about them!"
Graham Richardson

How do the great and mighty fall? And yes they do fall. Executives can, and often do, derail. How often? Actually quite frequently! Statistics indicate that in Australia, the average CEO lasts 3 years where as in the USA the average CEO lasts only 1½ years. Eighteen months—that is not very long. So what's happening with executives that they are moving in and out of the executive suite so often?

Richard Kilburg (2000) in *Executive Coaching* quotes statistics that indicate that 50% of executives will derail, that is, fail in their efforts to advance in their careers. Regarding this staggeringly high number, he identified the organization's design and culture at the heart of the problem:

> "Organizations are woefully unprepared to help managers perform well in their jobs and succeed in their careers." (2000, p. 104)

What accounts for the derailing? If the numbers are this high, why do individuals who consciously desire to succeed and do an excellent job, who bring energy and passion to their work, who put in long hours and sweat the details, and who possess superb educational foundations and technical backgrounds for their jobs, manage to fail so often?

"It Was Just an Off-handed Comment"
Before answering these questions, a review of the story of Tony Haywood, CEO of BP (British Petroleum) and what happened to him might be enlightening. It all happened when there was an explosion on an oil rig in the Gulf of Mexico off the shore of New Orleans. The explosion that started it all killed eleven men and broke open a pipeline deep under the ocean. Then with the oil flowing from beneath the ocean, the open pipeline contaminated ocean, and land with millions of barrels of oil. The contamination of thousands of gallons of oil went on for weeks. In the aftermath of the catastrophe, thousands of people lost their jobs and the whole area went into an economic distress which set in and lasted for years.

Into that disaster, the CEO of British Petroleum came to look into the problem of the spill and the effect it was having on the area. They studied it and set out to communicate to the public that BP was on it. BP promised to solve the ongoing spilling of oil into the ocean, bring relief to those suffering from the aftermath, and assume financial responsibility for the clean-up and recovery. BP promised billions of dollars for the recovery and delivered billions for the clean-up and relief of those impacted by the disaster.

Yet in the whole process, it only took one off-handed remark by Tony Haywood to end his career and send him racing home. That happened one afternoon, after spending two weeks in the New Orleans area. It happened when he was walking through an affected area and a reporter caught him in an off-moment. The reporter asked him an irrelevant, and yet politically explosive question about what he felt, and about getting things back to normal. He commented that he was ready to "get his life back."

"Oh, he wants his life back! His golfing!" That comment aired on all of the major television, cable news networks, and radio broadcasts that evening. And when it did, it didn't play well. It made him sound as if he was uncaring and selfish. As if he was dismissal of the situation. Eleven men had died, thousands lost their jobs or income, the ocean was being polluted with hundreds of gallons of oil every minute which lasted weeks, and he wants his life back! In spite of all that BP was doing, one off-handed comment was his undoing. The board immediately called him home and the last we heard, he was sent off to Siberia or somewhere!

Derailment

There are so many ways to go off the tracks—to derail. There are the obvious derailments—by illegal or immoral behaviors that violate the law or the ethical practices of an organization. Then there are the questionable activities that are not wrong in themselves, but certainly questionable in being risky. Of course, the more any person gets into a state of stress, the more risky become the behaviors. That is, when in a period of high stress, these behaviors are more potentially risky in terms of the danger of derailing.

What are the areas of derailment? What causes executives to fail? We can list the different causes and factors that lead to executive derailment into numerous categories.

1) Failure in one's own Personal Development:
> Ego-driven so that one is dominated by the fear of being wrong, so that one *has* to be right.
> The impatient quick-fix mentality that demands solutions immediately if not sooner. This tends to make one uncoachable because one cannot slow down and actually listen.
> Fear that creates the lack of courage so that one holds back and is over-nice to the point of not speaking up when necessary.

2) Failure in and with Personal Relationships:
> Sexual misconduct, sexual harassment.
> Not listening to people, dismissing people, putting people down.
> Railroading over others, being over-demanding in one's requirements.
> Failure in patience—impatiently listening and communicating.

3) Failure in Leadership:
> Failure to exhibit appropriate leadership behaviors.
> Failure due to being too ego-driven, over-valuing one's own opinions to the neglect of others.
> Failure due to being over-devoted to external relationships such as

government meetings, community events, celebrity golf tournaments.

Failure due to being over-confident and/or over-optimistic and not balancing the perspective with what could go wrong.

Failure to change or adapt to a required transition.

Failure to treat people right and so unnecessarily creating enemies by mistreating and dismissing people. Then, with the existence of enemies—there are people present who want to see you fall and who may work to see you derail.

4) Failure in meeting Business Objectives:

Failure to assimilate the culture of the company.

Failure to assimilate organizational politics, power, influence, etc.

Failure to reach the company's financial goals.

Failure to "watch the store."

Failure to sufficiently understand expectations of the board.

5) Failure to Build and Lead Effective Teams:

Failure to work effectively with groups and teams.

Failure to create high performance teams.

Failure to show openness to the opinions and ideas of others.

Failure due to over-valuing one or two trusted advisors and not listening to multiple perspectives to get a fuller perspective.

The problem of derailing may involve corporate theft, mishandling of funds, fraud, betrayal of trusts—the big problems. It may just as well involve little things like an insensitive comment at the wrong time or a trail of ruined relationships. People derail due to a personal weakness or a blind spot that trips one up. The person then fails to see a problem and so walks right into explosive situations. Obviously there are a lot of Executive Coaching challenges when coaching executives regarding derailment.

1) Coaching Executive Weaknesses

2) Coaching Executive Blind-spots

3) Coaching for the Lack of Executive Accountability

1) Coaching Executive Weakness

Obviously you will want to find and address potential mines for executive derailment. In spite of that, you will not get far if you go after it too directly. So, for example, if you start the coaching session by asking: "What are your personal weaknesses that could derail you?" "What weak spots in your leadership style would you like to be coached on today?"

That approach seldom works. The reason for the ineffectiveness of this too direct approach is not hard to discover. That's because when it comes to a weakness or a weak spot, just about everybody feels vulnerable. Executives also will feel exposed and vulnerable. So no wonder when someone points out a weakness, most of us will not be very open to talk about it. This is especially true for those in the highest positions of organizations—people who have power, status, and reputations to protect.

For this reason, you usually have to gently nudged executive weaknesses out into the open and you have to do so slowly and gently. Most often the weaknesses are best revealed by a 360-feedback. That makes it more objective and less like a personal attack. There's another factor that also contributes to this reluctance. Namely, most of us tend to protect ourselves from the awareness and knowledge of a weakness. We do so by the defense mechanisms of denial, justification, intellectualization, etc.

What are we talking about when we speak about a *weakness* or *weak spot*? A weakness could be:
- An under-developed understanding or skill.
- An area of understanding or skill that we find especially difficult to develop. It's as if we are not "wired" for that area (i.e., language, mathematics, music, athletics, etc.). It's one of the natural multiple intelligences in which we are not strong.[1]
- A skill that is mis-placed and so used inappropriately.
- A strength of personality (knowledge or skill) over-done or over-played.

For under-developed skills or knowledge, the solution is easy— focus on it, learn it, and give oneself to deliberately practice, and sufficient time for development. For those capacities wherein a person has less capacity due to one's neurological wiring or disposition (where a person scores very low on the multiple intelligence tests), the solution is to manage by delegating or communicating so others understand and can supplement with their strength. For capacities or competencies that are inappropriately misplaced, coaching can help identify appropriate responses— how and when and with whom in applying the skills.

Often a weakness is to found in the shadow of a strength or an impressively powerful skill. Someone who is strong at the high levels of strategy may be weak at the details, or vise versa. Someone who is a great people person, may be poor at holding people accountable. Someone who is fabulously charming may simultaneously be phobic of conflict. Someone who is fastidiously reliable may be seen as a perfectionist, or even a bully, to those who are less concerned with turning out results, or without a sense of urgency. Inside of strengths are weaknesses. It's these weaknesses that we are usually blind to.

What do you do as an Executive Coach for this common area of executive derailment that involves a strengths over-played? First, help the executive realize that executive leaders are often derailed by over-playing to their strengths. This leaves them exposed to their weaknesses. A senior manager who prides himself on his energy may over play it and work him or herself to the point of burnout. Over-playing a driving value or a perceptual filter (e.g., meta-program) typically creates problems by devaluing or suppressing its opposite.

Once you have facilitated an awareness of this problem, then keep posing quality control questions about it. The design of these questions is to begin to create a focused intention to counter-balance the strength.

> "Does this serve you in the long-run?"
>
> "Does this over-playing to your strength empower you or does it undermine your effectiveness?"
>
> "How does the shadow weakness inside this over-riding strength fit in with your professional values?"

2) Coaching Executive Blind-Spots

Blind-spots— we all have them. Everybody is blind to certain facets of themselves. No one is so totally self-aware so that they have no facets of their own way of being in the world that's unknown to them. Yet how do any of us come to *see* what we are *blind* to?[2]

Blind-spots are those areas where we are simply not aware of ourselves— what we are doing, how we are coming across, and the affects we have on others. The solution for this is obviously: Become more aware, make the unsaid said, make conscious what has been an unconscious response or behavior.

The Johari Window (developed by Joe Luft and Harry Ingham) identifies two kinds of blind spots.[3] Yet the really *deep blind spots* are those which occur at a higher level to belief frames. We are often blind to the frames that govern our most outside-of-conscious assumptions. Because we live inside of the frames, we can't see them. That's why we need others to help us see ourselves.

```
┌──────────────────────────────────────────────────────────────────────┐
│  Johari Window                                                         │
│                                    SELF                                │
│                       Known to Self          Unknown to Self           │
│                      ┌──────────────────┬──────────────────────┐       │
│    Known             │                  │                      │       │
│    to Others         │   Public         │   Blind              │       │
│                      │   Public Self    │   Self-Blindness     │       │
│  OTHERS              │                  │                      │       │
│                      ├──────────────────┼──────────────────────┤       │
│    Unknown           │                  │                      │       │
│    to Others         │   Private        │   Unknown            │       │
│                      │   Personal Secrets│  Deep Blindness     │       │
│                      └──────────────────┴──────────────────────┘       │
└──────────────────────────────────────────────────────────────────────┘
```

If you or your executive client are a life-long learner, a person committed to your own growth and development, then you undoubtedly know the experience of studying and understanding far more than you do. In this case, *you know far more than you do.* That is, there are areas of life or work that you *know* what to do, yet you are not *doing.* You have a knowing–doing gap.

It could be that you are *over-informed* and simultaneously *under-reflective* about how to translate the information. When this happens, because you "know" something, and because you know that you know, *you never revisit it.* This is the problem. When you think you"know," you never question your knowledge. So you become less and less open to updates or to new knowledge. This is what makes a person under-reflective.

From there the problem of being *over-informed* about something *and* under-reflective about one's knowledge, the person does not take the time to think about what they know. The temptation then arises to trust one's knowing without paying attention to one's doing. As a result, the person may not act on what he or she knows. And executive clients are often caught in this dilemma.

Unless this changes, the person will continue to become better and better educated about his or her original knowledge, less reflective, and therefore less competent. The person can have good intentions, even noble aspirations, yet the results will become increasingly disappointing. Why does this happen? Because in the end, the previous knowledge becomes less relevant to the ever-changing territory.

There are two reasons for why this happens. First, perhaps the person does not know *how* to close the knowing-doing gap. If that is the case, use the Mind-to-Muscle pattern to create the needed quality of integrity and congruency. This pattern enables a person to translate what he or she knows intellectually into muscle memory so that the person knows it in one's body and neurology. (See Appendix B)

Second, perhaps the person has a hidden self-conflicting system. This means that there may be a self-organizing system within that is structured and designed to prevent one from activating the change that is consciously wanted. So ask, "Could there be within you a self-organizing system that effectively, systematically, and dependably prevents you from achieving what you think you want?"

Coaching to Prevent Executive Derailment
The best prevention for executive derailment is first to secure from the executive a commitment to continual growth and development. Within a commitment like this is the capacity to be a continual learner and to openly and transparently accept one's fallibilities. This includes the willingness to look clearly at oneself. When this intention is robustly present, a person will be fully open and coachable for recognizing and shoring up one's weaknesses and to search for and accept blind-spots, to set up structures for accountability.

Your Executive Coaching Take Aways
Executives can and do derail. No matter how skilled, how competent, the level of expertise, status, influence, etc., executives can and do get off track. Executives do fall and fall mightily. *For discerning executives the solution is prevention and risk management.* It can happen to the best of people and it can happen, not only due to personality and character flaws, it can happen given the very nature of the executive position in today's world.

The secret to all forms of executive development and, in particular, to blind spots and derailment is regular, objective and constructive feedback. Seeking and accepting feedback requires an inquisitive mind, a hunger for learning, humility, the strength to be openly vulnerable, and an open mind to continuous improvement.[4]

- How much time and effort have you put into flushing out your own blindspots or dealing with your weak areas?
- Coaching an executive on a weakness or blindspot requires lots of courage. How is your courage for bringing up these things?
- What frames do you need to set with executive clients so that when these facets of life and personality arise, you can bring them up in service of your client?

End of Chapter Notes:

1. Howard Garner's Multiple Intelligence Model. You can find this is the books *Frames of Mind: A Theory of Multiple Intelligences* (1983) and *The Unschooled Mind: How Children Think and How Schools Should Teach* (1991), and *Multiple Intelligences: The Theory in Practice* (1993).

2. For a pattern for addressing Blind-Spots, see the article on www.neurosemantics.com / Articles. For more about Blinds Spots, see Claudia Sheldon's book, *Blind Spots: Achieve Success by Seeing What you Can't See* (2007) or Madeleine Hecke's book, *Blind Spots: Why Smart People Do Dumb Things* (2007).

3. See *Management of Organizational Behavior* (1988) by Paul Hersey and Kenneth H. Blanchard for a description of the Johari Window.

4. See TED videos, Brené Brown: The Power of Vulnerability and Listening to Shame who says that the greatest act of courage is being open and vulnerable. She uses the term "shame" as equivalent to conditional self-esteem, low self-esteem, self-contempt that one wants to hide from others, the fear of being seen as real. The fear of not being good enough is what she calls "shame."

PART III:

EXECUTIVE

COACHING

CONVERSATIONS

Chapter 14

COACHING CONVERSATIONS

FOR EXECUTIVES

"The coach's job is to ask questions,
not to give answers."
Laura Whitworth, *Co-Active Coaching* (1998)

"It is all about communication—
80% of all issues are dominated by communication factors."
Angus McLeod, *Performance Coaching* (p. 11)

Now that you know the challenges that commonly face executives, what are the unique coaching conversations that you can use when coaching? What are the fierce conversations that enable you to get to the heart of things and address these challenges?

When it comes to the relationship between an executive and an Executive Coach, *the conversation is the relationship.* That is, the conversation between them creates the relationship, determines the quality of the relationship, and ultimately, *is* the relationship. That's because the conversation is the coaching. We coach via the conversation.

Given this, *the quality of the relationship,* as well as the quality of the coaching, is a function of *the quality of the conversation.* No wonder your coaching conversations are so critical, so powerful, and so central. They are powerful and determining even though when engaged in them, they almost never feel that way. When you and I are within the conversation, it only seems that we are talking. But no. It is much more than that.

Coaching is Not a Normal Conversation
Coaching is conversing. That's why dialogue lies at the very nature of coaching. What happens in the coaching room is a dialogue between coach and client. But (and this is a critically important "but") *it is not a normal conversation.* It is a very unique and special conversation; it is a conversation like none other. There are several factors that make the coaching conversation different and not "normal."

First, the conversation is one-sided. "Normal" conversations are two-sided. You talk about your view and opinions and then I share my view and opinion. You tell your story and that reminds me of something similar in my own experience which I then share. But in coaching, the conversation is one-sided—it is all about the client. The sharing does not go back and forth. The focus stays exclusively on the client— what the client wants, thinks, believes, feels, etc.

Second, the conversation is intensely focused and intimate. "Normal" conversations stay pretty much on the surface. They are typically shallow. Only occasionally do they drop down into some personal and intimate areas. Yet in coaching conversations, this is precisely where the conversation lives—at some of the deepest aspects of the client's experience. That's makes the conversation seem very direct, "fierce," confrontational, and intimate.

Third, the conversation goes for the self-reflexive thoughts-and-feelings. These deeper (or higher) thoughts are mostly outside-of-consciousness. In Meta-Coaching we call them the person's inner matrix of frames of meanings. "Normal" conversations typically deal with first level and maybe second-level thoughts. Coaching conversations go much deeper (or higher) to the thoughts-behind-the-thoughts, to the feelings-behind-the-feelings— to the *meanings* (e.g., assumptions and hidden beliefs) from which the person is operating as the person's map or model of the world. We also go to the kind of thinking by which the person has created the experience.

Fourth, the conversation is challenging and even personally confrontational. Because the purpose of the coach is to stretch the person beyond his or her current experience, by its very nature, coaching is challenging. It invites the person into a more intimate and intense self-awareness. It does this by mirroring to the person the responses that one might want to refine and/or develop.

All of this explains why the coaching conversation is like none other. It is definitely *not* a "normal" conversation and therefore unlike the conversations we have at the dinner table, in the pub, in the boardroom, or even at the water cooler.

The Nature of Coaching Conversations

When it comes to conversations, there are many different kinds of coaching conversations and each with different effects. Via a conversation, we can express our opinion and hear the opinions of others, we can connect mind-to-mind and even heart-to-heart. Via a conversation we can learn from others as well as from ourselves. Via a conversation, we can forge bonds, discover new insights, negotiate win/win arrangements, and many, many more things.

I like how Susan Scott (2002) in *Fierce Conversations* describes conversations and what she says about the power and the surprise of a conversation:

> "Our lives succeed or fail gradually, then suddenly, one conversation at a time. While no single conversation is guaranteed to change the trajectory of a business, a career, a marriage, or a life, any single conversation *can.* We effect change by engaging in robust conversations with ourselves and others" (p. 7)

Through *real conversations* we change and through them also we can facilitate change in others. This is the heart of coaching and Executive Coaching. It is also the power that the executive leader will utilize to lead or stabilize change in an organization. The kind and quality of these conversations make a difference and herein lies the art of Executive Coaching. Your ability to hold a robust conversation, a fierce conversation, is your ability to get to the heart of things, invite transformation, awaken vision, evoke solutions to problems, and much, much more.

Among the basic Coaching Conversations that we have identified in Meta-Coaching are the first six. The first six describe the most common coaching conversations— the core conversations.

1) The Clarity Conversation
2) The Decision Conversation
3) The Planning Conversation
4) The Experience (or Resource) Conversation
5) The Change Conversation
6) The Confrontation Conversation

The next set of six coaching conversations are those that occur with groups. These conversations are describe much more fully in the book, *Group and Team Coaching* (2013).

7) The Mediation Conversation
8) The Meta-Conversation
9) The Rounds Conversation
10) Problem-Solving Conversation
11) Collective Learning Conversation
12) Conflict Resolution Conversation

What then are the Coaching Conversations that an Executive Coach will have with an executive? These include the following six:

13) The Sounding Board Conversation (or Clarity Conversation)
14) The Outcome Conversation (or Clarity Conversation)
15) The Feedback Conversation
16) The Systems Conversation
17) The Paradox Conversation
18) The Potential Conversation

Coaching Conversations in the C-Suite
If the kind and quality of conversation is that powerful in our lives, then when you change the conversation, you change your thinking and feeling, your actions and responses—you change your life. As an Executive Coach, as you engage clients with different conversations, you invite new learnings, a change of intentions, new resources, possibilities, etc. Herein lies one of the great leverage points of change of an Executive Coach. The questions you ask and the way you ask the question drives the kind and quality of answers that emerge. All of this requires a slower, more demanding, and more deliberative approach. In Executive Coaching, as in all forms of coaching, the way you frame a question determines where and how the client looks for an answer.

If coaching, and especially Executive Coaching, is all about the relationship, then to match you will want to aim to go as faster or as slow as your client is going. What is best is to spend time seeing the world through the client's eyes to deepen our own understanding of his or her experiential world.

You as an Executive Coach

Who do *you* need to be to function effectively and optimally as an Executive Coach? What *identity* or role do you need to develop or step into? What *quality of character* do you need to access to be able to engage an executive in one of these coaching conversations?

1) Strong – Yet Compassionate

First and foremost, you have to be strong in yourself and in your skills, that is, confident, firm, and definite. You cannot be passive, weak, hesitant, or insecure. You have to know your stuff, trust yourself, trust your skills and competence ... and then be present to flexibly adjust in the moment. If you are insecure in yourself, the executive will detect it. He or she will smell your fear and hesitancy. And that will undermine the person's trust in you.

Having said that, you also need to have a soft side, a heart that is caring and compassionate. This means caring about the person, wanting the best in him or her, and respecting the person above and beyond the behaviors and responses that your client produces. Combining strength and compassion requires a unique synergy. As you do that, that combination will then become your style as a coach. It will describe how you carry yourself, and therefore part of your personal brand.

With those who live and work in the C-suite, you cannot be a "Yes" person. You cannot be awed or intimidated by those in the executive roles nor by their status, position, money, or power. They are just people. Fallible human beings. While they are often bluntly direct, and may even use language that strikes you as intimidating or even threatening, you will not allow yourself to be put off or intimidated by that. And just as important, you will also not allow yourself to be seduced by flattery or charm. As an Executive Coach, it's just their way of talking.

Being robust in your own skills and processes, you will aim to be friendly, good natured, empathetic, and operating from a sense of equality and democracy. As you come to know and trust your style, it will be in that manner that you will give tough yet fair feedback. Holding firm standards, you will simultaneously be human and humane.

Your "strength" as a coach is your self-efficacy. Efficacy is your sense of personal effectiveness for handling challenges. It is your "power" to know what you are doing and why as you work with and through others. This self-efficacy comes from a heightened sense of your own self-awareness and enables you to have a sense of self-control and self-discipline.

2) Stable Yet Creative

Your stability will be your inner gyroscope that allows you to know and operate from your center. Your center will be your own dignity, self-value, values, beliefs, principles, etc. To further ground and center yourself, you will want to have sufficient emotional intelligence (EQ) with yourself to know what you're feeling, how you are creating your feelings, how to manage your stress, fears, angers, anxieties, uncertainty, ambiguity, attraction, etc. All of this is entailed in E.Q. and is a demonstration of emotional mastery.

E.Q. speaks about the ability to tolerate emotions both in yourself and in your client. It speaks about embracing the emotions of discomfort when you are uncomfortable or in the presence of different or strange emotions. This is crucial for those times when your client becomes emotional. At that very moment, your own emotional intelligence requires that you embrace the reactivity in another person as when a leader might lose his or her cool and become emotionally reactive.

Moments like that provide you a tremendous window into the person. So if you treat the emotional reactivity as *information,* in fact, great information, you can then explore how the person creates that experience in that context. Your own emotional intelligence, as demonstrated in your ability to cope with your emotions, provides a model and example for the executive. Then as he or she develops an inner peace within self, the person can then engage in healthy and appropriate thinking, deciding, and creativity.

From your state of emotional stability, you can then temper and texture it. You can meta-state your emotional stability with creativity, playfulness, or even teasing. Doing this enables you to invite new potentials to emerge in yourself. After all, because leaders and organizations grow by innovating new things, they need to be creative and to elicit creativity in others.

3) Courageous Yet Appropriate

For Susan Scott in *Fierce Conversation,* "A careful conversation is a failed conversation." This describes how executive coaching can fail and often fails—the coach is too careful, too cautious, or too timid. This tends to be characteristic of novice coaches, who fear about going very deep with clients. They do not dare ask the potentially upsetting questions. Fearing to challenge their clients, they accept superficial answers without digging deeper. All of this calls for courage and explains why courage is such a critical as a state for an Executive Coach.

Courage is needed because without courage, you will chicken out and fail to provide the rigorous coaching that you have been hired to provide as an Executive Coach. First you need the courage to be direct with your executive clients rather than wishy-washy, timid, hesitant, and non-assertive. This is needed so that you model how the executive also can be direct and compassionate. Many executives tell about how they actually learned courage by seeing it modeled in the coach.

In *Co-Active Coaching* (1998), Laura Whitworth writes about the courage that a coach needs. You have to have courage, she writes and to be . . .

> "... courageous because clients need to find the courage in themselves to make significant change in their lives. The environment needs to be safe enough for clients to take the risks they need to take and be courageous. In this they can approach their lives with curiosity, interest, power, creativity and choice." (p. 15)

Next courage is needed in order to ask the questions and/or provide the feedback that no one else will dare to ask or provide. Most executives have all too many "Yes" men (and women), people who pander and brown-nose and say what they think the person wants to hear. Executives do not need another person doing that. They especially do not need that from their Executive Coach. They need (and many want) someone who will stand up to them and call their hand on things that they are doing which could mess things up.

You will need courage to courageously champion the changes that the person needs to make in oneself or in the organization. Again, this is often not easy and can be very challenging. You will need courage when the executive you're coaching gets cranky, grumpy, and/or impatient.

Then there is the courage to challenge as you hold an executive accountable. That too can be scary. After all, will that upset the person? Will you be fired? Will the person receive the challenge? Obviously, to do this you will need a robust sense of self, an ego strong enough so that you can set personal boundaries and hold them firm. Are you courageous enough to ask your client such questions: What topic are you hoping I will not bring up? What responsibilities are you avoiding?

4) Pacing Yet Leading

Coaching always begins by calibrating to the client, pacing or matching his or her verbal and non-verbal expressions. This gains rapport and describes how we connect to a person. Then we lead. So first you come into sensory awareness to identify the person, in all that the person is offering you—words, gestures, behaviors, etc.[1]

So you match the person physically, linguistically, and psychologically so you really get a deep understanding of who the person is, what the person is about, his or her dreams, hopes, fears, challenges, goals, etc. Because the coaching is not about you, but completely about the client, getting to know the client on his or her terms is quintessential. What keeps this person up at night? What does she want? What does he fear?

As you match, you will ask the Well-Formed Outcome questions to specify the person's objective in the coaching. You will be setting frames for both yourself and your client so that your focus is entirely on the client. In doing this, you are not trying to impress, only to connect. As an Executive Coach set the client's objectives as the relevance frame for the session and use it to challenge whatever distracts from the objective.

5) Collegial Yet Respectful Honor

Start from the premise that you, as an Executive Coach, are an equal to the executive. Whatever your title, status, financial income, etc. or whatever the executive's rank, title, and status—all of that is beside the point in the coaching relationship. It is *not* relevant in Executive Coaching. Speak and deal directly as you would to an equal, a colleague.

In the book, *The NLP Coach* (2001), Ian McDermott and Wendy Jago emphasis that the client is the expert regarding him or herself as well as regarding the challenges, problems, issues and the solutions. So as an Executive Coach, coach from the perspective that the client is, and will be, the architect of his or her own success. Coach to the client's self-expertise.

When you do this, you'll then be able to bring a humanizing humor into the

7session. It will be humanizing because the humor will enable the client to lighten up and be able to laugh at his or her foibles and imperfections. It will be humanizing in that it breaks the stranglehold of seriousness that creates unnecessary stress and pressure both on self and those who one leads.

6) *Present Yet Seeing Patterns*
The power of feedback lies in the immediacy of the feedback, and more particularly in the ability to give feedback in real-time. This means giving it in the moment that the response occurs. This is an advanced skill and one that typically requires some years of experience. Being present in the moment allows you, as the Executive Coach, to pick up on what's happening while seeing patterns. Does this seem paradoxical? You are able to both be fully present and, at the same time, able to step back and from a higher level recognize recurrent patterns.

When presenting the detected patterns, do so respectfully and provisionally. After all, you could be wrong. So make it tentative as you check with the client. As you present the pattern, while it may be there, the client may not recognize it. Blind spots are especially like that, so let it go. "Well, I thought I detect that pattern, but perhaps not." No worry. If it is a pattern, it will return. And when it does, bring it up again. In this way, by repeatedly highlighting behaviors, that client will come to recognize the pattern. He or she will personally discover the ah-ha moments.

7) *Doing yet Being*
With executives, the problem will seldom be getting them to *do* things, they are already great at that. The problem will be getting them to *be*. *Doing* is their strength. Typically it is how they have arrived at their current position in the organization. *Being*— that's the challenge. So if the conversation *is* the relationship, then simply getting the executive to take the time out to reflect is the first challenge and success.

At the heart of Executive Coaching is *relationship coaching*. That's because most executives, whether middle, senior management, or CEOs do not need coaches for business issues. After all, most of them have MBAs and are well informed about business. It is relationships that they need to learn how to handle more effectively, the relationships that they have with their board, their colleagues, their reports, committee, leadership team, stockholders, public, groups with vested interests, etc.

Skills for the Conversation
Now if the quality of your communications is the quality of your coaching, then raising the quality of your communicating enhances and enriches the quality of your coaching.

At the most basic level of coaching this means your skill of supporting: acknowledging, confirming, complimenting, praising, checking in with person, listening deeply, connecting to challenge, etc. It means exploring, detailing, and interrogating. It means asking questions and meta-questions to ground an experience and then interrogate the person's layers of frames of meaning as you mine the hidden knowledge within their system. It means mirroring as you receive and give feedback and especially as you mirror the here-and-now conversation. And it means evoking state in that you invite the person to feel and embody the experience.[2]

At a more advanced level it means empowering your clients so that as you facilitate them taking full ownership of their powers. You hold them accountable for their responsible-ability. It means challenging them as you confront them to stretch themselves in terms of their objectives. Your role is to be a supportive skeptic so that they can think through issues in a thorough and sound way and make high quality decisions. You will ask:
> What's at stake for you? What are you pretending to not know?
> In what areas are you selling yourself or human nature short?
> In what ways could you be playing yourself small?
> How are you hiding behind a persona and not being real?

As you hold these robust conversations, you engage them in such a way that the conversations are unique. They are direct, practical, tough, open, trucking with no secrets, and truth oriented to deal with the real issues. Your conversations with them are outcome-oriented so that they can achieve the practical results that they want. Typically, executives are focus on others, rather than themselves, so you challenge them to become more balanced in that orientation.

Powerful Questioning
By now, you will have probably noticed that the coaching conversation described here focuses primarily on asking questions. Nor is it just any question. The questions focus on putting the client into deep reflection. These are questions that bring about the emergence of beliefs, worldviews, paradigms, and opinions that may or may not be useful to the client. These

questions evoke learning by bringing awareness to the conversation so that the client can pay attention to what is germane to his or her development and growth.

We could say that your job as the coach is to evoke the client to articulate the answers to those questions in a way that brings the person's innermost frames out into the open. Once that happens they can then be examined and reconstructed to serve the client in a more and resourceful way. When this happens, the answers can be installed to become self-organizing attractors in the person. Doing this deliberately and purposefully puts them at the person's disposal instead of operating outside of awareness.

Your brain is an answering machine. Ask a question and no matter how simple, "What's your phone number?" "What did you have for breakfast?" your brain automatically and immediately goes into action processing the question to generate answers. If you have established requisite rapport with your client, and you ask a question that explores his or her inner reality, your client will be processing the question and generating answers.

If a person says, "I don't know," take a breath and hold that moment in suspense, because at that very moment, magic is in the air. So pause, hold the silence. Let the person's brain keep searching. Graham says that for him:

> "It's as if I can see the cogs turning and spinning as a virtual metamorphosis goes on within the client at the mind-body level as they keep processing the question as an instruction. Then oftentimes, mysteriously, the answer emerges."

Yet many people, perhaps most, miss it. That's why you will need to be listening very carefully. Even most clients do not, and will not, realize the moment when they have expressed an answer. That's when you play back the answer to the client that you've heard. Then, presto! Suddenly the person experiences a surprise—*you* know the answer to their challenge! "How did you do that? You are so brilliant to come up with that!" Also, very often the person will not realize that they spoke it and you are merely mirroring their own words. Yet when they discover that, this will generate a second 'Aha!' moment.[3]

Your Executive Take-Away
Coaching is all about *high quality conversations*— dialogues that engage a mind and heart and that enables an executive to come out from behind him or herself to be real as a human being. This is the conversation like none other because it is deep and authentic. Because it is authentic, it is transformative.

While there are numerous Coaching Conversations, there are some coaching conversations that are uniquely designed for Executive Coaching— which is the subject of the next chapters.
- If the conversation is the relationship, how does that change your perspective of the coaching conversation?
- How familiar are you with the 18 kinds of coaching conversations? Which kinds of conversations will you be wanting to learn more about or practice to become more skilled with?
- Gauge yourself on the character qualities of an Executive Coach presented in this chapter. What are your next learning steps?

End of Chapter Notes
1. The structure of rapport was one of the first things modeled in the field of NLP. It was discovered that to create rapport, one needed to match or pace the person. See *Influencing with Integrity* (1984) by Genie Laborde and *User's Manual of the Brain, Volume I* (1997).

2. All of these skills assumes that you have permission to engage a client and ask these intimate questions. If the client is not up for these fierce conversations, the coach will either be ineffective or will do damage. Graham notes that in this regard, Professor David Clutterbuck has quoted European research which suggests that 70% of the coaches that organizations allow through their doors are either achieving nothing, or doing actual damage.
3. There are many ways to answer the "I don't know" response. In Meta-Coaching we have a list of 15 ways to respond.

Chapter 15

THE SOUNDING BOARD

CONVERSATION

*Simply listening to another human being
is never a simple task; it is one of the most complex on the planet.*

"Be present and prepared to be no where else."
Susan Scott, *Fierce Conversations*

Sometimes people just need to talk out-loud. Sometimes all I need and want is for someone to just listen to me, and be with me, as I try my best to put my thoughts into words and to find the words that express my actual thoughts and feelings. Sometimes when this happens, and I get clear about what I'm actually thinking and feeling. All I really needed was someone to be a sounding board to me— someone to just listen, to be present, and to *not* try to do anything except listen with interest and respect. This describes one of the most basic Executive Coaching Conversations. And there's a reason for this.

The reason is due to the political nature of organizations. It is not uncommon for an executive to feel that he or she has no one to talk to. Then, without that kind of conversation, there is also the sense that there is no one who understands. And one can also not understand oneself. Understanding and feeling understood is the purpose of the Sounding Board

Conversation. Yet the amazing thing is that when a person can freely talk out what's on his or her mind, insights emerge much more freely as do solutions to problems. So also higher level understandings which a person could not have accessed by silent thinking or reflecting in a quiet meditative way.

We have all had the experience of coming to really understand something as we talked. It is as if the very process of talking out-loud in the presence of an empathetic listener enables us human beings to think better. How often have you had that experience? At times when I have caught myself talking something out loud in the presence of a colleague, I have actually been surprised at what I was expressing, and then I thought, "Someone ought to write that done, that was good!"

As simple as this sounds, it is much harder to do as a coach. Few people have learned how to *just listen.* Normally when we hear someone describe a challenge, a problem, or a struggle we can hardly resist the temptation of jumping immediately into problem-solving mode. Then we are off on the mission to find and to offer our brilliant advice. We then ask, "Have you thought about X?" "Have you tried Y?" Actually, these questions reveal our anxiety and challenge us to embrace uncertainty and ambiguity. It reflects *our* needs. That's why it can harmfully interfere with the process of our client.

Conversely, if you *just* listen, if you make yourself fully present with no objective other than to be present—you make possible the Sounding Board Conversation. Actually, and surprisingly, this is one of the most common conversations that Executive Coaches have with their clients.

The How of the Sounding Board Conversation
As this is a very different conversation from what's normal, how do you pull it off? As an Executive Coach, how are you to think about this Conversation? How are you to frame it so that you can use it as your way of deeply engaging your client? Where can you focus your attention to facilitate this conversation?

1) Focus on Awareness
To have this conversation as an Executive Coach, first set your intention to *just listen.* Without setting that intention, the need to intervene, to act, and to do something can quickly arise and take over. Yet once you've set the

intention, then when the need to "make things better" arises in you, you can just notice it, and let it go. Simply let the executive download stress, confusion, and talk things out. Simply encourage the person to talk, and as you do so, ask clarification questions to fill in your know-nothing frame of mind. Your not-knowing helps their clarification.

Focus on becoming and staying in sensory awareness so that you can just notice. The fact is, we humans are only able to control what we're aware of. Conversely, what you are unaware of is much more likely to control you. Awareness gives you choice. Awareness puts you at choice point. And sometimes, awareness *per se* is curative.[1] Raise awareness with awareness questions— raise awareness for increasing sense of responsibility.

- What's happening around you?
- How are you holding your body? How are you breathing right now?
- Which way does the person move his or her eyes?
- How are you smiling or not smiling when listening?

Invite your own awareness about the person's multiple systems— the biological systems, the inter-personal systems, the business, spiritual, linguistic, cultural, etc. Then simply ask questions that invite more awareness and then awareness of that awareness. Since questions empower people, in contrast to telling (which actually saves people from thinking), focus on asking questions that allow the person to think aloud about things that are typically in the back of his or her mind.

2) Focus on Learning

If you want to activate learning through the Sounding Board Conversation then focus your awareness questions on facilitating learning. Then let the person think out-loud about his or her learnings.

> "As you've been talking aloud, what have you discovered? What have you learned? And now, given that, what will you take away from that?"

This facilitates not only first level learning, but second-level learning as well. It invites the person to keep stepping up the levels of learning.

> "And if you step back from this, what have you learned about your ability to learn? What enables you to benefit the most in terms of learning?"

In facilitating learning, as a coach simply invite the client to make explicit what is latent in his mind-and-emotions. This develops the client's *meta-*capacity for stepping back, inviting discovery and insights, and claiming those insights. Without such self-awareness, the inner world is like a world of shadows. It's a dark and shadowy world hidden from the light of day and that only occasionally sparks of awareness emerge.

As you focus on learning, when you hear significant points or realizations, give expression to it— smiles, nod, utter "hmmm," "ah," or punctuate with, "What was that again?" "That sounds pretty significant, what do you think?" "Is that the solution you've been looking for?" As a coach, the way you respond can reward insights and discoveries and help make them more memorable. The way you respond can also discourage such discoveries.

You can also, at the end of the session, ask what has been learned and, "What will you take from this that will support your commitment, or take you to the next level of development?" "What's been the best thing?"

3) Focus on Reality

Because reality is not always self-evident, it needs to be interrogated in order to get it to release its secrets. Sometimes you have to question reality intensely to get to its hidden secrets. So, take reality into the backroom and like a CIA agent interrogate it thoroughly. Question it vigorously so that you can distinguish what is externally real to yourself from your perceptions of it. What questions do you have and will you ask about the executive's reality?

Once you have grounded a topic by indexing it in terms of what (subject), who (person), where (space), when (time), process (how), etc., and you have a good idea of the subject and have heard the thoughts and emotions about it, you can then explore the source of that information. You can also explore its validity and reliability. You can explore the person's understandings about it, the person's assumptions, implicit frames, etc.

*   You can explore its ecology: How well is this reality working?
*   How well is it working with regard to your health, fitness, wealth-creating, relationships, etc.?
*   You can explore the person's epistemology: How do you know that you know this?
*   You can explore the person's emotionality: What do you find as boring or irritating about it? What do you find scary, fearful, or intimidating?

While reality is never our enemy, what is real can be challenging, unpleasant, and even painful. Some of the constraints of reality can block us from our goals and we can feel frustrated, angry, or controlled by forces we cannot affect. Yet if there are constrains and factors that are real, and over which we have little to no control, then the beginning place for handling them is in facing them for what they are and accepting them. From there we can figure out how to influence them to whatever degree that such is possible. This is the wisdom of the Serenity Prayer:

> "God grant me the grace to accept what I cannot change, the courage to change what I can, and the wisdom to know the difference."

4) Focus on Change and Commitment
From a focus on awareness, learning, and both current and future reality, now move to focus on your executive client's response.

> So what? What needs to change? When does it need to change? How will it change? What can you do? Are you committed to making that change? What will the cost be if you do? What is your responsibility in this? Are you ready to step up to this responsibility?

Now it's possible to misuse these questions. In the context of a Sounding Board Conversation, you have to ask these questions slowly, thoughtfully, and gently. Just plant a question and see what happens. Pause. Be silent. Let the person be with the question in a reflective way. Ask the person to just talk aloud without censoring any of the thoughts and emotions that might arise. "Just let them arise and just notice them." These are not questions to facilitate a change conversation or an action plan conversation, these are still questions that allow the person's focus to shift to wondering what response to make and just listening to how this activates the person thinking.

Your Executive Coaching Take Aways
Sometimes what you offer the person in the executive role in Executive Coaching is to be a sounding board to the person. You present yourself as an empathetic listener so that the executive can talk out-loud, hear him or herself speak, and gain clarity about what he or she truly thinks, feels, values, understands, etc. This is increasingly true the more there are negative politics going on in the organization. That's because there will be fewer and fewer people with whom to talk who do not have political agendas.

It may seem simple and you may wonder how much good or how much value you are really doing by just listening and not offering your brilliant insights. Yet if you are fully present and actively listening— you are offering an incredibly important service that the executive can get nowhere else.

- What is your best state for *just listening* to someone? Experiment with calmness, peacefulness, playfulness, curiosity, relaxation, learning, etc. until you find your very best state.
- What state of mind do you need?
- How will you focus your attention so that you can be fully present and attending with your client when you are facilitating this conversation?

End of Chapter Notes:
1. ""Awareness per se is curative" is a formulation that comes from the old psychologists, Freud, Adler, Jung, etc. See *The Crucible* for the importance of awareness in change and in unlearning.

Chapter 16

THE OUTCOME

CONVERSATION

"If you want to build a ship,
don't gather your people and ask them to provide wood, prepare tools, assign tasks.
Call them together and raise in their minds the longing for the endless sea."
Antonie de Saint-Exupery

W herever there is coaching, there is a conversation about the direction, focus, outcome, and objectives of the client. Wherever there is coaching, the first question that the effective coach will ask, and ask every time, "What do you want? What do you really, really want?"

This is the Outcome Conversation and absolutely essential in coaching. It's essential because the client sets the agenda in the coaching, not the coach. The type of expertise that the coach brings to the coaching is not an expertise about what the client needs or wants—that's the content. The coach's expertise is in process—in facilitating the discovery, autonomy, empowerment, and unleashing of potentials in the client.

So the first conversation is about the future and, in Executive Coaching, it is about the leader's vision and direction whether for the executive personally or for the organization or for both. It is this conversation that forecasts with your client what he or she wants and how to reach that desired outcome. In Meta-Coaching we use an advanced Well-Formed Outcome Pattern which is comprised of eighteen questions. Within this process there are four sections and each one identifies the one of the four essential elements which is within a goal that is well designed.

The 18 Questions for Designing an Outcome

Theme:
   1) What do you want?
   2) What you see, hear, and feel when you get what you want?
   3) Why do you want that? What will it get you?

Contexts:
   4) Where do you want this?
   5) When is it possible to achieve this?
   6) With whom will you do this, if anyone?

Processes for Achieving:
   7) What do you have to *do* to obtain what you want?
   8) Are *you* able to do this?
   9) Can you do this?
   10) Have you ever done this?
   11) How many steps and stages are there to what you have to do?
   12) Do you have a plan or strategy for your actions?
   13) Does anything stop you or interfere with you doing this?
   14) How will you monitor your progress and what feedback will you want?
   15) Do you have the external resources?
       Do you have the internal resource you need?

Checks:
   16) Is this goal ecological, holistic, and realistic?
   3) Is it still compelling to you?
   17) Are you going to do this? Have you made a commitment to this?
   18) How will you know you have achieved it?

Section #1: Relevant Theme

The first three questions focus in on the client's theme and makes that theme ultimately relevant for the client. "What do you want? Why do you want that?" *What* targets the subject. It identifies the area or domain wherein there is something that the client thinks as desirable. *What* generally identifies the end-result from exerting oneself in taking the require actions to obtain something that will improve the quality of life. Many clients don't know what they want. If that's the case, ask, "What do you *not* want?" "And when you no longer have that, what will be present?" When the client tells you want they want—see if you can get an empirical description of it. That is, a description that is stated in see-hear-feel words. This VAK (visual, auditory, kinesthetic) description makes the goal specific and orients it to the real world. "What will that look like or sound like or how will you sense it in your body?"

While this may not be what your client really wants (because the presenting goal is frequently not the real goal), it is a beginning place. So lock it down. Use testing questions to do this. "So this is what you want? Are you sure?" Then link it to the kind of coaching conversation they seem to be calling for— "So you are wanting a Clarification Conversation to get really clear?" "So you're wanting a Change Conversation to change a limiting belief?"

Next, ask about motivation: "Why do you want that? Why is that important to you?" This calls forth the person's values and intentions. And with each value spoken, test it, confirm it, and holding that value in place, invite your client to rise up to the next highest value and intention. "So that's important to you? And when you get that, what does that give you that's even more important for you?" In this way, you discover the relevance of the theme. You discover the client's *big why* that lies in the background for wanting whatever he or she wants.[1]

Section #2: Grounded Contexts
The next three questions contextualize the relevant theme that you've co-created with your client. With the contexts, you ground the objective that your client *wants* with time, space, and personnel coordinates. So you ask, "When, where and with whom?"

The *when* gives you a rough time-line for the completion or achievement of the outcome. If it is sometime beyond the time frame of the session, then what you'll do in the session is in service of the larger outcome. If it can be achieved within the coaching session's time frame, then is the person ready for it? Ready for the change? And is it realistic? Here you jump down to the Ecology question (Question #16) and use it to check if the objective can be achieved in that time frame?

The *where* positions the outcome spatially to home, relationship, career, health, friends, and so on. In what domain is the outcome? Spatially where will the outcome occur? Depending on the outcome, does the location matter? If it does, what does the goal require in terms of space or location? If a goal is, "I want to move into a new home." does your client have any idea of where that new home would be? Does it matter?

The *with whom* identifies the social context if there is one. Does the goal itself require others? Starting a coaching practice certainly does. Who will you coach? Where is your market? Starting a company with one or more partners certainly does as well. Do you currently have a collaborative partner? If the outcome can be achieved in the session, then the answer to "With whom?" is you as the coach.

Section #3: The Processes for Reaching an Outcome
The third section is the section that describes *the how to* for the goal achievement. "How will you reach your goal?" The answer lies in what you have to *do* in order to get the results that you want. From the *awakening* of the first part and the *contextualizing* of the second part, this is the part where you get down to the details with your client. That's why people who think in very general terms (the global meta-program) find this challenging and have a tendency to skip this part. Yet this is *the how to* which will or will not actualize the goal. Without this part, the person can dream and hope and wish ... but will never make it real.

The key word in this section of questions is *do.* This is Question #7, "What do you have to *do* to obtain what you want?" *Doing* implies all of the actions that are required to reach one's desired outcome—action, responsibility, proactivity, and planning. For this reason the questions here begin to put the client *at cause* for making his or her dreams come true. This is where the effort of specifying the outcome enables us to have a precise target to aim for and work toward. Dreams just don't come true without effort. They don't just magically appear. They are the result of focused, disciplined, and planned effort.[2]

First, explore to check if this *doing* lies within the realm of the person's ability: "Are *you* able to do this?" "Is it within the person's power or does it lie within the realm of someone else's actions?" Then explore capability to see if the person has the skills, competency: "Can you do this?" If it is in the person's power—but she has not developed the skill—then developing the skill will be a first, and smaller, objective within the larger objective.

You can then check out the person's history: "Have you ever done this?" Perhaps the person has already done it, but quit before achieving it. Or that when the person attempted to act on his goal, he lacked the persistence, resilience, belief, or some other essential quality. Here a post-event review may identify hidden resources and/or key factors for the outcome.

The complexity of the doing is explored with the next question:
> "How many steps and stages are there to what you have to do? How many things does a person have to *do* in order to reach the desired outcome? Are there a lot? Are there natural stages that the person will have to go through?"

When there is a lot of complexity and numerous stages, then people usually need a plan, hence the next question: "Do you have a plan or strategy for your doing what needs to be done?" And if a person creates a plan, then following that plan requires monitoring how one is doing and the milestones along the way. It also involves identifying what feedback the person will need to determine where one is and how to keep improving.
> How will you monitor your progress and what feedback will you want? Will the monitoring be hourly, daily, or weekly? From whom will you want feedback? How do you want to get this feedback? In what form?

All of this exploration into the process is to full discover *the how to* for goal achievement. Once you have identified that, then you can ask: "Does anything stop you or interfere with you doing this? What's holding you back, if anything?" If there are lots of interferences, perhaps this will become the focus of the coaching session. To deal with interferences that could stop the person from achieving his or her goal. Or you could make a list of the interferences to be dealt with in another session.

If what stops a person is due to the lack of sufficient resources, then the next question will play a crucial role. "Do you have the external resources? Do you have the internal resources that you need?" If resources are needed, then the current coaching session or a future on could be used for a

Resource Conversation.

Section #4: Checking the Quality of the Desired Outcome

The final questions for designing a well-formed outcome are meta-questions. Because of that, they invite the client to take a meta-moment, step back, and reflect on the quality of the outcome that you have been exploring. The first step back is to gain a wider perspective about the required resources: "Do you have the internal resources to make this happen?" A menu lit of these include: willingness, courage, self-efficacy, patience, responsibility, etc.

The next question invites a further step back to a wider perspective about how the outcome fits or does not fit into the person's whole life: "Is this goal ecological, holistic, and realistic?" If it passes those checks, then the *why* question again: "Is it still compelling to you? Do you still have a big enough why to go after this?"

Next, the commitment question: "Are you going to do this? Have you made a commitment to this? Are you ready to make a commitment to this knowing more about the process and the form of this outcome?" This moves from the Clarity Conversation to the Decision Conversation. With the clarity that your client has experienced through the exploration of the outcome, is he or she ready to go for it?

The final question calls forth the sensory evidence that will convince the client upon completion of the outcome: "How will you know you have achieved it?" This epistemological question explores the client's convincer strategy: *"How will you know* that you have achieved your goal?" By means of this question you and your client will be able to measure the difference between where the client is today and where he or she wants to be.

There is a trickiness in the *how-will-you-know* question. That's because with every *kind of conversation* there will be a different kind of evidence.
- For a Clarity Conversation— the convincer will be the person's understanding or clarity strategy. How do you know you are mentally clear?
- For a Decision Conversation— the convincer will be the person's strategy for when and how to make a decision. What meta-programs does the person use? What values and standards does the

person use? What time-frame? Etc.[3]

- For a Planning Conversation— the convincer will depend on how the person plans, how the person strategizes, the person's style and convincer that he or she indeed has a plan that he can use as a blueprint for building his future.

- For a Resource Conversation— the convincer will involve the person's internal "tests" that lets the client know that a resource has been accessed and is now available.

- For a Change Conversation— the convincer will similarly involve an internal "test" of some sort. In both the Resource and the Change Conversations, you will *test* the client repeatedly by asking, "Can you do it now?" If the answer is yes or no, ask, "How do you know?" This enables you and the client to begin to discover *how* the client knows when she has or has not made the change.

Making the Outcome Questions Really Work

You now know the series of questions to ask. Yet how do you use these questions powerfully? To create a strong personal impact with them—ask the question and notice if the person answers your question. And if not, then notice *what* question the person does answer. If the person's answer is an answer to some question, what is that question? If not, acknowledge that, and then repeat the question. It is common that people do not answer questions which are asked. So simply be on the alert, notice, and feed that back to the person.

To really get some mileage out of the questions, *refine the questions*. How do you do that? Refine each WFO question with the *testing, checking, clarity, and exploration questions*. This is illustrated in the diagram as the penetrating arrows (**←**). Use these questions to *refine* the WFO questions. This creates clarity, focus, and the relevant details.

If you move too fast with these questions, you will get superficial answers and the questions will not really work to call forth an outcome that the client wants. If also you race down the list of these questions, you won't know what the hell you're talking about. So *refine* the answer by checking questions, testing questions, clarity checks (for how the person is using the terms), and exploration. As you do this, you will be *grounding* the conversation. Every "yes" answer that you get, move down to the next WFO question. Every "no" move up to the "What?" question again and go from there.

In this way, the WFO questions can be used as a system. You can then use the question systemically as a guide for your questioning. Using the four sets of refining questions enables you to ground and detail. This will help you move the client down to the ground of reality so that both of you have sufficient specifics. Then both you and your client will know precisely what you are talking about. If you notice the penetrating arrows (**←**), these are the key places where you need to get a sensory-based description.

When you put this together, you will now have the ability to truly work over the answers of your client so that they create clarity—insight, awareness—and then decision. It will take practice, deliberate practice, to thoroughly learn this. So practice. Keep checking with your client to see how he or she is experiencing the exploration. Doing that and you will become a powerful questioner.

The Outcome Conversation in Executive Coaching
Whether for a single coaching session or for an entire program, the Outcome Conversation provides a fundamental structure for thinking strategically about the goals and outcomes of the coaching program. When used for a single session, you can use it to establish what is, and is not, relevant as you set a focused direction with your client. It also allows you to test and measure the effectiveness of the session. When used for a coaching program, it sets out the entire coaching contract regarding what is to be accomplished and how to measure it.

With executive coaching, unless you are coaching the most senior person in an organization, the client will usually have both development needs pertinent to themselves and to the organization. Typically, because the organization will be paying for the coaching, there will often be an additional objective for the executive. The client may also have his or her own agenda. In these cases, you could be working with a double set of objectives— one from the client and one from the organization.

If there's a conflict between the person you are coaching and the organization, where should your allegiance lie? The answer arises from the fact that you will first set up an agreed-upon outcome in a three-way meeting between yourself, the organizational representative, and your executive client, you have the organizational KPI. This goal will be externally measurable. Because it is, it can be measured by the client and the organizational representative (a senior manager or HR manager).

Subject/ Theme	**WHAT? ?**	←TEST← Can You? This is what to talk about?
Motive	? *Why? ?	
Time	When? _____ ?	←CHECK← Really? Sure?
Space	Where? ?	
Personnel	With Whom? ?	←CLARITY← VAK? Def. of word Meta-Model Q
Action	**DO? ?** ?	
Control/ Influence	You? ?	←EXPLORE← Tell me more? What do you mean?
Capacity	*Can? ?	
Memory	*Have? ?	Code: * Meta-Questions ←check VAK clarity Arrow down if "Yes" to Q Arrow up Go back to "What"

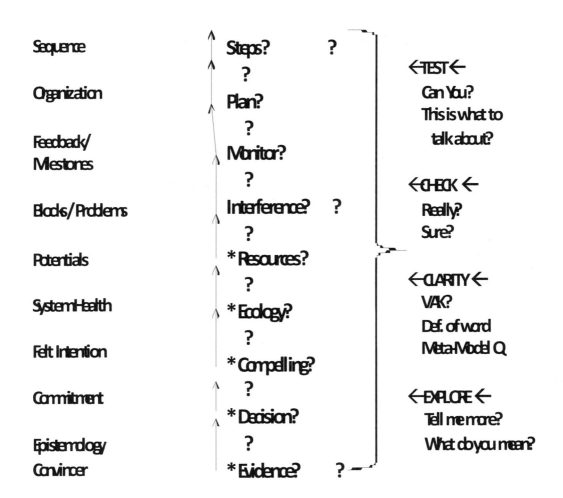

Sequence

Organization

Feedback/
Milestones

Blocks/Problems

Potentials

System-Health

Felt Intention

Commitment

Epistemology
Convincer

Steps?   ?
?
Plan?
?
Monitor?
?
Interference?   ?
?
* Resources?
?
* Ecology?
?
* Compelling?
?
* Decision?
?
* Evidence?   ?

← TEST ←
Can You?
This is what to
talk about?

← CHECK ←
Really?
Sure?

← CLARITY ←
VAK?
Def. of word
Meta-Model Q

← EXPLORE ←
Tell me more?
What do you mean?

Code:
* Meta-Questions
← check VAK clarity
Arrow down: if "Yes" to Q
Arrow up: Go back to "What"

Then, given that when you are in the coaching session with your client, you can focus exclusively on serving the client. While it is true that the goal which has been mutually set is the organization's goal for the executive, your commitment is to your coaching client. You are there primarily in service of your client's needs, not the organization's. Is there a potential dilemma here? Yes, of course.

How will you navigate this issue of the dual objectives? However you navigate this will determine the success of your coaching program. How willing or open is the client to the coaching? Even though the person agrees with the organizational goal, does the person really want to work on that? Is the organization using the coaching to determine whether to keep the executive on board? Is the client using the coaching to prepare him or herself for leaving the organization? These things happen and it's not that uncommon. Will you want to contract with the client organization so that it will not be your role to either assist the client to remain in their employ nor to influence the person to leave? Lots of questions and lots of places where an Executive Coach could become embroiled in numerous ethical (and even legal) issues. [I will return to this subject in chapter 25 under Caveat Empor, pp. 257-258.]

Your Executive Coaching Take Aways
The client sets the agenda— so first and foremost, as an Executive Coach, you have to find out what your executive client really wants. Does he even know? When she gets that, is that the ultimate outcome or just a step to the final one?

Use the Outcome Conversation for those situations when a client is confused or torn between goals. Use it when the executive's language is vague or fluffy about objectives to precisely prescribe what one truly wants. This conversation is designed to help both coach and client understand *what* one to achieve and what it will take to achieve that dream.
- How familiar are you with the 18 questions of the Well-Formed Outcome template? If not, what will you do to thoroughly learn these questions?[4]
- There's an art in making these questions really work so that they enable your executive client to access their highest vision. The secret is to refine the client's answers by using the testing,

checking, clarifying, and exploring questions. Spend time with some of your own goals using the interplay of these kinds of questions to get a real sense of how you can use them together to create the power and synergy of a compelling outcome.

End of the Chapter Notes:

1. This is the Intentionality Pattern in conversational form. See *Secrets of Personal Mastery* (1997) or the APG (Accessing Personal Genius) Training Manual.

2. The book *Achieving Peak Performance* (2009) is the fifth book in the Meta-Coaching series of books and primarily addresses performance.

3. For more about the Meta-Programs Model see *Figuring Out People* (1997), for more about time and time lines, see *Adventures in Time* (1997).

4. See *Coaching Conversations* (2004; 2010) for more about the Outcome Conversation.

Chapter 17

THE FEEDBACK CONVERSATION

"When you give feedback, you become like a mirror.
You receive what your client gives out and mirror it back.
The cleaner and straighter you are as a mirror, the cleaner the feedback."
L. Michael Hall

"Mistakes are toothless little things
if you recognize and correct them.
If you ignore or defend them, they grow fangs and bite."
Dee Hock (1999, *Birth of the Chaordic Age, p.* 280)

The Feedback Conversation is designed to give the coaching client a mirror so that the executive can see him or herself accurately. Without feedback, none of us can clearly and accurately see ourselves or sense how others are experiencing us. If we are going to be truly open and transparent we need mirroring feedback. If we're going to lead people, we need to learn to be clear, candid, and considerate with people. So like it or not, we need feedback. We need it to see ourselves as we are. But the problem is getting it. And an even greater problem is receiving clean and clear feedback not contaminated by judgment, evaluation, or mind-reading.

As has been mentioned, true feedback is one of those essential ingredients in effective coaching. *Yet truly high quality feedback is rare.* The truth is that most people have not been trained to offer it. This is also true of many coaches.[1] They do not know how to offer it. What's needed is accurate, clear, useful, sensory-based, and reflective feedback which will assist a client in attaining accurate self-awareness, in tuning up skills, recognizing the way that others experience us, and incorporating new response patterns in adapting to life's changes. That's a lot.

This especially is true for executives and people who live within organizations because organizations tend to do the very things that counter-act high quality feedback. They tend to "keep the peace," to just get along, to conform, to not rock the boat, etc. Those at the top are especially liable to suffer from only getting highly filtered information. This is the executive disease of being shut out from ground truth.

In the Quality Movement, Edwards Deming emphasized the critical importance of high quality feedback at every step and stage in production and delivering. That's because we can only change and make corrections when we know specifically what to change to improve the quality of our products and responses.

High Quality Feedback
While defining feedback is fairly easy, there are three things that operate as pseudo-feedback to be wary about. This means that to truly be effective in giving feedback, as an Executive Coach you have to know what *not* to do as well as what to do. The three forms of pseudo-feedback are evaluation, judgment, and mind-reading.

So while your executive clients need feedback, they do not need your evaluations, your judgments, or your mind-reading of their states or intentions. Feedback frequently masquerades as evaluation, hiding behind "expert advice and insight." But because it does not come from the client, that is not feedback. It comes from the coach.

Feedback is mirroring back to the person what you receive. That's why it is not evaluation or your interpretation. Nor is it your guess, intuition, or mind-reading of what your client is experiencing. That comes from you, not your client. Even learning to distinguish your stuff from their stuff is a highly refined skill. Feedback is especially not judgment. It is not the application of criteria of standards to your client— even if it is their standards.

So what is mirroring feedback? *It is precise and specific sensory-based information that accurately feeds back to your client what you receive from them.* The metaphor is that of a clean mirror receiving an image from the person who stands in front of it. The mirror only gives back what it receives.

The Skill of Cleanly Mirroring Data

For yourself as an Executive Coach, your skill in giving feedback that's as clean and clear as a new shiny mirror determines the quality of your Executive Coaching. So, as an Executive Coach, how skilled are you at appreciating and celebrating feedback as mirroring your responses? How skilled are you at giving feedback that performs the functions of high quality feedback?

In Executive Coaching, many executives are not ready and/or not skilled for receiving feedback. There's several reasons for this. Perhaps they associate feedback with criticism and feel that they are being criticized. So they go into strong negative states when they receive feedback. Perhaps they have never linked feedback with learning, progress, and development. Perhaps they have never thought of feedback as a way of measuring progress against the standards that they have set. For these reasons coaches generally have to coach their clients on how to effective receive feedback.

Enabling Clients to Receive Feedback Graciously

The fact is, almost no one has been trained in taking feedback effectively. No wonder then that most of us simply do not know how. Most executives do not know how. So how does a person receive feedback like a pro? How does a professional receive feedback in order to shape skills into expertise? As you explore this question, there are factors to consider:

- What do I need to understand about feedback so that I can both receive and give it effectively?
- Am I ready to step up to a new level of development and receive feedback like a professional Executive Coach?
- Have I created a *receiving feedback matrix* for myself and designed it so it is well formed and enabling me to give feedback?[2]
- What state or states do I need to be in to most effectively receive feedback?

Among the key skills required to effectively receive feedback are the following:

- Listening in an open way to the feedback data as just *information.*
- Exploring in a curious and non-defensive way the facts and meanings.
- Distinguishing language that is evaluative and that which is sensory-based.
- Asking for examples.
- Asking about the person's positive intention.
- Accepting words as the other person's perception and mapping without confusing it with the territory. Words are just *words.*
- Patiently persisting to translate the feedback so that it fits the criteria of well-formed high quality feedback. (See the section on High Quality Feedback)
- Having a healthy relationship to vulnerability.

The last item mentioned, "having a healthy relationship to vulnerability," is especially important. It is important that we do not equate vulnerability with weakness. Instead, vulnerability is being human, being real, being authentic. Then you can see feedback as a contribution self-awareness, to having an impact on others, and to opening yourself up for personal growth and development.

Start with your own intentions. Do you have some high level intentions for receiving and giving feedback? With your clients, do the same by asking about and setting empowering intentions for receiving feedback in the most positive way possible:
- Why do you want to receive feedback?
- How will it help you? For what purpose?
- Have you decided to refuse to let another's incompetence in giving feedback deprive you of the feedback?

Check your meanings. Update your meanings and current frames about feedback.
- When you think about someone informing you that you made a mistake, error, messed up, did something wrong, etc., what thoughts and feelings come to mind?
- What state does that put you in?
- If your thinking does not put you into an open and receptive state— a state of robust openness, then what thinking, believing, memories, etc. do you need to deframe?
- What old frames or meanings undermine your competence for

receiving feedback effectively?
- What do you now want to think about feedback so you find it acceptable and even valued?
- Have you the frames set to texture your state for receiving feedback with the most robust set of frames?

Distinguish person and behavior. Separate feedback from the person and even the style. Most people simply do not know how to give *sensory-based feedback.* Rather than feedback, they give judgments, evaluations, and mind-reading statements. These are pseudo-forms of feedback. Given that, will you let their incompetence deprive you of useful feedback? Or will you refuse to let that happen? You can overcome a person's incompetence in *giving* feedback in several ways. One way is to translate their judgments into sensory-based referents. To do that use the questions of specificity. "What are you speaking about specifically?" "What specifically do you mean by delegating?" These indexing questions specify the when, where, with whom, how, in what way, etc. of a subject.

Set higher texturing frames. If your state for either receiving or giving feedback is not of the highest quality and fully robust, then meta-state yourself.[3] Use the meta-stating process to texture your state with the qualities and resources for a robust feedback state.
- What do you need to texture your feedback state with? (Patience, interest, curiosity, good will, kindness, etc.)
- Do you need more patience, acceptance, appreciation, recognition of positive intention, commitment to yourself, to your learning, to your budding genius, etc.?
- How hungry are you for feedback? Enough? Do you need more motivation about the values and benefits of feedback?
- Are you able to invite another to specific the feedback in precise sensory-based behavioral terms?

Coaching Executive Receptiveness

As you might suspect, many executives are not open and receptive enough to receive feedback when the coaching begins. The first objective of the coaching program then would be to coach him or her to develop a highly refined and effective style for receiving feedback. First set that as your coaching objective and then invite the person to test where he or she is in receiving feedback. Here's one way to do that.

1) Identify a subject, problem, or issue that the executive wants to work on. As you do that, specify the context sufficiently so that it is grounded in terms of what, when, where, who, etc. Ask, "What deficit would you like to work on?"

A menu list could be anything like the following: defensive under fire, difficulty delegating, undisciplined, late, rushed by time pressures, dominating, can't release control, lack in interpersonal skills, abrasive, large knowing-doing gap, etc.

2) Next begin to explore with the person both the strengths and weaknesses of that response. Do that by asking a series of questions like the following:
> What went well? What was excellent about it?
> What are you good at? What are your strengths?
> What could be improved?
> What could be enhanced, made more elegant, smoother, powerful, useful, practical, etc.?
> What are your weaknesses? What could you do differently?
> What would be a stretch? What would take this to the next level?

3) Give feedback on the feedback to enable the person to reflect on it. To do that, here is the next set of questions:
> What have you learned as a result of this conversation?
> Was the conversation useful? How are we doing?
> What would you like for us to do differently?
> What did you like about the conversation? What did you not like?
> Would you like to shift to a different kind of conversation?

4) Move now from feedback to an action plan. The final step of feedback, of course, is integration. This means using the feedback for change and developing an action plan to specify what you are going to do about the feedback.
> Do you have an action plan?
> Does the plan have a timetable for improving your performance?
> Why measure this performance? What are your values about it?
> What standards will you use? (Your criteria and guidelines)
> What variables will you measure? (Your critical variables)
> How accurate and relevant are your measuring tools? (Your tools)
> Who should measure performance?
> When should the measure be done? (Time Frame)

High Quality Feedback

True feedback that is accurate begins with the clean reception of the actions, words, gestures, patterns, etc. that come from the client. If it is precise, it is immediate and empirical. The following further describes high quality feedback that we use in Meta-Coaching.

1) Rapport-Based

The condition that's required for giving feedback is *respectful rapport*. It is based first on connecting with another person and gaining rapport with him or her. It is unwise to even begin giving feedback until you have rapport. Questions for your competency in giving feedback:

> Are you and your client in a resourceful state?
>
> Have you set a context of support that's backed up by your non-verbal signals?

2) Outcome Relevant

From time to time someone will ask me to give them feedback. If I'm willing to do that, I immediately ask, "About what and by what standards?" If I don't ask these questions, I won't know what feedback content they want or the standards and criteria that they want to be measured by. So first, in giving feedback, you have to identify the object or outcome they want to achieve. Once there is rapport, feedback requires a clearly established outcome for what feedback to give and the criteria to use.

> "In light of your desire to become more people oriented as a manager, I noticed that you used the first name of four people who were in the meeting today and I also noticed that you did not do that with the other three."

Questions for your competency in giving feedback:

> What is the outcome, design, or objective?
>
> Have you tied your feedback to the person's outcome?

3) Tentative

Feedback has to be offered tentatively rather than in an absolute manner and all the while seeking the person's validation or dis-validation of it. High quality feedback is tentative—it is tentative to your point of view, your perspective, and to the situation as best as you know it. If you offer it as absolute—absolutely true as if you could not be wrong or mistaken —you are playing God. It will also feel imposing and so create pressure for the person. This will more than likely put them on the defense. To present it tentatively, use open questions which encourage the recipient to try on the feedback. After presenting the feedback, ask for the client's thoughts about it. That is, check with your client to see how the feedback fits or doesn't fit. Ask if the mirrored response seems accurate and valid to him or her.

> "In view of eliciting a stronger motivational state in John, I heard you ask what he wanted to achieve this quarter in his new position. Then afterwards I didn't hear you confirm his goals with him or explore what they meant to hm. I would suggest that would take your skills to the next level."

Questions for your competency in giving feedback:
> Have you made your feedback tentative?
> How does this feedback fit for you?

4) Timely
Effective feedback is timely. In fact, the most effective feedback is in the moment—*in real time.* For feedback to be of the highest quality, offer it in the moment. You have to be quick, alert, and on your toes. When you do, you are giving *just-in-time feedback.* Doing this will give the feedback an undeniable quality because the reflection just occurred.

Questions for your competency in giving feedback:
> Did you present your feedback when the action or experience was happening, when it was fresh?
> Was your feedback timely rather than waiting days, weeks, or months before presenting it?

Timeliness also means that sometimes feedback needs to be taken off-line or to a different time when the person will be in a more resourceful state for receiving it. Graham writes:

> "I find that, on occasion, it may be better holding back one's need to intervene. It can be quite magical when the opportunity to give the feedback presents itself quite gracefully at an opportune time and in a very different way to what I might have previously, if I had dived in spontaneously in a timely way."

5) Person / Style Distinction
Given that you feed back to your client what you receive from him or her, you receive behaviors—actions, gestures, non-verbal expressions, linguistic patterns, etc. All of these expressions are not the same as the person. They are expressions of that person. Yet so many people identify themselves

with what they *do*. They confuse self with behavior and achievement. This is how they *personalize* and hear feedback as insult, attack, or threat. To enable the person to receive the feedback, clearly as just information, separate the feedback from the person.

Questions for your competency in giving feedback:
> Have you invited your client to recognize him or herself as more than behavior?
> Have you set the frame that distinguishes person from behavior and feedback?

6) Sensory Specific

When you see yourself in a mirror, you see the specific and precise sensory qualities of your image. That's why the best feedback is sensory specific. To do this, use empirical terms, neutral words, and precise action words. This will eliminate any semantically loaded word or phrase that could carry evaluations and judgments. Feedback that is completely in see-hear-feel terms is framed so that it is empirical enough to catch on camera.

> "I noticed that you quickly engaged your staff this morning by excitedly raising your voice and stressing certain words about the importance of the meeting as you said 'essential' twice and 'critical' once. As I experienced it, however, it seemed to me that you moved a little too fast when you cut John off and didn't allow that exchange to finish. What do you think?"

Questions for your competency in giving feedback:
> Is your feedback sensory-based— in see, hear, feel, etc. format?
> Have you communicated using neutral words rather than semantically loaded words?

7) Actionable

Actionable feedback is information about what a person did or said that the client can do something about. If the person cannot do anything about the feedback, it is not actionable. To be actionable requires that your suggestions identify something that the person can *do* to refine his or her skills or response. It offers one or more steps for improving things.

Questions for your competency in giving feedback:
> Is the feedback actionable?
> Is there anything that the person can actually *do* with the feedback?

Creating the Safety for Feedback

Regarding safety, make sure that you keep the coaching session completely confidential or that the degree of confidentiality is explicitly agreed upon. This sounds simple, obvious, and easy; it is not. It takes courage to keep confidentiality and that's because there will be numerous temptations to break that confidence and share personal information from the session.

Politically, however, it would be career limiting to give your evaluations about an employee to the manager. Set your own policy that you will not to answer any question that any manager or executive asks you about the details of coaching a manager or employee.

If you do, then when your client find out that you shared an evaluation of his performance with the boss, he will lose all trust in you as his coach. Suddenly the coaching session is no longer safe. From that day forward, that client will be guarded and politically aware that you also operate as "a secret police" for the administration. As the Executive Coach, it is your job to facilitate the ongoing relationship between the manager and the direct report. Making evaluations of your client undermine the manager's responsibility to evaluate his direct report himself through direct experience.

In the end, receiving feedback effectively can accelerate learning, inspiration, motivation, and planning. Effective feedback streamlines the learning and incorporation processes. This works as we use feedback to develop *an action plan* for changing our responses:
- Do you have an action plan?
- What is the timetable of the action plan?
- What is your first step? When?

Your Executive Take-Aways

Giving feedback so that it is effective lies at the heart of coaching and yet it is one of the most challenging things for any Executive Coach to do. It is not easy and can quickly become contaminated by the pseudo-forms of evaluation, mind-reading, and judgment. It can be learned and when it is, you become as it were a mirror for your executive client in such a way that he or she can begin to truly see him or herself.
- How well have you cleaned out all of the cultural myths and misbeliefs about feedback so that you think and feel it as neutral, as just information?

- What belief changes do you need to complete to be able to fully embrace feedback as information and not as insult or attack?
- How well do you know the distinctions for high quality feedback?
- How skilled do you currently gauge yourself for giving high quality feedback?

End of the Chapter Notes:

1. An example is in the book, *Group Coaching: a Comprehensive Blueprint* (2011) by Ginger Cockerham who is a MCC (Master Certified Coach) with the ICF, in fact a board member of ICF. In the few examples of a coaching conversation, there is advice given, corrections about the client being wrong, rhetorical questions leading to where the coach wants to go rather than the client. She quotes one group member "giving feedback" to another, "You thought Harry had had enough time, and you were determined to get in." Of course, this is not feedback, it is that coach's evaluation. How did he know what he "thought" or that he was "determined" to do something? Those are examples of what we call mind-reading (p. 57).

2. In *Coaching Mastery,* the ACMC training of Meta-Coaching, we facilitate every participant to construct a customized matrix of frames that enable them to fully access the ability to cleanly and openly receive feedback. You can do this by taking the questions of the eight dimension of the Matrix Model and answering them. See *The Matrix Model* (2003).

3. If the process of *meta-stating* is new to you, a *meta-state* is a state-about-another-state. Joyful learning is the state of joy (delight, fun, humor) about the state of learning. By linking one state to another we *meta-state.* See *Secrets of Personal Mastery* (2000) or the book, *Meta-States* (2007).

Chapter 18

THE CONFRONTATION

CONVERSATION

"Come out from behind yourself into the conversation and make it real. In any situation, the person who can most accurately describe reality without laying blame will emerge as the leader, whether designated or not."
Susan Scott, *Fierce Conversations* (2002)

"The truth spoken in public is a rare commodity in most institutions."
Peter Block, *The Flawless Consultant*

When it comes to communication in companies, in corporates, and even just between friends, the big question and the most critical question in people's mind is the one about truth and truthfulness:

- Are we getting the straight story?
- Or are we being duped, lied to, conned, and getting the "official line?"
- Is someone "playing politics" and withholding information and telling you only what they think you want to hear?

Nobody likes being tricked or deceived. Yet all too often this is "the way we do things" on planet Earth. We do not tell the truth, we tell our version of the truth as if it was The Truth. We tell people what we want them to think, what we think they can or cannot handle, what will serve us best, or what we hope will become real. In these ways, we attempt to impose our truths on others. Telling the truth, giving the straight story, and communicating things that do not put us in the best light is hard. We fear the consequences. So also it is challenging to both allow and respect others to have their own truths and to speak them. We tend to follow cultural expectations because "it is the way we do things around here" and because we may feel that it's not be safe to do otherwise. Cultures have a way of dealing with outliers when they threaten the status quo.

Now when it comes to trust in management, trust does not depend on whether management is right in their view or position as much as whether they are *willing to tell the truth*. Whether they are willing to explore for the full truth. Willing to adjust when new facts are discovered. These are the things that build trust. Yet this takes tremendous courage and skill.

When one tells the truth, when one probes to get to the truth, when one pushes through the cover-ups, the distortions, the PR, the image, etc., then the conversation becomes fierce. It becomes real, intense, and therefore dangerous. Dangerous even though it is simultaneously full of possibilities. This is as important as it is essential. It is crucial for health, well-being, effectiveness, etc. and that's why the Confrontation Conversation is so essential to coaching. That is why it so often lies at the very heart of the coaching process.

Confrontation — What it is and Why it is Important
Confrontation means to bring up something that could be interpreted and experienced as unpleasant, upsetting, painful, even insulting. Yet while that's what it means, that's *not* the purpose of confrontation. The purpose is precisely the opposite. We confront to enable resourcefulness. We confront a person to deal with something that could undermine one's well-being or effectiveness. We confront when things are small and manageable before they become serious and destructive. We confront because we care and because we want the best for people. The truth about confrontation is that confrontation is actually an act of care and intimacy.[1]

When I first interviewed and modeled Graham Richardson (2002), I asked him about his style. "What's your style as an Executive Coach?" His answer was shocking, "Ruthless compassion." At first I didn't know how to understand that meta-state. So I inquired further. It turns out that the *ruthlessness* is about the *compassion*. It frames and qualifies the compassion as strong, persistent, and patient.

In other words, the compassion is not soft, weak, mealy-mouth, "mothering," smothering, etc. No. The compassion is strong. It is committed. It is a compassion that will persist and that will challenge and confront. It is a compassion that typically causes the coach to believe more in the client than the client believes in him or herself. It is a compassion that does everything in service of the client's long-term skills, empowerment, and success.

Later I got to see *ruthless compassion* in action as I observed Graham coach one person after the other in numerous contexts and over several years and in different countries. Graham said that he didn't experience himself that way, but that others described him as being ruthlessly compassionate. And after observing him repeatedly, I came to understand that description. He will not let a client sell him or herself short. He will not let them hide, pretend, play games, or discount themselves. He confronts.

In part, we confront because people get stuck in patterns and are unaware of it. This sometimes happens when they find that something is wrong in their lives. Sometimes a person knows that he or she is stuck in a pattern, and may have tried to deal it yet to no avail. When they do that repeatedly without success, it's typical for a person to become frustrated or defeated. One may become stressed, discouraged, or angry. All of these emotional responses are *symptoms* of a pattern which is not working. Yet often one thinks that the negative emotion is the problem and has no awareness of the pattern itself. To become unstuck a person then needs awareness of the pattern, not just the emotion. This is what confrontation offers.

Confrontation is misused when a person waits too long so that the problem becomes so large it becomes overwhelming. When that happens and we then confront, the person is usually far too upset, angry, or scared. And when we try to confront something so big, we also may do so too strongly. Then our confrontation will be filled with too much emotion. No wonder that such confrontations are ineffective and seldom do any good. At that point many people draw a fallacious conclusion: "Confrontation always involves strong negative emotions and only makes things worse."

Given that description, confrontation works best when we bring up something that is potentially unpleasant while we are in a pleasant and resourceful state. Bringing something up when you are calm, relaxed, clear, caring, empathetic, and sufficiently skilled makes all the difference in the world. Then you will be able to deal with the strong emotions of another person. You also confront best when you are proactive, and not reactive. You confront best when you do so in a matter-of-fact voice. Then you will be able to manage destructive emotions, access your best resources to be compassionate as you confront in a way that respects yourself and the other.

Confrontation in Coaching

As an Executive Coach, the questions for you about confrontation are these:
*   What are you to bring up to your executive client?
*   When do you dare to bring something up to address it?
*   What is worth bringing up which may be upsetting?

The answer: *Anything that undermines the person's well-being, effectiveness, development, or self-actualization.* When is this appropriate in Executive Coaching? Primarily whenever there are blind-spots, incongruencies, or excuses. Obviously, these are things that undermine healthy humanness and could lead to executive derailing.

In fact, if you are listening acutely, your client is almost always telling you what to confront in their language and behavior. How can you tell? By observing very carefully. If you do, you will hear, see and sense when your client is challenged internally. At this point be sure to calibrate the time and nature of your intervention. If your level of rapport is strong and congruent, you can go almost anywhere with your clients and they will let you know if they are up for it.

As you do this, set it in your mind that when your client says "No, I'm not up for it now," that *no* means *no.* Respect that. Don't push a confrontation if your client truly is not up for it and doesn't want it at that moment. Let it go. As a good and compassionate listener, say, "Thanks for letting me know, I appreciate your honesty. Let's wait until you are in a much more resourceful state to deal with it and resolve it."

The What to Confront

What do you confront as an Executive Coach?

1) Inauthenticity. Being authentic is the challenge for a leader to get real and to connect with his or her

> We confront in order to enable a person to deal with something that could undermine the person's well-being or effectiveness.

people at a deep level. Confrontation takes this on. It challenges the executive to have authentic conversations with people. Why? Because leadership is about being real, about speaking one's truths, and enabling people to hear them without defensiveness. Many will consider this to be a fierce conversation. As an Executive Coach, have you been too polite in your questions? Have you been too hesitant and timid in bringing up issues around the presence of inauthenticity?

2) Defensiveness. Being defensive is our natural tendency. All of us easily and quickly and naturally cover-up, protect ourselves, lie, excuse ourselves through blaming, and use whatever defensive routines we know. Executive Coaching inevitably has to challenge this. As an Executive Coach you confront to challenge the executive when he or she hides behind one of these protective devices.

3. Anonymity. Sometimes those in executive roles have learned to hide as an anonymous person. So they use language that keeps them or others anonymous— "they," "someone," "the organization," "the board," "the report says..." etc. In doing this no one is held accountable or responsible, especially the speaker. This also shows up in *triangulating*—talking about someone with those other than the person that we need to be talking to. Anonymity often takes the form of gossip and typically this involves things said that diminishes the reputation of another person. As a communication process anonymity creates and keeps secrets, cover-ups, and deceptions.

5. Incongruencies. When an executive is not being congruent in his or her behaviors, this undermines his or her credibility and trust. When a leader speaks, affirms, or promises but does not follow-through, this incongruency sabotages that leader from being credible and trustworthy. For these reasons, you will want to challenge and confront incongruency.

Incongruency has numerous contributing factors. Typically it arises from conflicts within the person and often from a lack of self-awareness. Sometimes one has simply not been held accountable for one's actions and for following-through on one's word. As a result, one has developed a habit of living with the incongruencies and not dealing with them. As a result one has become unconscious of them. Yet problem is that incongruency invites questions about what is real and authentic in a person. It questions what you can and cannot trust in a person.

To confront incongruency obvious brings us things that are very close to a person's very center. No wonder many cultures devalue confrontation. If a person has been trained in a culture to fear confrontation, if the culture values "being nice" over being real, then incongruency could be part of the cultural expectation for how to be.

6. Blind spots. As noted before in the chapter on derailment (chapter 13), we all have blind-spots. It is part of the human condition. The value of coaching is that it enables us to identify these and bring them into perspective. Then we will no longer be blind to these areas. As an Executive Coach, when you bring up to your client what is outside of his or her awareness, expect him or her to first experience a shock to awareness and then a denial. This is just part of the process of confrontation.

7. Irresponsibility. To lead each of us have to recognize and own our own responses. This develops a strong sense of our ability-to-respond (literally, responsibility). To fail to do this is to fail at leadership. True leaders are responsible and proactive. Yet many leaders fear this and avoid this. This generates irresponsibility. The person will then feel powerless, incompetent, and helpless. Not a good place to be! A leader in that position will feel like a victim and that will inevitably lead one in the opposite direction. He will then engage in blaming, making accusations, and shifting responsibility away from himself. This obviously needs to be confronted.

8. Poor performance. Lots of factors can lead an executive to a poor or even a failed performance. It often happens that the person has simply failed to come through on what one said or promised (incongruency). It may happen because the person did not take responsibility to do what needed to be done. It could occur through failing to develop a competency —having been promoted to a level of incompetency and then hiding that fact for the sake of one's image.

Poor performance can have at its origin in a number of factors which need to be checked out.
*   Is the person in the right role for his or her skill set?
*   Is she being asked to do too much with too few resources?
*   Is he being supported by colleagues, or structures which undermine his performance?
*   Is she under personal stress with health, financial, or relational

issues?

Often the executive is having problems with a difficult boss, or matrix structure. Sometimes the person may be unhappy with human resource issues, like remuneration, promotion, succession or other employment conditions. There are a great many reasons that an executive may be stuck in poor performance.

9. *Inappropriate and unuseful conflict.* Conflict can be positive or negative; it depends on how one thinks about conflict and the skills one applies in resolving conflict. Sometimes an executive can create unnecessary conflict (conflict without a positive value) simply due to that lack of personal development. This is the conflict that arises from being personally vindictive, living in hostility, operating from the win-lose attitude, being too rough or aggressive in one's approach, etc.

Obviously, it takes courage and lots of it to challenge and to confront executive clients. It requires courage to ask questions which challenge people, to explore risks, to tell the truth and especially bold truths. It even requires courage to call attention to real-time feedback in the session.

From Challenge to Confrontation
Challenge comes first as it is the very nature of coaching. After all, coaching is about challenging people to be better and more than they are. It is about continuous self-improvement one step at a time and sometimes involves remedial development as when an executive faces a potential, or real, career derailer.

Challenge can refer to setting stretch goals, about stepping up to a challenge, and about actualizing more and more of one's potentialities. One challenge for every Executive Coach is to not be a "Yes" man to the executive. It is to *not* simply rubber-stamp whatever the executive says. If you do that, then you become complicit in, and a part of, the problem and that will exacerbate the situation. The result will be that you will do damage to the client, the client's organization, and to your reputation. So your challenge—bravely speak up.
- How do you challenge?
- What is your style? How direct or indirect are you?
- What state are you in when you do challenge?
- Is that the best state and a state that brings out your best?

How to Confront

When you challenge, your challenges are actually small confrontations. The first thing you challenge or confront is *anything that contradicts the truth*—any falsehood, deception, lie, or anything less than the whole truth. This level of honesty stands in contrast to what we can call "truth management." Now, of course, speaking the truth in the executive suites and in the board will not always be liked or appreciated. In fact, it will seldom be liked or appreciated in the moment. Yet with people who care about the truth, it will be respected, if not now, then later.

Alan Downs in his book *Secrets of an Executive Coach* (2002, speaks about truth management:

> "Truth management is denying expression to the unique truth of oneself. The unvarnished truth stings, exhilarates, and infuriates. Dissatisfaction, frustration, anger, disappointment and unhappiness well up inside you and refuse to be managed. "

In the book *Co-Active Coaching* (1998), Laura Whitworth writes:

> "Truth telling refuses to sidestep or overlook; it boldly points out where the emperor is not wearing clothes. There is no inherent judgment in telling the truth. The coach merely states what he or she sees. Without bold truth serves neither client nor the coaching relationship. It is not based on being nice, but being real."

In some contexts, an employee feels that he or she cannot tell his or her boss the truth. They are unable to level and tell the truth that needs to be told because of fear of retribution or due to the lack of competence in trusting oneself to speak up. Yet as we know, the quality of information being communicated determines the quality of the company. Obviously, one facet of challenging and confronting is giving honest and straight forward feedback (the subject of the previous chapter).

Regarding feedback that is often experienced as confrontative, the best and the most challenging feedback is calling attention to whatever is happening in the moment. To do that, simply highlight what is happening right now. Focus on what is occurring right here-and-now between you and your executive client. When you can deal with real-time data in the moment, while it may be uncomfortable, it will also tend to be profound. This *just-in-time feedback* is what makes it so powerful.

Challenging and confronting finds its fullest expression in *shadow coaching.*   Shadow coaching involves following, or shadowing, an executive to observe what he or she is actually saying and doing in real time with others.   This shadowing may be for just an hour in an important meeting, it may be for an average day of work, or it could be for an entire week to pick up larger level patterns. After intense and focused observation of the executive in his or her environment for a period of time comes the feedback session. Here the Executive Coach will give feedback about the executive functioning to whatever criteria they have selected. The content of the shadow coaching is usually planned as the objective and criteria are discussed and identified.

Via the shadowing process, you invite the executive to become aware of his or her responses, how people seem to be experiencing them, and what is needed to take communication, leadership, delegation, inspiration, etc. to the next level of development.   The challenge as an Executive Coach, is to get your clients to take ownership of what they are doing, saying, and how they are affecting their organization. The design is to get them to say, "I am responsible for my life and for the things that happen in my life."

Your Executive Take Aways
You cannot coach without confronting. If you attempt Executive Coaching without an effectively refined and robust ability to confront, you definitely will not be successful.   Executive Coaching inherently involves both challenge and confrontation.

Effective confrontation involves knowing both *what* to confront and *how* to carry out the confrontation so that it serves the development of the executive, his or her work and leadership.
- What are the beliefs and meanings that have informed you about confrontation in life? Which of those are helpful? Which ones are not helpful? Which ones create limitations to you in developing the skill of elegant confrontation?
- How aware are you of the nine items listed here for confronting? Do you recognize them when they arise in the coaching?
- What are your next steps for developing your skills and/or state for more effective confrontation?

End of the Chapter Notes
1. For more on confrontation, email the author to receive a PDF file of the Neuro-Semantic Confrontation Model (meta@acsol.net).

Chapter 19

META-CONVERSATION

"Training in the meta-position facilitates a higher perspective
leading to higher achievements and wisdom—
that's why we call for a Meta-Moment."
L. Michael Hall

"People can simply solve their own problems if the problem is externalized.
When the problem is internalized (personalized) it is much more difficult to solve.
Use the Step-Back skill to externalize the problem and invite the client to figure
out the solution."
Angus McLeod, *Performance Coaching*

If only there was a meta-room—a place where Executive Coaches could
invite executives to step back from life's everyday stresses and activities
and access a loving mindfulness about life, self, relationships, and
business. Wouldn't that be grand? A meta-room for a meta-conversation!

Well, one of the early graduates from Meta-Coaching created just that.
Shortly after graduating, Silvia moved to a new apartment on the 35th floor
of an apartment building in the CBD of Sydney Australia. It was a two-
bedroom apartment, and one of the rooms overlooked the Sydney Bridge
and Opera House and it was that room that she turned into her Executive
Coaching Room. And there, as an Executive Coach, she invited executives

for a time-out in the middle of the day or a week. With chairs set to give a person a broad and expansive view, executives spoke of the room and the experience as a mental-and-emotional vacation in the middle of the day or week.

Now you may not have an actual meta-room like that, yet if you know how to facilitate a meta-conversation, your clients will have a similar experience. It will be as if they had spent time in the penthouse of their mind and spirit and developed a broader perspective about their lives.

The Meta-Conversation is the conversation whereby you invite an executive to step back from self, from one's thinking-and-feeling, and from one's experiences in order to take stock of where one is, where one is going, and the quality of one's experiences along the way. This is the purpose—to step back and gain perspective about values, direction, blind spots, one's strengths, weaknesses, and to gain an accurate assessment of goals and progress.

The Meta-Conversation gives you a penthouse view of life. It's like taking an elevator all the way to the top of your visions and values. This then creates, as it were, an island of reflection in one's life. The following is how Kilburg described it in his book, *Executive Coaching* (2000):

> "The most effective thing that coaches do with their very able and largely successful clients is to provide a safe environment and a process that forces both parties to be reflective about the situation facing the leader. The life of the modern executive has become so packed with activity, information, and pressure that there is virtually no time available to examine the work being done, the performance of the organization being led, or the individual's cognitive, emotional, and physical responses to life on the leadership race track." (71)

> "A properly executed coaching agreement and process creates a structure through which the coaching client can safely explore as many dimensions of his or her life as time, motivation and resources permit. I'm both amazed and pleased at how refreshed, renewed, and relieved my clients become as a result of spending a little as an hour thinking, feeling, and talking about what they are doing and how they are reacting to their experiences."

Keys to Effectively Engage in a Meta-Conversation
The first key to an effective Meta-Conversation is safety. Create a safe

zone as an Executive Coach that's predictable, reliable, and respectful, and confidential. Then in this place every executive will know that he or she will experience empathy, understanding, and respect while becoming more open and vulnerable to his or her inner truths.

This safe space provides safety even for what an executive may consider to be dangerous feelings (i.e., anger fear, fatigue, sadness, timidity, etc.). You can then use those feelings to lead you to the source of the problem and its solution. In this, as a coach you are like a bounty hunter of the executive's frames and feelings. The emotions may or may not be accurate or useful. Whether they are or are not, they express energy in the person's system. So you can use them to follow the trail within the person's inner matrix of meanings.

To get there you may have to identify and arrest the tactics of "image management" that the executive may use for hiding from his or her emotions. As a coach you know that feelings often hold important information about a person's inner world and mental maps.

A second key to an effective Meta-Conversation lies in your own understanding and realization of the power of stepping back to a reflective stance. The ability to think and work reflectively enables one to make better decisions. It enables one to cultivate and then operate from wisdom. That's because "wisdom" results from multiple perspectives held together in a broader perspective while taking the time to think something through thoroughly.[1]

Levels of Reflection
When it comes to the skill of stepping back and "going meta" to reflect on things, there are several levels whereby a person can reflect. Here are the principal levels of reflection for a person to pay attention to:

1) *Action Learning*

> The first level that you can step back from is from whatever you are immediately *doing*. This gives you the ability to become self-aware as you perform a task. This does not describe much reflectiveness as it does simple awareness. It invites your client to see, hear, and feel the sensory components of an experience.

2) *Reflection on Learning*

> The next level is to step back to become aware of your learning as

a process. The awareness is not about *what* you have learned, but *how* you are learning. What are the ways that you approach a task? How are you approaching things in real time? How were you thinking? What was the quality of your thinking? Any cognitive distortions? Cognitive biases? This level of awareness can enable you to then modify things as you perform the task. Your reflection here focus on the kind of thinking that creates your experiences.[2]

3) *Reflection on Reflection on your Action Learning*
　　Next is the ability to be aware of the multiple levels of complexity, paradox, and polarities in the situation. This expands your ability to review all of the many variables of the experience: the initial conditions, environmental variables, personal responses, strategies, tactics, and behaviors that you used, their results, and the outcomes that you generated. Your reflectiveness here becomes systemic as you view the whole system in action. It also allows you to view the assumptive frames that holds the system together.[3]

Recognizing and Using Meta-Comments

A third key to an effective Meta-Conversation is to *discover and use meta-comments*. Penny Tompkins and James Lawley offered some valuable insights about meta-comments in an article in the peer reviewed journal *Acuity*. The title of the article was, "The Role of Meta-Comments."[4] What's important about meta-comments is that you can use them to set a frame with a person or prime a context for a frame. Meta-comments also enable you to hear layers in your client's mind of his or her categories and conclusions. That is, by identifying the meta-comments, you can detect and point out the meta-levels of a client's meta-states and frames of mind.

What is a meta-comment? It is a comment that either you or a client make about your communications and experience. "I don't know why I said that. I don't think I even believe that." Hearing meta-comments requires careful listening. With practice you can begin to hear the meta-comments of your client as they reflect on their own statements. "I've said that before, haven't I?" When this happens, the person is either interrupting or observing his or her train of thought for a moment to—

　　"... pass a judgment, reflect on their knowledge, give notification of a change, or in some other way reveal something about the current state of their inner world."

What does a meta-comment reveal about a person's current state of mind, of the person's inner world or matrix?[5] Penny and James note several features about such client generated meta-comments. The meta-comment of clients in a coaching context are characterized by the following:
- They are embedded in their narratives.
- They are somewhat hidden and therefore easily ignored. They are momentary shifts in perspective.
- They give evidence that the client has just "stepped back" to another awareness.
- They can be important signposts for how best to proceed in facilitating the client.

A meta-comment indicates that a person has shifted perspective or at least expanded perspective. The person may have moved from a descriptive narrative of their experience to a higher level perspective— a self-reflective perspective.
> "Because we are remarkably consistent beings and we cannot not be ourselves, the structure of what we do in the micro (seconds) is often isomorphic with what happens in the macro (days, months, years)."
> "Since meta-comments are about the client's *relationship with their interior landscape* they often reveal something about the degree of significance or insignificance they attach to a part of their experience."

Here is the amazing thing about meta-comments: while this is so common, *unless you know how to listen for it, this whole meta-realm of communication will be invisible to you.* In Meta-Coach trainings, or supervision of coaching sessions, I hear many, many meta-comments by clients. They comment on their own comments, states, experiences, even on their own meta-comments(!). Here are examples of meta-comments:
> This is important.
> Why did I say that?
> That makes me wonder if that's what I really want.
> No, that's not what I meant. Let me see if I can say what I really mean.
> Do I want to go there? That's a hard question.
> Does that make sense?
> I know I shouldn't say this but ...
> It just occurred to me ...
> I can't believe I just said that.

Pattern-Level Comments
There's another thing that makes meta-comments important to you as an

Executive Coach. Meta-comments can indicate how a person is internally organized at a pattern level. That is, the structure and patterning of the person's matrix.[5] So when you hear a meta-comment like one of the following, the likelihood is that it indicates a valuable insight about the working of his or her system. To effectively respond you first need to do is hear it and then to follow it to its sources.

> That's like my whole life.
> I'm back to square one.
> I can't stop running round in circles.
> How long am I going to complain about this?
> I realize it's never going to work.
> Here I go again.
> It's the same problem in a different guise.

About such meta-comments, Penny and James write:

> "Comments like these are especially important because they mark out that the client is perceiving at a pattern level. With skillful choice of questions, a facilitator can help keep the client attending to the pattern and effectively working with all the examples at once. By transcending and including the multitude of lower level components and examples the client is working strategically."

Using Meta-Comments

After you hear an executive make a meta-comment, then what? How do you use it? How do you trace it back to its source? There are actually many chooses about how to use a meta-comment. James and Penny use a model which they developed called "Clean Language."[6] So they ask questions like: "What kind of..." "What is it like..." "What's about that..." etc. these open-ended questions enables the client to focus on the internal landscape of their ideas and metaphors.

> Unless you know how to listen for it, this whole meta-realm of communication will be invisible to you.

In Neuro-Semantics we ask a different set of questions. We use questions designed to enter into and/or open up the person's Matrix. These Matrix questions opens up another set of possibilities.

First, for any meta-comment, first of all, repeat the meta-comment as you hear it. Doing that acknowledges the statement as it confirms to the person that you have heard him or her. Then pause as you hold the space and time for the person to consider and reflect. After that, ask: "And is there anything else about that comment?" This continues to hold the space and invites further expansion of it. After that you can use any of the following questions to further explore the person's matrix of meanings.

"There's something else I can't quite grasp."
- How do you know that?
- If that's true, what then?

"I'm trying to do this in bits."
- Is that your strategy?
- Is there a belief that drives that?

"Both elements are important."
- And so you need or want both?
- So how can you embrace both? What do you understand about embracing both simultaneously?

"I know this pattern."
- And the pattern is what?
- What belief holds this pattern in place?

"If I'm honest ..."
- Is that the question— being honest?
- Does that mean you are tempted to not be honest?

"[Laugh] I've been here before."
- And that means?
- If that's true, then what?
- What do you believe about that?

"I kind of know that I want something, but [client sits back] I don't know what I want."
- Kind of? But not really? What do you mean?
- So there's an urge?
- What does the sitting back mean? Is there also an urge to *not* know?

If meta-comments are everywhere and, if everyone makes them, then we have to be circumspect in using them. We also have to be careful to not over-use them. There's a reason for that:
> "Attending to their own meta-comments is likely be an unusual experience for a client. While it can encourage them to become even more adept at self-reflection and open up areas that were out of their awareness, if you overdo it clients are liable to become self-conscious. Therefore you need

to be selective and to calibrate how useful the client's responses to your questions are to them – given their desired outcome."

Yes meta-comments are everywhere when you tune your ears for them. So it is simply a matter of learning to hear them and then using them by graciously exploring them. Meta-comments can be categorized so that we can distinguish different classification of meta-comments.

Knowledge category— kinds of knowing
　　　– The first thing that comes to mind is ...
　　　– I'm guessing it must be just a kind of ...
　　　– I'm imagining ...
　　　– No, that doesn't actually feel right.
Scaling Experience by making comparisons
　　　– It's a big deal for me.
　　　– I just don't like that (judgment)
　　　– I would rather have ... (preference)
　　　– That's odd.
　　　– That always happens (persistence)
　　　– Actually in some ways that's new.

Classifying by using a Time Frame:
　　　– At the moment ...
　　　– I'm at the stage where...
　　　– I feel that's the end of it.
　　　– Let me think about that.
Classifying as searching for the right words– a linguistic frame:
　　　– Let me rephrase that.
　　　– I can't verbalize it.
　　　– The question is ..

Categories of Experience– kinds of experiences:
　　　– That's the pattern.
　　　– I've no new ideas.
　　　– My outcome is ...
Classification of Conditional or Potential Contexts:
　　　– I *would like* that to be true.
　　　– *If only* I could get some new insight.
　　　– I *might* do something about it.

Classifications that are physiological or Non-Verbal:
　　　– Laughter at
　　　– Tears about

– A sigh

Your Executive Coaching Take Aways

The primary conversation is not the only conversation going on in a coaching session. While it is occurring, there's constantly another and higher conversation occurring—the meta-conversation. As an Executive Coach you can facilitate your clients to go there. You can also detect when clients are at the edge of that perspective by their meta-comments.

• How are you at avoiding "getting caught up in content," in the story as a coach? What do you need to do to stay alert to the structure and process of the conversation?

• What meta-comments do you common hear? Which meta-comments mentioned here do you almost never hear?

• What will you do to improve the frequency and quality of hearing meta-comments and responding for the benefit of your coaching?

End of Chapter Notes:

1. "Wisdom" in Gregory Bateson's definition arises from multiple perspectives all held simultaneously. See *Steps to an Ecology of Mind* (1972).

2. Thinking about thinking in Neuro-Semantics focuses on critical thinking skills so we can move beyond "dangerous thinking," clean up our thinking skills, and engage in *real* thinking. Colin Cox and I are currently developing this.

3. Systemic thinking is central to NLP which grew out of several systems models and especially in Neuro-Semantics, see *Systemic Coaching* (2012).

4. Acuity Journal is edited by Joel Cheal and published by The Association of NLP in the UK. joe.cheal@gwiztraining.com

5. *The Matrix Model* (2003) offers a systems model for becoming aware of and for working with the structure of an experience.

6. Clean Language arose from the modeling of James Lawley and Penny Tompkins, see *Innovations in NLP* (2011) also the website, www.cleanlanguage.co.uk.

Chapter 20

COLLABORATIVE LEADERSHIP

CONVERSATION

"A culture of collaboration must start at the top,
but it must also be owned at the bottom."
Ron Ricci and Carl Weise, *The Collaborative Imperative*

"Collaboration will be the point of differentiation between the companies
that grow successfully into the next decade and those that don't."
McPhaill, CEO of Best Buy

All leadership is not the same. There are many, many forms, kinds, dimensions, and levels of leadership. This is true inside and outside of organizations. Without going into the multitude of variables regarding leadership, there are two primary leadership dimensions inside of organizations—one of *the dimension of vision* and the other is *the dimension of performance.*

The leader in the vision dimension sees trends, visits the future, and sets out the direction and focus of the company. The leader in the performance dimension integrates this vision and set of values into the organization. The language that we generally use in distinguishing these two groups ("leaders" and "managers") is obviously inadequate and lacks precision. But it is what we have to deal with.[1]

"The leader is no longer the one who works on his own, comes up with ideas, and then communicates them to others. He is at all times obliged to co-construct solutions with others. The pdetermining factor is his capacity to generate teamwork." (Vincent Lenhardt, 2004, p. 10)

Two Dimensions of Executive Coaching

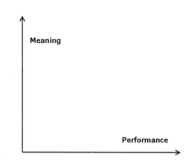

These two dimensions actually apply equally to us as individuals and to organizational leadership. Whether individually for yourself or for a company on the individual level, we all need *visionary leadership* just as we all need *managerial leadership.* When this relates to you as an individual, the two aspects generate *self-leadership.* This is where you first set your vision and direction for your life. Then you exercise self-management. This is where you apply the vision and values to yourself so that it becomes real and actual in your experience. Neither aspect of leadership is better or more important than the other. Both are required, and each is different. To dichotomize these into a superior/ inferior framework fails to see the synergy of the two and creates organizational pathologies.

Jim Collins in *Good to Great*; *Built to Last* (2001) says that a great company requires both great leaders and great managers. What then are the actual differences between leaders and managers? Some people think that managers are just junior leaders who do the same thing as leaders except at a lower level. But that's not it. These roles are not the same—not at all. The expertise required in leading and in managing radically differ from each other. That's why merely getting the label or status of "leader" doesn't make you one, nor does calling yourself a manager make you one. Each involves a different set of skills and dispositions and a mere role does not create the reality.

- How can we tell which leadership role is for you?
- How can you tell if you are truly leading or truly managing?
- What's involved in each of these roles?
- What core skills make a person a skillful leader?
- What core skills make a person a skillful manager?

John Kotter answers these questions in his classic book in the field of leadership, *A Force for Change: How Leadership Differs from Management* (1990). Kotter clearly distinguishes between the differences leadership and management identifying three distinctions about the core of each form of leadership. This gives us "leadership" in two dimensions: leaders who create the change and leaders who integrate and stabilize the change.[1]

Executive Leaders	**Managerial Leaders**
Creating Change:	*Integrating and Stabilizing*
New Adaptive Solutions	*The New Adaptive Solution*
Handles Change & Chaos	Handle Complexity
1) Direction setting: Vision, frames, meaning: purpose.	1) Planning: Detailing the vision, creating a business plan.
2) Aligning people: Team creation, continuity and stability.	2) Organizing: Creating consistence and order via staffing, and delegating.
3) Inspiring solutions and enabling problem-solving	3) Controlling: Monitoring, measuring, system homeostasis.

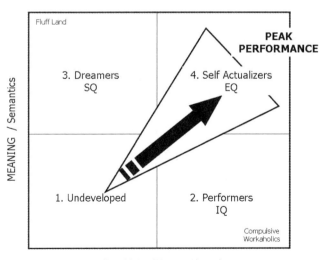

The

Self-Actualization Quadrants
On the Meaning-Axis, the SQ stands for *spiritual quotient* which highlights one's quotient of meaning and meaningfulness— what inspires a person above and beyond the materialistic world. EQ stands for emotional quotient and, of course, IQ for intelligent quotient.

Executive Leaders
1) Direction Setting: Visionary
An executive leader is needed, first and foremost, when we need a sense of direction and vision. These leaders live in the future. They work to invent a bright and compelling future. This establishes *direction setting* as one of the most important roles of an executive leader. Central to leadership is direction setting which involves developing and communicating a vision of the future for solving some problem or fulfilling some dream. Setting a direction involves motivating, inspiring, and awakening people to compelling meanings. This calls for the framing and reframing skills of a leader. There's a reason for that. A leader sets the vision and the direction by framing meaning.

What does vision and direction setting entail? It involves framing the meaning and meaningfulness of things, awakening people via how one communicates, giving meaning to change, creating a goal oriented and purposeful direction, awakening needs and wants to prevent complacency.

2) Aligning and Engaging People for Commitment
The second core aspect of leadership is *aligning* people gathered by the vision. A leader not only points out new possibilities, articulates a clear vision, and inspires new meanings. Leaders also align people to work together for the vision. Aligning people to a vision involves getting them to understand, accept, and cooperate *as a team*. All of this involves communicating the direction and vision to elicit cooperation as well as to create coalitions that will facilitate the achievement.

Involved in this is aligning and unifying people, collaborating and uniting people is creating community by co-mingling needs, goals, aspirations into a common enterprise. Doing this creates a movement. This requires articulating the values and then using those values to inspire people. The purpose here is to sustain the alignment, mobilize commitment, build collaborative relationships, and share power. Executive Coaching frequently focuses on calling forth these skills and the frames that support them.

3) Enabling Problem-Solving of the Vison.
On the way to achieving a vision will be lots of obstacles and plenty of conflict. Whatever vision a leader sees and whatever direction a leader establishes, there will be barriers. Typically there will be political, bureaucratic, communicational, organizational, financial, time, energy, etc. barriers. Often it takes a herculean effort to deal with and/or overcome these barriers. All of these things require the third core skill of a leader: providing ongoing inspiration so people will keep moving toward the vision. With that inspiration they will also keep accessing the resources they need to handle the obstacles.

What does this involve for the executive leader? It involves problem solving, reducing obstacles, resolving conflicts (managing conflicts relevant to the vision), and enabling organization capacity. These are the common conversations in Executive Coaching.

Where people rise up to provide inspiration for a vision this is leadership. It is this kind of leadership that adds value to people showing them how they make a difference. In doing this, it aligns people to join in on an adventure.

> *Leaders work with and through people to achieve goals far too large for a person to achieve by him or herself.*

In this role, leaders work as problem solvers of the vision. They make things happen by empowering others. Then through the magic of collaboration people feel that they are a part of something bigger than themselves. Such leaders inspire people to face difficulties, adversities, and to push through the constraints and challenges to make a vision real. No wonder then the executive looks to their coaches to help them have the inspiration for this.

Managerial Leaders
The success of a system depends on *how well* that system is managed. Are the managers working systemically and holistically? Is there an openness in the communication flow?

Great Managers turn potential talent into actual performance!

While leadership has been around for millennia, management (and especially modern management) is a more recent invention. Kotter says that it was invented to help the new railroads, steel mills, and auto companies in the nineteenth century. The legendary entrepreneurs of that age set out to do things on a massive level that needed management processes if they were to produce a high degree of consistency and order. This called for a new role and a new set of skills different from visionary leadership. It needed those men and women who could work with people and processes in a way to *solve consistency problems of the system.*

What is the core of modern management? Setting up all of the processes necessary to detail the larger vision and direction of change, as set by the visionary leaders. The three key skill sets that make this happen are *planning, organizing, and controlling.* Managers play a most vital and critical role as they translate the vision to the craft people and feedback from the craft persons to the leaders.

Success as a system depends on how the system is managed. Is it managed from a systems perspective so it works holistically with the whole system? Does it seek fit for the parts, for cooperation, effective flow of information through the system?

1) Planning and Budgeting
By the core competency of planning management is able to detail the vision into plans with targets and milestones so it happens over time and on time. Managers establish the detailed steps for achieving those targets. They establish the timetables, the guidelines, and the structures and processes for allocating resources. *Planning* for a manager differs radically from vision setting. As it involves detailing the plan, it generates *how-to-knowledge* — presented in step-by-sep instructions. It also involves detailing a budget so there are the finances to pay for the operations.

As an Executive Coach, you do not need to know or even have experience in these areas. Your contribution are the awareness questions. Ask them in Socratic fashion to enable the executive leader to find his or her own answers. After that ask meta-questions to enable them to become aware of these skills and their importance for being effective as a managerial leader.

2) Organizing and Staffing
Management's second core competency is *organization.* Here the manager takes the vision of the leader and establishes an organizational structure of a set of jobs to accomplish the plan. This involves staffing the jobs with qualified individuals, communicating the plan to them, delegating

responsibility for carrying out the plan, and establishing systems to monitor the implementation of the plan. This *organizing* aspect of management differs radically from what a visionary leader does when she aligns people.

This involves system building. That is, getting the right people on the bus, training to develop the required competencies, creating fit by getting the right people in the right jobs and roles. It requires the ability to match for sameness and to engage in systems thinking. It requires a system for accountability. Coaching a senior manager in being able to play this outer game requires the necessary frames for the manager. This is where you are most needed as an Executive Coach.

3) Controlling and Problem Solving
Third, *management controls and solves problems.* "Control" refers to taking action, staying involved, and aware of what's happening. It means doing what you are response-able to do.

If the plan, structure, and implementation isn't controlled, but out-of-control, there will be a lack of consistency and order. Reliability and credibility then weakens. This undermines the process of empowering a company to create quality products or services. In controlling, a manager monitors in detail the actual results against the designed plan. He checks who is accountable for what. The manager meets with people to identify any deviations from the plan. Every deviation is a "problem." The manager then reports the findings in order to create a plan to solve the deviation. All in all, a manager manages the homeostasis of the system.

> "In all of this the basic function of management is homoeostatic. It is to keep a system alive by making sure that critical variables remain within tolerable ranges constantly. And an important aspect of any homoeostatic process is control. After a target has been established and a system has been designed that can achieve that target, a control mechanism is created to monitor continuously system behavior versus plan and then to take action when a deviation is detected." (Kotter, p. 62)

In controlling and problem solving, the manager has to do two very different things on a single continuum. First, *sort for differences* to detect deviations. Simultaneously, *match for sameness* to the plan. No wonder great managers think in terms of following procedures. They have to care about the precision of details that make for quality. And they have to aim for fail-safe and risk-free structures. If a visionary leader thought that way, he or she would be overly cautious and poor at envisioning new possibilities. Yet this is the talent of a manager who seeks to minimize deviations from the plan unlike the visionary leader who is wired to seek for new deviations.

Summarizing the Difference
Executive leaders focus on creating change—what is changing in the world and marketplace and the organizational changes that are needed to cope with those changes. Managerial leaders, by contrast, focus on following procedure and producing predictable results (non-change). Some leaders create meaning as they see the vision and set the frames. They articulate the opportunities. They inspire the dream. They explain the outcome and purpose. They generate the energy of the excitement. These visionary leaders operate on the Meaning Scale—the vertical axis.

Managerial leaders focus on managing, solidifying, stabilizing, and integrating the change. These processes create and keep the change. A covert manager masquerading as a leader will run a company in a very cautious and conservative way which, in the long run, will make the business less effective, less adaptive, and less relevant to its marketplace. Managers translate the meaning into performance— they turn the vision into specific action plans. They articulate the strategy into tactics that are actionable for the opportunity. They establish a time-line as they schedule the work that will realize the purpose. They monitor the people engaging in the actual performances and enable them to comply with the plan.

In the dimension of *meaning,* the executive is a visionary leader responsible for the vision and values of the organization, the framing, culture, change, and effectiveness. In the dimension of *performance,* the executive is the managerial leader responsible for the company's productivity, profitability, results, efficiency, etc.

Coaching the Leadership Team
Vincent Lenhardt (2004) *Coaching for Meaning*, notes that leadership is a plural process, not a singular one.
> "The leader is no longer the one who works on his own, who comes up with ideas and then communicates them to others. He is at all times obliged to co-construct solutions with others. The determining factor is his capacity to generate teamwork. The leader who leads in the swirl of change." (page xxi)

Co-leading for executives, whether visionary or managerial leaders, means working together as *the leadership team.* Then as a team of leaders, they together create a synergy between meaning (vision, values, etc.) and performance.[3]

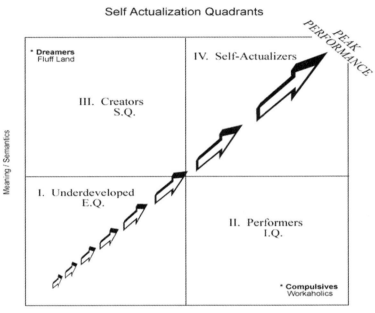

Self Actualization Quadrants

\What emerges from this synergy is *an engaged work force.* In fact, the engagement level of the employees is the best benchmark we have for determining effectiveness of a leadership team. In Meta-Coaching after I mapped out the twin-functions of meaning and performance for self-actualization, we began applying that to groups—to companies, organizations, and to corporates.

The diagram of the Self-Actualization Quadrants gives in quadrant one those who are undeveloped, in quadrant two those who focus almost exclusively on performance (the performers), in quadrant three those who focus almost exclusively on visions and dreams and inspirational meanings (the dreamers, creators), and then in quadrant four those who integrate these for the synergy of actualizing one's highest meanings in one's best performances. Quadrant IV is where the highest quality emerges.

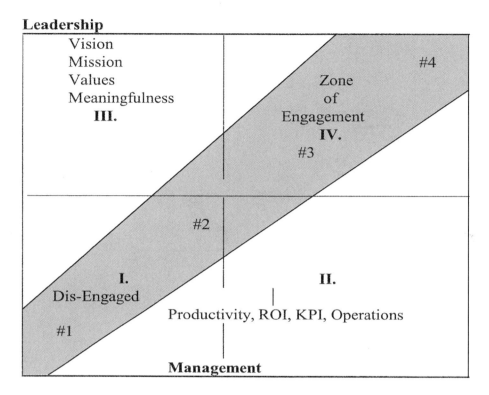

Applying that to the twin-dimensions of leadership we have the visionary and the managerial dimensions. Next, let's ask some challenging questions:

How do we benchmark the leadership's team performance?

How do we know that the leaders, as a team, are doing their job and being effective in what they are doing?

The answer? The employee's level of engagement in the business. That is *the leader's benchmark* of effectiveness. "What is their engagement level?" The higher their engagement, the better the leadership. The lower their engagement, the more ineffective the leadership.[4]

Working Together as a Team

Collaborative leadership is a tremendous challenge and for that reason it is a high development and relatively rare. A great deal of the challenge is developing the *collective abilities*—thinking together, learning together, deciding together, and performing together. Facilitating that kind and level of collaboration requires leaders in an organization working together as a team and getting beyond the silo mentality of inner competition.

Your Executive Coaching Take Aways

Leadership is not a "long ranger" job. It involves being part of a leadership team and co-leading with others leaders. To unify the required competencies of visionary and managerial leadership enables executives to operate as a highly effective collaborative team.[5]

The very best benchmark for the quality of leadership in any company is the engagement level of employees. When employees are not engaged—mind, body, and spirit—someone is failing in their leadership competency.

- When coaching executives, there are two very different dimensions of executive leaders: those who are visionary and those who are managerial. How well do you know the difference and know how to coach to those differences?

- Attempting to groom a managerial leader to a visionary leadership role requires a lot of changes. It requires changing the person's focus, time allotment, values, and skills.

- The lack of alignment between those on the executive leadership team is often *the big hidden problem* in many organizations. Yet if the visionary and managerial leaders are not on the same page, then all of the worse symptoms of bureaucracy— secrecy, dirty politics, mis-communication, dis-information, silo thinking, competition between departments, etc. arises. How ready are you for these things in your Executive Coaching?

End of Chapter Notes

1. See John Kotter's work, *A Force for Change: How Leadership differs from Management* (1990), also the Training Manual, *Unleashing Leadership*.
2. See the set of questions for the visionary and managerial leadership skills, Appendix B.
3. See *Group and Team Coaching* (2012).
4. See *Unleashing Leadership* (2011) and chapter eight for an entire discussion about engagement in an organization and the leader's role in facilitating employee engagement.
5. I'm currently completing a book on this subject with Ian McDermott, *The Collaborative Leader.*

Chapter 21

THE UNLEASHING POTENTIALS

CONVERSATION

"Think of potential as the work one can do in the future."
Charan, Ram, et. al
The Leadership Pipeline (p. 169)

The Unleashing Potentials Conversation is the conversation where you are either awakening a realization in an executive of a potential or assisting your client in developing and refining a potential. When you do this you are grooming people to be the best they can be. You are focusing on bringing out the best in people– which is the heart and soul of true "leadership."

This conversation is bold. It is audacious. After all, it is by this conversation that people can identify and develop the potential talents and competencies that are not now actual, but which can become in the future. Yet is this really possible? Can a conversation do all of that? If so, how? What goes on in a conversation that can do that?

It's true enough that most conversations cannot unleash or develop potentials. Most of the time the way we converse and chat and argue and complain to and with each other has no possibility for unleashing hidden talents and potentials. Many conversations, in fact, may actually do the opposite— they may smother, dampen, kill, sabotage, undermine, and destroy potential. How do we do this to each other? Mostly by judgment. To kill dreams all you have to do is judge, condemn, mock, be sarcastic, discount, insult, laugh at people. You can dishearten people. When we talk together and one walks away dispirited, frustrated, confused, fearful, feeling guilty, etc.—she has probably become less open to change and renewal. He has shut down and put a "Closed. Out of Business" sign on his heart.

Judgments, insults, put-downs, criticisms, mockery, sarcasm, and the like take a tremendous toil on the human spirit. For many people it doesn't take a lot of this to throw cold water on their dreams and visions. Their big exciting idea that makes them come alive is now crashing and burning due to neglect or criticism. They can then become stuck in the world of the actual and feel so stuck there that they begin to believe, "The only real world is what is actual. What isn't actual is only imaginary and unreal." So they don't even consider it.

Others may have once believed in actualizing a potential, but were then traumatized by a failure or rejection. Now for them, to even give a potential a moment of possibility in the mind, it is just too painful. All of this puts more demands on an Executive Coach in being able to gracefully and effectively handle the Unleashing Potential Conversation.

The Art of the Conversation
As an Executive Coach, how do you lead this conversation so it has the possibility of awakening your client to the things within that are clambering to be released and so that the real self can emerge?

1) Awaken possibilities.
This conversation begins either with an awakening of a possibility or by dealing with the inhibitions that a person has from entering the domain of the potential. In this case, ask about potentials—about dreams, visions, hopes, things that enliven, and stepping up to become one's best self. Or one's best leader. The conversation may arise from possibilities within the company that the coach could then champion. This conversation may arise from talking about stretch goals or any desired outcome (The Outcome

Conversation, chapter 16). Many Unleashing Potentiality Conversation begin here.

To awaken possibilities, get into the habit of thinking of people in terms of potentials. Refuse to look at people through the lens of their title or status, not their current performance. What if, in the future, this person becomes a brilliant CEO? This will help you to believe that there is tremendous potential within people. Keep asking yourself, "What's actual (current) and what's potential in this person that has a likelihood of becoming or developing?"

2) Reframe Semantic Hurts
Beyond merely asking about potentials, coach the executive's meanings. How does the person interpret the idea of potentials? Here you coach to the leader's or manager's semantics (meanings) about potentials. What you find could very well require therapy rather than coaching. So be sure to check out how much damage the person has experienced. The keys that therapy is needed are: The person lacks the ego-strength to face reality as it is, the person is not okay in oneself, he or she lives in the past, the person feels helpless and hopeless.

Now if hope has been only dampened and belief discouraged, then you probably only need to discover the semantic inhibitions and work with those frames. Most of the time the solution lies in acceptance. Enable the person to give him or herself permission to accept what was forbidden and tabooed. Identify the frames that are doing the damage and then deframe and/or reframe those frames.[1]

3) Inspire people for Reaching their Potentials
Once a person is free from negatively interpreting things and has taken charge of his semantic frames, he or she is ready for inspiration. This is the next stage and that's because it takes a lot of spirit to take on the unleashing of potentials. And, of course, the skill of inspiration is also a leadership skill par excellence. How well has your executive client developed this skill? How well can she inspire herself? Here you can be a model for your executive client this core skill of leadership as you coach inspiration.

What inspires? What puts spirit in a human being? Hope. Desire. Excitement. These are the emotions of inspiration and they arise when values are accessed and visions are expressed. So go there. Spend time enabling your client to discover and explore his or her own values and dreams. Once you have those, you can use them to inspire him or her to raise one's hopes and expectations about what's possible. This art involves seeing small seeds of possibilities that can grow into wonderful potentials. The art includes believing in your client and communicating that.

A cautionary note: Be careful that you are listening to the desire deep in the client that wants to emerge. If you are trying to put your need for the client to realize some potential which you want for them, you will be forcing the issue. That will seldom work. In effect, this violates the rapport and trust of the relationship.

4) Develop and Refine the Person's Potentials
Once a potential is identified, it has to be developed, shaped, and reinforced over time. No potential ever appears fully developed. Begin by enabling your executive client to identify and call forth the component pieces of a skill. Then sequence them so they comprise the best structure (strategy) of the skill.

This works because every skill is made up of our four fundamental powers —the power to think, feel, speak, and act. The baby steps of any great potential begins as just that—baby steps. While they are small steps, they are also significant steps. Make sure you give them significant meaning, then take action to perform what can be performed at this moment, no matter how small. Refining a potential will also require feedback. Lots of it. Feedback will accelerate the learning and development of the skill.[2]

5) Call the Person to Become Real
A self-actualizing leader is a leader who is authentic, transparent, and approachable. He or she is real. And being real means getting beyond one's roles, status, title, and the glamor of the position and remaining a growing and developing person who is open and learning. He is open to his humanity and therefore fallibilities. She is learning as an ongoing progress. This kind of person is what Jim Collins called a Level 5 Leader—one who is simultaneously ambitious and humble, determined and modest.

The Unleashing Conversation
As a coach, these are the central questions about unleashing potentials:
• 　　　How do you coach an Unleashing Potentials Conversation?
• 　　　What questions do you ask in facilitating this conversation?

•   What steps are involved in the process of mobilizing a client's resources that will enable potentials to be identified, released, mobilized, and developed?

In answer to the question about what unleashes potentials, there are many processes. The good news is that you have already read about many of these processes in the earlier chapters. What follows comes from the processes that are detailed in the book, *Unleashed!* (2007).[3] As you recognize these mechanisms and begin to use them, you'll empower yourself with the required skills for *unleashing* your powers and potentials.

1) Self-awareness. You cannot unleash what you're unaware of. So self-awareness is first. Because human potentials come from within, enabling a client to turn inward to develop a more expansive self-awareness helps the person to become aware of him or herself—his or her hidden talents, strengths, and potentials. This is intra-psychological intelligence. It enables one to get in touch with one's real self and with one's deepest passions. And Executive Coaching, by its very nature is designed to increase one's intrapsychic intelligence.

2) Vision of Actualizing Potentials. A person can have lots of potentials and never actualize them. The actualizing process is not automatic. It especially does not operate without vision, action, decision, commitment, and practice. It does not occur apart from a person's choice and action. It only occurs through the personal commitment and responsibility. Yet it all begins with vision—with awakening to the possibilities. The vision carries the person forward.

3) Ego-Strength. To unleash potentials requires the ability to face reality for what it is without falling apart or going into fight-flight responses. We call this experience and state of mind "ego-strength." With regard to coaching, ego-strength is required as a beginning prerequisite. Of course, it is also strengthened, refined, and enhanced in the process of coaching. Coaching has this dual relationship to ego-strength; it is required and it also develops through coaching.

4) Releasing Judgment. If there's any one big thing that inhibits the identifying, unleashing, releasing, and developing of potentials—judgment is the villain. The person who judges himself or herself and the world and others creates all kinds of inhibitions against the unleashing process. Judgment trashes effort; it defeats hope. Judgment discounts first steps and treats them as worthless because they are small steps. Judgment blocks learning and inhibits creativity.

5) Meaning. Without a rich construct of meaning and meaningfulness about a potential, the potential will not develop or be unleashed. It is not just a vision that we need—we need a *meaningful* vision. Meaning is what makes a vision great. Therefore the more your coaching enables a client to recognize and own one's meaning-making powers for creating one's sense of reality, the more the person can activate and develop potentials.

6) Quality and Quality Controlling. As it is not just meaning that unleashes potential, but meaningful vision, what makes it *meaningful* is when the meaning is high quality. This explains why the ability to quality control one's own meaning-making powers and processes is so crucial. Every client needs to be able to enrich his or her skills in detecting and reframing meaning. Then they can set quality meanings that are robust and enlivening. After all, the quality of life is a function of the quality of one's meanings.

7) Synthesizing. To actualize any potential so that it becomes fully developed, a person has to synthesize two things—one's meanings and one's performance. That's because self-actualization is the synergy of meaning and performance. This is also why we use these two factors or variables as the axes of self-actualization. This explains the construct of the Self-Actualization Quadrants. When put together they identify the pathway to self-actualization—that central path between meaning and performance, the path wherein one synthesizes both.

8) Synergizing Opposites. This describes the skill and process for overcoming the limitations of dichotomizing polarities which thereby creates false and paradoxical conflicts. To facilitate self-actualizing, coach people to create synergy between any conflicting forces and especially perceptual patterns. Do this by expanding limited meta-programs.[4]

9) Need Gratification. There are some pre-conditions to unleashing one's potentials. One of those is the basic gratification of one's *deficiency needs*. When a person gratifies the lower needs sufficiently so one can get by, new needs and drives emerge. This is the process for moving up the levels of needs (Maslow's Hierarchy of Needs) which creates the foundation for moving beyond the lower needs to the higher needs.

10) Esteeming Self. If a person's "self" is weak, undeveloped, or conditionally valid (conditional self-esteem, even if it is "high"), then one's self is always in the way. That will undermine the unleashing process. Healthy self-actualizing requires that you validate your own *unconditional* value, worth, and individual uniqueness. Begin by distinguishing your person (what you *are*) from your behavior (what you *do*). Then declare as a positive assertion that your humanity (your person) is *unconditionally* valuable. Assert that it is beyond rating it either low or high value (that creates conditional esteem). Doing that gets your ego out of the way. Now you will experience your value (your *being*) as a given and detached from your achievements (what you do).

11) Centering Self. Having creating a solid sense of self through unconditionally valuing yourself, now you can focus on your skills (what you can *do*) thereby developing your social, relational, and career self. With this solid sense of self, you will be able to create personal and social safety nets for what you *do*. Doing this then enables you to take smart risks and to courageously stretch beyond the familiar comfort zones that hold you back.

12) Transcending. To self-actualize one's highest potentials requires transcending the lower needs. That's obvious. What is not so obvious is that it also requires that one transcends one's *sense of self* to gain higher level perspective. When a person transcends the animal drives to the highest human drives, she experiences the drives and needs of *being*. You now transcend the deficiency needs and live in the *being* needs and values. Here the *meaningfulness* of your passions develops fully. Here a miracle happens. It is the miracle of getting over yourself (a big miracle!) So that you become self-forgetful.

The miracle is also that one's motivation completely changes. It changes from deficiency to abundance. As you transcend all of the lower needs that are driven by deficiency, you transcend *getting* motivation. You move to a higher level, to the self-actualizing or *being* needs where you experience *giving* motivation: making a difference and contributing.

13) Stepping Back Awareness. To transcend, in part, means to be able to "step back" from oneself and one's experience. At this point you is able to observe yourself with a non-judgmental awareness. Unleashing this power unleashes the richness of your self-reflexive consciousness. Now you can flexibly move out of an experience and back into it at will and for the purpose of gaining multiple perspectives.

14) Robust Active Powers. Unleashing one's potentials requires an active and responsible response-style. Therefore it involves the processing of finding and taking complete ownership of one's innate powers (thinking, feeling, speaking, and acting). This enables you to then use your core powers or capacities to play to your strengths, manage around your weaknesses, and take an active role in unleashing your potentials. Ultimately, actualizing your potentials depends on your performance. Potential is not equal to performance. You can have potential without performance. A coaching client can have potential yet fail to develop it. And if it is never developed, then the person will live and die with his or her music still within—unreleased.

15) Choosing. Given that unleashing doesn't happen automatically and that it occurs through the process of choice, clients must choose. Unleashing requires the ability to choose and decide to step up to one's executive power of choice. Only then can a person take control of his or her focus, meanings, emotions, identity, attitude, and direction in service of unleashing potentials. As Morpheus said in *The Matrix,* "I can show you the door, but you must walk through."

16) Engagement. The final state of self-actualizing your potential *and* the process for getting there is one and the same. It takes the expression of being *fully engaged* in a passion or love. By accessing the "flow" state of being totally present in an engagement, you will coach your executive client to take his or her performance to ever higher levels of excellence. This is the "genius" state which one can then take charge of and turn on and off at will.[5]

17) Stretching. The process of unleashing potentials inevitably also requires setting compelling goals that stretch a person. In the stretching process you move to the next level and actualizing your highest self and best performances. Outcomes and visions obviously facilitates this process. So does challenge. In fact, this explains the importance of challenge to move a client out of comfort and familiarity and into the adventure of growth and change.

18) Receiving Feedback. The process of being able to see yourself and your actions as if in a mirror—cleanly and clearly, enables you to make coarse corrections moment by moment as needed. To unleash new potentials, the receiving and welcoming of that feedback information facilitates adjusting more quickly and flexibly to needed changes.

19) Capitalizing Problems. Potentials not only lie in one's strengths and talents, frequently potentials hide in the form of problems. That's why it's important to welcome and capitalize on one's "problems." Then clients can put them to good use for energizing, releasing, and unleashing of new possibilities. Many men and women became great because of a problem that they faced and eventually overcame. In the process of facing and winning over the problem, they became more than they were. We could say that, to some extent, they needed that problem. It was a valued trigger by which they unleashed hidden potentials.

20) Loving. Love is an ultimate unleasher. Unleashing potentials occurs by learning to love—love life, love oneself, love others, and love developing and contributing. Activating one's fullest sense of the mind-set and attitude of love enables a person to care, to really and deeply care. So we coach to this. We coach so that our clients grow in love and fall in love with the adventure of life.

21) Playing. While unleashing potentials is a lot of effort, it doesn't have to be "work." Not at all. It can be play. A person can be joyfully playful in the whole process of unleashing potentials in the adventure of self-actualization. So we coach to this as well. We coach our client to bring more play and playfulness into the process. We do that because we know that more joy in the unleashing experience, the more one's development accelerates.

22) Valuing. At the heart of meaning-making is that of seeing and creating value and doing this everywhere. This powerful process directly unleashes potentials. In the field of money and wealth-creation, appreciation (or valuing) unleashes the entrepreneurial spirit. In the field of personal development, appreciation (or valuing) unleashes the transcending *being-*values and makes them "the meaning of life." This explains why discounting is like a cancer to the self-actualizing process.

23) Culture. The process of unleashing potentials both leads to and creates culture. It creates a new culture in every context— home, work, organization, etc. So when we coach for people to *cultivate* mind, heart, and interactions with others, we create more and more of the good conditions required for self-actualization. From that a new culture emerges. Actualizing a person's potential depends on being in the right job, at the right level, and within the right environment.

Your Executive Coaching Take Aways

Executive Coaching in its highest form is about coaching clients so it unleashes an executive's highest and best potentials. To achieve this, the coaching identifies those potentials, calls them forth, and then develops them. All of this is designed so the person becomes more of his or her real self.

The good news is that there is a structure to this unleashing process. As you learn the science that governs that structure and give yourself to practice it, you increasingly become skilled in the art of facilitating self-actualization.

- How well acquainted are you with the mechanisms and the processes by which a person identifies and unleashes potentials?
- What mechanisms do you primarily rely on when engaged in Executive Coaching?
- Which of the processes mentioned in this chapter will you explore further to enhance your coaching skills?

End of the Chapter Notes:

1. I have written extensively about the skills in *Mind-Lines* (2005), and in *Winning the Inner Game* (2007). Also see *Meta-States* (2007) which addresses the subject of resilience.

2. See *Achieving Peak Performance* (2009). *Secrets of Personal Mastery* (2000).

3. See *Unleashed!* (2007) which offers a detailed presentation of how the unleashing of potentials occurs. Also the workshop, *Unleashing Potentials.*

4. Our meta-programs are our learned perceptual patterns, and if learned, they can be unlearned and relearned. We can expand these perceptual patterns thereby reducing our blind spots and unleashing new potentials. See the pattern for Expanding Meta-Programs in *Figuring Out People* (1997).

5. The genius state is the state of focus where one is completely engaged with an activity outside of oneself. It is a state of being "in the zone' and being able to turn it on and off at will.

Chapter 22

THE INTEGRATING & INTEGRITY

CONVERSATION

"The secret is integrity—learning to *do* what you *say* you will do.
When you're honest with yourself and others,
it leads to trust, consistent results, and higher performance
and from that comes congruence and trustworthiness."
Graham Richardson

If *a conversation* can unleash potential (chapter 21) that would be an incredibly dramatic and powerful conversation, would it not? Well another equally profound coaching conversation is the Integration Conversation. This is the coaching conversation that enables a person to integrate conflicting parts (or aspects) which are not aligned? This is the conversation that addresses what is not fully integrated or aligned to be in harmony within the person.

Sometimes the Integration Conversation is really easy. Sometimes you can pull it off successfully simply by bringing up and discussing aspects that are not integrated. Sometimes all you have to do is ask, "What are the unintegrated aspects of your life?" Ask about the relationship between work and life, between work and play, between responsibility for making a living and the creativity to live it in your unique way, and so on. Sometimes just asking about the link between things, and the quality of that link, is enough. The person may have an immediate "Aha!" and link these aspects of life together.

At other times, the conversation that facilitates integration may occur by planting the questions of integration and let them slowly develop in the person's mind. As an Executive Coach, you can using any of the following questions to initiate that inquiry:

- What needs to be integrated?
- What is not integrated? How do you know?
- What let's you know that there is a conflict between different aspects of yourself?
- Where do you feel pulled apart as if pulled in two different directions?
- In what aspects of your life would you want to have a more harmonious relationship?
- What feedback have you received that suggests that there's a lack of integration or alignment or integrity?

There's another way to initiate the integration conversation. Simply invite a vision about the integrated life. Or you could talk about an extraordinary leader or executive who exudes with integrity and alignment. That could elicit your executive client to begin considering a new level of personal unity in a way that he or she has never considered before.

What are the steps within the Integrating Conversation? There are three:
1) Identify what needs to be integrated.
2) Set a higher frame to facilitate the integration.
3) Use an open-ended conversation or follow a formal process like *the Intentionality Pattern* or *the Meta-Alignment Pattern*.
4) Develop a robust integrity.

Identifying What to Integrate
With a great many things, the process of integration normally works as an automatic process in human personality. Normally you take something that you have learned— some new idea, skill, pattern, role, etc. and make them part of your way of thinking, feeling, talking, and acting. Typically that's how you *integrate into yourself new learnings*. Along with the process you also develop supporting beliefs, values, identities, and understandings. These form the hidden or unconscious framework that enables you to feel

fully aligned with the new learning.

But not always. Not infrequently when you learn something new, sometimes you find it difficult to integrate into yourself. Why is that? What's happening in those circumstances? Typically there is some other aspect of yourself that opposes it. That's why it doesn't seem to fit. To some extent it fits, but to some extent it does not. If this results in internal conflict then you become aware of that lack of alignment. Yet just as often, if not more, it results in uneasy feelings of discomfort.

> "I just feel uncomfortable when I do that." "It's just not me when I speak up in the boardroom, or lead the discussion, or disagree with the executive team."

That's one scenario—what's newly learned and developed conflicts with another part of yourself at the same time. There's another scenario. If the new learning is applied in one context, and then later, in some other context, an opposite set of behaviors prevails, you may have the structure of *sequential incongruity* rather than *simultaneous incongruity*. In the first, you sense it and feel it. Not so in the second. In the second, other people sense it about you.

This gives us three signals for the lack of integration and alignment. First there are the conscious signals: inner conflict and discomfort. Then there is the blind spot for self which shows up as others sensing that at different times we think, talk, act, and relate in contradictory ways.

- What patterns of thinking, talking, acting, or relating do you have that you sense are in conflict with each other? That may not be aligned and that may cause you to be lacking integration?
- What patterns seem to be pulling against another part of yourself?

For example, you might learn some of the principles and processes for wealth creation and then feel bad about wanting money or talking about money when people around you are struggling with poverty. Is there a conflict pulling you in different directions?

- Polar opposites creating a sense of an either–or choice.
- Judgments that forbid you to go in a certain direction or experience something.
- Dominance of one side over another side.
- Growth and development that has out-grown an old expression so it now feels uncomfortable yet, "Who would I be if I let it go?"

- A limiting or even a toxic belief, decision, understanding, etc.
- An incongruence that occurs either simultaneous or over-time.

As you identify the inner conflicts which may be preventing the integration, you'll know what to clear out. When a conflict continues and behavior does not change even when you have a strong motivation, there is probably a blind spot of internal conflict present.

Now for a warning about integration. Everything should not be integrated even though it is "part" of you. *Some things are best released.* Could it be time to release it? If it is a limiting belief, decision, or identity, perhaps it is time to eliminate it by changing it. This raises the question: What should you do— integrate or release (eliminate)? If the solution is not to integrate, then release it. You can do this in a number of ways: by suspending, by letting go, by doing your necessary grief work, by refusing what does not serve you, by updating your programs for your identity, values, etc.

Feeling like an Executive Fraud

As an Executive Coach be aware that many executives feel like a fraud. In spite of the person's outward confidence and way of handling him or herself, inside the person may feel the very opposite. This frequently happens when a person has been labeled a "high potential" and is fast-tracked through the intermediate roles to a senior position. As a result, the fast-tracking robs them of getting a real solid sense of the company and of his or her skills.

The fact is, normalizing to a role and position takes time. How long? It depends, of course, on many things. It is relative to many factors in the person and in the context. Yet it is not unusual for it take two to five years. In terms of integration, this may be the content of an Integrating Conversation.

Stepping up to Set a Higher Agreement Frame

Warring parts often war because they are not sorted out in terms of *when* and *where* each is useful. When should an executive be supportive and understanding? And when firm with rules and boundaries? In such cases, a higher agreement frame can end the war and become the peacetime treaty. A higher frame can negotiate the treaty between the parts. The higher frame of committing yourself to a balanced life can help integrate the conflict between work and family.

When we set a higher agreement frame between aspects of ourselves, that higher frame can hold different aspects together. That's the power and usefulness of an agreement frame. We take two or more conflicting "parts" as valid aspects of ourselves and put them all inside of a higher classification or category.

For the polarization of pride and humility, perhaps the higher frame could be "self in its experiences." After all, pride is not being superior or putting on airs. And humility is not shame and humiliation. Healthy pride speaks of acknowledging what one does well. You take pride in effortful achievement due to responsibility and in spite of being a fallible human being. In healthy humility you recognize that much of your good fortune and success is due to luck and happen-chance rather than your effort and skills.

To set a higher frame, identify and follow the positive intention up the levels. Keep doing this until you find a positive intention that will unify the conflicting parts.

- What is the positive intention behind each of the conflicting parts?
- Why is that aspect of yourself wanting what it is wanting?
- For what higher purpose or intention?
- What belief frames in the back of your mind support your thinking, acting, and relating? Which belief frames do not?
- What decision frames support you and which fight against you?

Use these same kind of questions for other meta-levels: understanding frames, identity frames, permission and/or prohibition frames, metaphoric frames, etc.

Integrating through Intentionality

In Meta-Coaching, one of the patterns we often use is *the Intentionality Pattern.* We primarily use it for generating a strong intentional purpose to create the motivational energy to go after an important outcome. This pattern can also be used to conversationally coach for more alignment and integration.

The premise within this pattern is that what we attend to, what gets our attention, and what interrupts our attention is often very different from what we intend to focus on. We have good *intentions.* We set good intentions. But then, somehow, we get lost in our *attentions.*

These two facets of consciousness, intention and attention, speak about two different dimensions and levels of consciousness. *Attention* is what is *on* your mind, what you think about, and what captures your focus. In a world where there are so many things competing for our attention, it is easy for your attention to be capture by a zillion things. *Intention* is what is *in the back* of your mind as our purpose, agenda, or goal.

When we are first born—we live an attentional life. We focus on whatever is loud, bright, moving, etc. This describes the life of an animal or small child. We respond entirely by reacting to the sensory stimuli in the environment. Yet to live humanly and at our best, we must live intentionally. Living intentionally is living on purpose. Intentionality means you respond according to your highest intentions. When attentions are aligned to your highest intentions, you develop a laser-beam focus of concentration.

The following steps (numbered and in italics) describe what you are doing in the coaching while the questions as an induction describing the process of integrating through using an executive's intentionality.

1) Identify an activity that's important which does not feel important.
For this pattern, begin with any everyday activity. It can be an activity that the person enjoys and loves, feels turned on about, or it can be a highly dreaded activity—yet one a person knows is important. As a coach use the elicitation questions to facilitate the process.
- What are some of the tasks that you engage in as part of your everyday life, career, etc.? What do you *need* to do, because it's important to your long-term success, *yet it does not feel important*? You don't feel motivated to do it?
- What important thing do you need to do but as you do, you find it hard to maintain your focus?
- What activity do you have good intentions to do, but then suffer ADD (Attention Deficit Disorder) when it comes time to actually do it?

2) Explore the importance of the activity by asking the "why" question.
- Why is that activity important to you? Is this activity important and significant?
- *How* is it significant? *Why* is it valuable?
- Why is it meaningful? In what way? Is anything else important about that?

Each time your client mentions a reason why, summarize as a value, and confirm it with him or her, "So that's important to you?"

3) Continue the exploration up the meta-levels.
Continue asking the value question of importance to discover the person's intentions. Do this until you flush out and detect all of the higher values. You'll probably want to write down this ascending list of intentions in order to keep track of them and repeat them back.

> "This activity is important because of these values (repeat the values to acknowledge them). And why is this important to you? What's important by having this? What is important about that outcome? And what's even more important than that? And when you get that fully and completely and in just the way you want it, what's even more important?"

4) Step into the highest intentional state.
> When you elicit a highly valued intention, ask, "Have you ever experienced that intention or value?" If yes, then say the following. If no, ask them to imagine experiencing it and say the following.
> "As you welcome in the good feelings that those values, be with and experience those values and feelings so that you register them fully in your mind and body. Do you like that? Let those feelings grow and intensify as you recognize that this is your *highest intentionality,* this is what you are all about . . . isn't it? Close your eyes and be with your highest intention and let it fill every fiber of your being."

5) Link to the highest state to the primary context.
> "Now in just a moment, when you are ready, I want you to open your eyes and look at the event that you started with, the event that you know is important, but has not felt important *and look at it with all of these higher intentions in mind.* As you now take this highest intention—*look at that event* and notice how it aligns your attentions so your attentions can now do service for your intention. With this in mind, notice how this highest intention changes those attentions. Will you now be able to focus and concentrate? Now imagine taking this intentionality and moving out into tomorrow with them. How is that?"

6) Commission your executive mind to take ownership.
> "There's a part of your mind that makes decisions, will that highest

executive part of your mind take full responsibility to access this intention of *your big why* whenever you are engaged in this activity so you can see the world this way? Imagine using this as *the basis of your inner life,* your way of being in the world. Do you like that? Would that make a difference? Would you be able to focus on this activity and complete it?"

As an option, you can invite other resources.
"Would you like to bring any other resource to this intentionality? Would playfulness enrich it? Would persistence, passion, love, etc.?"

7) Future Pace.
• Will you take this into your future?
• Will it enhance your life and align your attentions to your highest intentions? Will you keep this?

Integrity through Meta-Alignment
Another pattern that you can use to conversationally coach an executive to create a higher degree of integrity is known as *the Meta-Alignment Pattern.*[2] This pattern provides a way to align and use meta-level structures to create an overall sense or gestalt of integration, congruency, wholeness, and well-being. In doing this process you can turn it into a practice by standing and talking about each level so that you spatially anchor each level as you back up from the primary state of the behavior that you want to create more alignment with. If you spatially anchored each meta-state, go back to the highest level of metaphor and step from there to the next one and the next gathering up the resources and bring it down to the behavior.

1) Identify an experience in which the person wants full alignment.
Around any and every behavior we have multiple layers of frames of mind and meanings and sometimes these may not be aligned with each other or with the behavior. As a result, a person may not experience the full congruency and integrity with the behavior that he or she desires because of these other ideas. To achieve integration, we can access layers of frames (meta-frames) to support a greater alignment. To elicit the context for this pattern, ask one of the following questions:
• Is there any behavior that you would like to perform with more personal alignment, congruency, and integrity?
• What activity do you engage in that's very important to you, but

which sometimes lacks the full range of congruency, power, and focus that you would like to have?

2) Stand up and experience the behavior.
Find a place to stand and in that place, describe the behavior, skill, activity, or experience in sensory-based terms. What does it look like, sound like, feel like if seen from a video-camera (Behavior). Where do you do this? (Environment) Where not? When? When not? (Time).
•   Are you *fully aligned* with this activity in all of your higher levels of thinking and emoting? Are you ready to be?

3) Step back from that space into one representing the skills which enable this behavior.
Having experienced the behavior, step back one step to the capacities and skills that enable you to do that behavior. Now silently or out loud answer these questions:
•   How do you know *how to* do this? Can you pull this off?
•   How do you do that? Describe it for me briefly.
•   What strategy or strategies do you deploy in doing this?

4) Step back one more step to the beliefs that support this behavior.
Keep looking at the behavior itself and as you step back into a space that represents the beliefs that support that behavior, answer these questions:
•   *What* do you believe about that activity?
•   What belief or beliefs support you doing it?
•   What are some empowering beliefs that could support this behavior?

5) Step back one more step to the values that support the behavior.
This step back is into a space representing your values. Look at the space where the behavior occurs and answer these questions:
•   Why do you engage in this? Why do you believe this is important?
•   What are some empowering values that support this behavior?

6) Step back to your best identity for the behavior.
This space is your space for identity, your sense of self, how you identify yourself when you do that behavior.
•   When you do this, does it affect your identity?
•   Who are you when you engage in this?
•   What does engaging in this behavior say about your identity?

7) Step back to your meta-state of purpose.
This next space is your space for vision, mission, and/or spirit. It represents your purpose for the behavior. So focusing on the behavior, answer these questions:
•   Does this fit into your overall sense of destiny and purpose?
•   How does it? What's your highest intentions in doing this?

8) Step back now to your most empowering decision.
The next step back is into your space for a decision or commitment.
•   Have you decided to do this? You will?
•   Have you said "Yes!" to this? What decision supports this behavior?
•   Are you fully committed to this behavior?

9) Step back finally into a space for a metaphor.
This final step back is into a metaphor or story that gives you a sense of what the behavior is like.
•   What is this like? Let a metaphor or story encapsulate this matrix of your mind. As it emerges ...notice its sounds, colors, shapes, music, light, etc.

10) Step forward to integrate all of the levels.
Let's now walk through all of these steps and spaces to bring them all together. Are you ready to do that? As we do, you will be confirming each of the states that you have constructed and allow yourself to fully *feel* them.

Then walk from the metaphor space through all of the other spaces and end up at the behavior space where you began. Then repeat by quickly moving back up each of the steps, calling out the name (skills, beliefs, values, etc.) and when back to *Metaphor,* then walk forward through the spaces again. If needed, you can repeat until all of the levels become more and more integrated.

At the end say, "And with all of these meta-levels in mind—just enjoy thinking about this behavior and feeling it with all of the awarenesses that you created . . . and imagine bringing all of this into your experience of *doing that behavior* and notice how it enriches the behavior.
•   And how's that? Do you like that?
•   Do you now feel fully aligned in this activity?
•   As you let all of the levels fully coalesce into this behavior giving it quality and richness, how do you experience this behavior now?

• Do you want to keep this? Will you?

From Integration to Integrity

If you ask, "Is integration all that's required for integrity?" the answer is no. No it is not. A person could be well-integrated in the sense of being fully congruent and still be out of integrity. Integrity differs from merely being aligned and congruent.

Integrity is honesty. It is being honest with yourself; it is being honest with others. It is speaking and living your truth as you live from a set of values that are ecological for you and others in the long-run. Integrity means that you are a person who lives by principles rather than merely by self-interest and self-promotion. These principles are those that are ecological for all parties over the long-term.

When someone is not a person of integrity, he operates solely from self-promotion. In this case, if he doesn't get anything out of it, he's not interested. She lives from self-comfort and self-ease and if it requires extending self, exerting self, she's chooses avoidance. The person of integrity lives by principles of fairness, equality, kindness, cooperation, care, love, etc. and does so even when it costs. Even when it is hard. Even when it does not promote self-comfort or an easier way of life.

While integration is *necessary* for integrity, it is not *sufficient.* To be a person of integrity it's first required that you integrate within yourself what you say with what you do. What you promise with what you deliver. How you proclaim a value with how you live that value in a specific context. Yet merely being integrated and congruent does not equal being a person of integrity. To that we have to add honesty, truth-speaking, and truth-living.

> "The one thing that has become clearer than ever to me is that integrity is the most important characteristic of a leader, and one he or she must be prepared to demonstrate again and again."
> Warren Bennis
> *Becoming a Leader*

Warren Bennis writes, "Leader never lie to themselves, especially about themselves, know their faults as well as their assets, and deal with them directly." (p. 34). They operate by candor, by character, by earning trust by being trustworthy. Why? Because to look forward with acuity, you must first look back with honesty.

Coaching for Executive Integrity

If people today are requiring anything of their leaders, and leaders at all levels within organizations, it is integrity. With all of the scandals in business and government in recent decades, a leader who is *out of integrity* is a leader who is on his or her way out. That will no longer fly. If you doubt this, think Enron. Think Worldcom. Think Stanley Morgan. And what of all the dot.com businesses during the late 1990s? Or of the worldwide financial recession that began in 2008?

A leader or manager out of integrity is not a person who can be trusted. If that choice has to be made, he or she will do what's in self-interest over what's in the interest of the larger group. That makes the out-of-integrity person—a dangerous person. Who knows what they will do to promote their own ass? Who knows what information they will leak, what trust they will betray, or even what funds they may steal?

Graham Richardson on Developing a Robust Integrity

In my work around integrity, there have been two definitions that I have found very powerful. The one comes from Shakespeare and the other from the principles of engineering.

> Th is what Shakespeare said in Hamlet when Polonius said farewell to his son Laertes who was returning to university. "This above all: to thine own self be true, And it must follow, as the night the day, Thou canst not then be false to any man."
>
> In engineering integrity is this: "This thing does what it was designed to do, consistently, reliably and robustly."

The Challenge of Integrity

The more deeply you enquire into the distinctions of integrity, the more you are likely to discover how much of our lives are lived outside of integrity.

- Do you ever cross the road against traffic lights?
- How often do you tell little white lies?
- Have you ever dropped trash into the street, or left it in the park, or dropped a burned-out cigarette to the road, etc.?
- What about avoiding tax? Or cheating by advantaging yourself at the expense of someone else?
- Or doing something that affects someone else that you would not enjoy having done to yourself?
- When did you last gossip about someone? [Gossip can be defined as

anything you say or do that diminishes the reputation of another.] Wow! Where does this integrity start and end? And who could possibly live a life totally "in integrity?" Recall the chapters on culture and leadership (chapters 10 and 12). What organization on earth can seriously claim that it does not transgress integrity in some way or another? Probably none. For this reason dealing with integrity is a permanent issue for those in executive roles.

The next challenge is in the realm of ambiguity, or more accurately, moral ambiguity. *Moral ambiguity* refers to vacillation, that is, being unable to embrace the proper (ethical) course of action. Moral ambiguity is knowing what the right thing to do is and yet not acting on it because you are dithering. There's within you a desire to give into some temptation. Moral ambiguity also involves blurring the lines of integrity to validate or justify pushing the boundaries, and even crossing the boundaries. Any organization with its executives can do this. And many do. Actually, it is surprising the extent to which this occurs and in what ways.

Most organizations have their espoused values and valued behaviors like "respecting people." In spite of this we can watch how they "cut heads" to save on costs. How they treat more junior employees who are on lower salaries, yet they employ staff at higher rates in equivalent positions to leave the long termer on a lower rate. You can count on the sitting employee to either not know that they are well below the market rate or that they will stick with the job because they don't have a ready alternative. Or watch how they treat suppliers, making sure that they pay the absolute minimum for goods and services in the interest of price advantage, and/or profitability. Often this means sourcing from poorer countries, or exploiting the disadvantaged. We all see these things going on.

As an Executive Coach, the danger is that you may find yourself an accessory to these facts and therefore involved in the situation. When that happens, you now have a dilemma. That's because you are working with an executive as he or she deals with this moral ambiguity. What do you do?

My recommendation: Be very careful. On one side, avoid becoming the integrity police. Do that and you could do a lot of damage. You could do damage the executive's career, your reputation, the viability of the organization, and the livelihoods of many people and their families. On the other side, do you look the other way and avoid the needed conversation?

Ah, the horns of a dilemma! It is about integrity. And you are in a sticky position in terms of how high up the ladder of meaning you choose to go. You can stop at the level of what's best for this executive's career. You could go to the next level: What is best for the organization and its survival? You could go to the next level: What's best for the market? The community? The country? Humanity? The planet? Things look very different at every one of these levels of integrity. So, what do you do?

Aim to work at the level of the executive's meaning and integrity. If that offends, violates, or otherwise disturbs you, it's time for an evaluation. Consider whether you ought to be working with this person or this organization. Consider also if you should be working as a coach with people at all. Ultimately, your own personal integrity is in question. Are you taking the money *and* avoiding the fierce conversation? Are you justifying yourself? "Well, it keeps the wolves from the door. I need the business." Yes, even this is a matter of personal integrity.

Is this controversial? Yes it is. After all, you work in a field of controversy. And because of this thing called *integrity,* it cannot be otherwise. If you see it differently, what could you be over-generalizing, distorting, and/or deleting?

Integrity Coaching

Here's a recent example. A very talented young lady joined a company in a role related to finance. She had been employed to set up a new financial instrument that involved leveraging substantial high value assets which the company traded in. Although the board had approved the business case, political lobbying ensued by the other executives who did not want to release their coveted assets into the pool. This effectively blocked the initiative. Our lady, being intentional, focused, talented and bright went into battle—and lost. Not even the new CEO could unravel the nexus. That's when I got a call.

> "Can you please work with this feisty executive who has alienated her colleagues because she is too dogmatic and disdainful of her colleagues and can't build constructive relationships."

I'm listening to how she has sat in meetings, watching her colleagues present inaccurate documents qualifying and justifying their positions (actually, these documents were not just inaccurate, they were downright lies). When she then politely asked questions about the validity of these documents, she faced dark looks, invalidation, and veiled threats. There were also malicious whisperings down the corridors. This put her in tears and inconsolable frustration. She knows how to make the company a lot of money yet the other colleagues are hiding ancient mistakes, doing write-offs and losses into the future. Each one has each other's back. And it's "too dangerous to talk to anyone about it"—except her coach.

What's a poor girl to do? She had to handle the moral ambiguity. She took on "assignments" that diverted her from the main action and set about finding a new job elsewhere. That's not where it ends, though. She pointed out to me, as if I didn't already know, that it wasn't likely to be much different elsewhere— it's just like changing chairs. Each has its comforts as well as its little challenges, do they not?

All of this can induce a person to become cynical. And to a great extent, this is life in the human condition. Each of us tend to find coping mechanisms to handle this lack of integrity around us and still be able to make the difference we yearn to make as we leave our legacy.

As a final thought. Not long ago I was watching a video of Stephen Covey presenting his last book, *The 8th Habit*. That habit is, "Find your voice, inspire others to find their voice." He was comparing Hitler and Mahatma Gandhi as great leaders. He ended by saying "There is only one difference between these two great leaders—*conscience*."

Your Executive Coaching Take Aways
Personal power begins and ends with congruency and integrity. Both are needed. The Integration Conversation is required for the first to facilitate an integration of warring parts. A fierce Challenge Conversation is required of the second. This is to hold an executive client's feet to the fire when it comes to truth speaking and living up to the ethical values of business.

As an Executive Coach, if you truly want your executive clients to succeed, two conversations are required of you. First coach to enable your client to align all of his or her powers so the person is congruent. What she says and what he does is the same. What he promises and what he delivers is the same thing. Then coach for integrity. With integrity, then the person's leadership will be seen as credible and he or she will build trust by the trust-worthiness of actions.
•   How alert are you to incongruency when a person is either

simultaneously incongruent or when it occurs over time and is sequentially out of alignment with self?

- What skills will you develop to become more able to facilitate personal alignment and congruency?
- What resources (states or beliefs) do you need to work on as an Executive Coach so that you can have the fierce conversations that challenge your clients about integrity?

End of Chapter Notes

1. Intentionality, see *Secrets of Personal Mastery* (2000).

2. I adapted the Meta-Alignment Pattern from Dilts' Neuro-logical levels in which the first three distinctions are primary state variables (behavior, environment, and capability) and the next four are actually meta-levels (beliefs, values, mission, and spirit).

Chapter 23

THE SYSTEMS

CONVERSATION

"When there's resistance in a client, I ask myself,
'What is in me that's limiting my client.'"
Graham Richardson

Because coaching is systemic, it fundamentally requires a systems-oriented approach to be holistic and effective. This is required first of all because every human being is a system and secondly because every person lives within multiple layers of systems. To attempt to coach without the ability to think and work with these systems severely limits the coaching and reduces its effectiveness. Without systemic thinking, a coach operates in an over-simplistic way—thinking that human experience operates in a strictly stimulus-response way.

For this reason the ninth volume in the Meta-Coaching series focuses exclusively on systems and the processes for being able to coach systemically. While I have introduced systemic coaching in this chapter, I have not included practical coaching conversations. For those, see *Systemic Coaching* (2012) which has more than a dozen such conversations.

What this means in Executive Coaching is that you never have just one person to coach, there are always many, many other people in the room with you and your client. They may be invisible to the naked eye, but the client is able to see them with his or her inner eye. Your executive client is within a system and that system is within even more systems. There are layers of systems which all inter-relate to each other. And there's more. In addition to people, there are things and events in the coaching room as well. Many of them. And all of this gives you lots of variables to work with.

The Systemic Conversation starts whenever you begin exploring the variables at play in an experience and their relationship with each other. If your client tells you about an action or an emotion— then you'll explore it as an expression of the human system. You could start by contextualizing these variables:
•   Tell me more about where and when you did (or felt) X?

You could back up and explore the state of mind and the meanings that were activated which led to the action or emotion.
•   When you did X, what was on your mind?
•   You did X in response to what? What was the trigger?
•   What were the factors at play when you did X?

The Systemic Conversation opens up a larger perspective about things as you inquire about the various influences that are present to and within an experience. Then as the conversation proceeds so will the system. The client's system will operate in the way that it operates. It is and will be self-consistent. Because of this you will be able to identify new and additional connection between things. With practice, your skill will develop so you will be able to easily *follow the information—energy loops* around the system. As an Executive Coach you will therefore need to identify and attend to all of these systems that are at play regarding your executive client.

Preparing for the Conversation— Thinking Systemically
With a systems perspective, you are able to see the system as a system. You will be equipped to recognize the *systemic forces* that are at work within the life of the executive client and in the client's organization. Of course, to do that you will need two things.
       First, to know and understand these systemic forces.
       Second, to recognize and use them in the moment.

First, what are these systemic forces? The systemic forces within the human being are the communication dynamics that bring information in to be processed and transformed and then disperses the energy into one's person (as emotion, muscle memory, behavior, etc.) and through those means into the environment. These are the feedback loops of the system. In systems language—input, throughput, and output.

What we humans input is *information*. We do not bring the energy manifestations that are "out there" in the world. Instead we code it as data or information. Sights, sounds, sensations, smells, and tastes. As we then perceive this information, we represent it. Yet it doesn't stop there. We continue inputting information as we transform that representational information that it seems that we see, hear, and feel on "the theater of our mind" by abstracting it level upon level. With the representations we create our mental movies, and from those movies we input words, descriptions, propositions, beliefs, decisions, understandings, concepts, etc.—the logical or meta levels.[1]

We input in two dimensions. First there is *the external input* (feedback) into the system. Here you bring information about the world into yourself. The world itself never comes in. Bateson noted this when he said that there are no monkeys in the brain. No mothers, no green grass, no dogs, no yellow bananas. There are *symbols* of these, but not these entities themselves. There are *representations,* but no actual cars or cash or carrots. All we have within our mind are *symbols* of these things and events. And that's what we manipulate— our symbols of these referents.

The second input is our own *internal ongoing inputting*. The internal inputting is what we do when we draw conclusions and input to ourselves additional information about the first information. We call this "thinking" about our thinking. And we do this level upon level. This inputting is also known as "feedback." After we receive feedback from the world "out there," we give ourselves feedback, that is, we literally *feed-back* to ourselves the next level meaning. As we construct ideas *about* that first information, we feed-back our meanings to ourselves. We could call this the first part of the *throughput* as we process the information brought into the system.

The internal feedback that we give ourselves operates by the mechanism of self-reflexive consciousness. This infinite process never ends. Whatever conclusion we draw, we can then reflect upon it. In this way we build up layers of beliefs, decisions, dreams, hopes, etc., and these, in turn, become our inner matrix of meaning.

The output comes next. This refers to what we do with the information inputted. As we process the information, we transform it again now as signals to the body which activates our nervous systems, organs, and physiology. This activation creates emotions (*motions* that are *moving* us *out from* where we are) and so mobilizing us to somatize our semantics (our meanings). That is, we first feed-foreward into the body as emotions and somatic responses and then out into the world as speech and behavior. These are products of the human system.

Some of the outputting is fed-forward into ourselves and some is fed-forward from ourselves to others and to our immediate environment. These are expressions of our human system at work. A valuable way of thinking about these outputs is to realize that these are *symptoms* of the system.

Following the System's Energies
To understand a person systemically is to follow the *information—energy* of a system through the system. It is to recognize the information that is brought in from outside and observe how it goes through the insides, and then back out into the world again. Do that and you will be able to recognize and to follow what is happening and how it is happening. Now you can ask the person what he or she is doing with the information coming in. What kind of thinking patterns are being used to process the information. What new higher level conclusions are being created and how that interpretative schema or explanatory style is showing up in emotions and behaviors. How is it being actualized in the neurology and physiology?

Time plays a significant role in this energy system. After all, it takes "time" for all of this to happen. It does not happen instantaneously. Here then is another systemic force to be reckoned with. We have to anticipate the "time" it takes for the system to operate because different human systems work at different speeds.
- How long does the inputting and outputting take?
- How fast or slow is a given person's system in inputting information, understanding, interpreting, and then responding or reacting?
- Are there any slowing or distracting factors going on within the person?

Another systemic force that challenges you as an Executive Coach to follow the energy through the system. It is the reflexivity factor. By definition, a system has multiple variables and parts which interact to influence each other. The result is that what a system produces as an effect can then re-enter the system as a cause or influence.

> Yesterday I became frustrated with my manger of sales and then all of a sudden snapped out at him in anger and called him a total nincompoop! Afterwards I was surprised at my emotional response and even more surprised about the strength of my response. It was definitely too much. I over-reacted. And as I thought about that, it makes me question myself and my own competence. Then when I heard myself questioning and doubting my self, I wonder if I was projecting my own problems on Harry.

Products and effects of the system keep re-entering the system to influence the system level upon level. A system *cause* creates an *effect* which then becomes the next level *cause* and so the system goes round and round. It spirals or circles upon itself. So as you follow a person's inputting-and-outputting through the system, you will frequently find the person going round and round, or spiraling up and down. This is valuable information. As you follow a system, notice what and how much is inputted. This raises the question about the system's openness or closedness.

•   Are the feedback and feed-forward loops open or closed?
•   Is the person locked into a looping system with no exit?
•   Does the person have a way to step back from his or her own system to quality control it?

Sometimes instead of circling or spiraling a system will jump. It will jump a level or several levels and generate a new emergent property. An emergent property is a gestalt phenomenon that occurs because the variables or parts come together in a certain way and something new arises. This offers yet another system force to consider.

As a system operates, emergent properties arise. This mechanism creates gestalts—experiences that are *more than* the sum of the parts and *different from* the sum of the parts. In the human system this means gestalt states. These are very complex states which cannot be explained by identifying all of the parts. Adding them together does not explain them. There's a multiplying effect occurring. This non-linear process can generate solutions.

We see this in the human system with such states as *courage* and *seeing opportunity*. You cannot explain either of these by pulling apart the pieces (the thoughts, feelings, and physiology) that comprise it. When all of the pieces come together, something new emerges that is more than the sum of the parts.[2]

Systemic Self-Organization

Because systems go in circles and there's a spiral relationship of cause to effect to next cause to next effect, *this sets a bias.* Now when a bias is set in a system it will have a self-organizing effect. This is, it will operate as *a self-organizing attractor.* The bias will attract to itself what fits for the character and identity of the system. The bias could be a value, standard, criteria, belief, or almost any higher level that internally creates the system. That bias now works as the attractor that creates the context. As a systemic force, it governs the operation of the system— the range within which the system will move.

It's like a thermostat in a house. A thermostat sets the bias and range of the temperature. The bias of the system governs how much flexibly adapting there is within the system. This then gives birth to strange attractors, vicious and regressive spirals, virtuous circles and other unique system features. We experience and talk about these when we say that we are in a negative spiral.

> For example, someone may start by thinking about a mistake and then judge themselves for the mistake, and then feel ashamed for the judgment of the mistake, and then feel upset and frustrated about the shame of the judgment of the mistake, and then feel angry at the frustration of the shame, etc.

Then there are the enablers and inhibitors of the system. What are all of the enablers of the system? What are the inhibitors? What are the contributing variables that make the processing faster or slower? What causes the system to distort information? What causes it to be more precise and clear? These may be elements within the system or they may be some of the contextual factors.

The systemic forces make up the structure of a system. Yet this is not a static structure—it is a dynamic one. So a system itself will function as a structuring of these forces and variables. When you have a system, you have a patterning or ordering. This patterning puts the parts—dispositions (talents), skills, opportunities, situations, etc. to use. This refers to how the processes operate to generate the form or pattern of the system that we call the "structure." When we use this systemic perception, then how does an experience like "derailing" occur? So in coaching, we are forever asking system questions such as:

> "What's the system and how does it work?"
> "How does this or that experience work?"
> "Is it operating to achieve what objective?"

Systemic Executive Coaching

As an Executive Coach when you engage your executive client, you are encountering and entering a system. Before you, systemically, there are causes, contributing factors, and symptoms. It is the ability to distinguish what is happening in a system that gives you the ability to make critical distinctions. This will lead to insights about the person's functioning and possible solutions. Seeing how the system is working enables you to know how to classify any given experience. You will know if it is a cause, a contributing factor, an effect, or a symptom of the system.

The human system shapes the way a person thinks and feels and what one considers real. That's because the system operates from beliefs and premises which are key in coaching. Within them are the meaning frames which govern about everything– roles, expectations, understanding about what a thing is, how it works, its significance, etc. As an Executive Coach this is what you'll want to discover.

Coaching the Executive for Working Systemically

You are not the only one who needs to think and work systemically. Executive leaders also need to know and understand systems inasmuch as they are leading a system.

- How does the corporate system work?
- What are the organization's beliefs, values, and intentions that drive it to operate as it does?
- How open or closed is the company's system?

In systems thinking, we do not "control" a system. Rather we manage and influence it. We influence the system by accepting and working with the system. In fact, a powerful systems principle is that the person or factor within the system with the most flexibility will have the most influence to change that system.

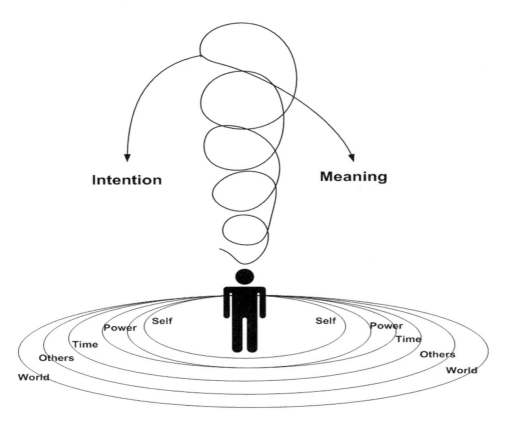

Another principle of immense importance you'll want to use is that *systems are self-organizing structures.* Systems self-organize according to the set bias or attractor and in human systems these attractors usually take the form of beliefs or intentions. You can tap this power by setting or inviting an attractor bias by setting a frame in coaching. By presenting a frame of reference you influence the meaning that a person constructs and refers to for understanding an experience. Via framing, you set the agenda of a session, guide the facilitation of a resource, and enable a client to unleash new possibilities.

Framing refers to classifying the class or category of something. By classifying, you set an interpretative category for how to understand something and how to interpret something. After it is set, the frame operates as a lens for perceiving. It filters and colors the world.

In your Executive Coaching, set frames for your style, for how you operate, your premises about the coaching relationship, and your expectations of your client. Set frames to co-create with your client the outcome of the session and to co-establish a KPI for knowing how you and your client will measure success. When you set frames for the direction of the coaching session, it establishes what is relevant and what is not relevant.

In thinking systemically you will want to be able to detect the larger invisible systems within which the client lives and operates. As a coach your job is first to detect the patterns of the system and then to enter and mirror them back to the client. For self-awareness or work with them to facilitate the client's goals.
- What are the systems? Family, business, religious, language, etc.
- How do these affect the person?
- How are you experiencing the system?

Coaching to the Matrix

The primary tool in Meta-Coaching for thinking and working systemically is the Matrix Model which is a systems model par excellence.[3] To learn this model, begin by using it as a checklist of eight of the most fundamental aspects of human personality. Three of these aspects are the dynamic processes by which we construct our sense of reality: Meaning, Intention, and State. The next five of these aspects are facets of Self: Worth, Power, Others, Time, and World.

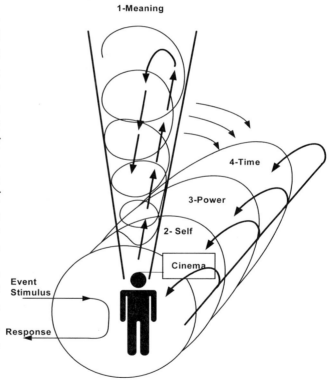

We use *The Matrix Model* as a systems model for thinking and working systemically with people, groups, and organizations and for working with the multiple layers of meaning frames that create and describe the client's world so that we can "follow the energy through the system."

The Matrix Model offers a multi-level and multi-dimensional approach for understanding how human beings function. It identifies the system dynamics and processes (feedback and feed forward loops, meta-level self-organizing frames) by which we create our sense of reality. With all of this dynamic complexity, the Matrix Model gives us a way to detect the way the mind-body system is working and how it could work.

The Matrix Model gives a way to organize a large field of information, distinctions, and patterns as you work with your clients who want to develop more expertise. To achieve this the Matrix Model is comprised of both process and content matrices. Together these make up the core of how we experience our personality, attitudes, and perceptions. They govern how we invent our identity (who we are) and our direction in life (where we are going and what at we are about).

1) The Grounding Matrix:
   State – the foundational matrix that grounds all frames
2) The Process Matrices:
   Meaning
   Intention (purpose, values)
3) The Content Matrices about one's Self:
   Self-Esteem (Your worth and value as a person)
   Power (Your capacities, talents, resources, assets)
   Others (Your relational or social self)
   Time (Your temporal self)
   World (Your world or domain of knowledge and skill)

Using the Matrix Model as an overarching framework for coaching, you can now orient yourself so that you will know *what* to do with a client, *when* to do that particular thing, *with whom* to do it, *how* to pull off that activity, and *why* to do that.

Coaching Executives Systemically
When you coach an executive and his or her inner neuro-semantic system of meanings and intentions, that matrix of frames is embodied (and grounded) in his or her states. That is obvious. What is not so obvious is the inside structuring that's behind it and that creates it. Behind *state* is a whole set of meaning-frames about the executive's sense of self. Knowing this and recognizing it as you coach gives you the ability to now follow the person's information—energy loops. Then you can discover how the person's unique personal system works.

This enables you to explore the person's unique system in which the executive lives and how it operates in the various contexts of life—home, work, career, recreation, spirituality, etc. You can also now check the ecology of the executive's system to make sure that it is functional, effective, and enabling him or her to fulfill their highest meanings, values, and intentions.

Your Executive Coaching Take Aways

People are not simple— *they are a living, dynamic system* which is dynamic and forever changing. Because human beings are themselves systems, effective and holistic coaching is by its very nature systemic. This explains why effective coaching requires you to learn to think and work systemically if you want to develop expertise in the field of Executive Coaching.

In spite of all of the many, many variables that make up a system, there is a dynamic unity within it. This systemic unity enables you to work effectively with the human system as you following the input—output energy loops.

- To what extent do you think systemically when working with yourself or when coaching? What aspects of systemic thinking are you best at? In what aspects are you weak?
- How aware are you of the information in—energy out communication loops during the coaching conversations? What practices will you give yourself to become more present to and aware of these loops?
- Spend the next week looking for and identifying self-organizing attractors in the mind-body-emotion system of your clients.

End of the Chapter Notes:

1. See the book, *Neuro-Semantics* for a full description of the meaning making processes; also the book *Meta-States* (2005) deals with this.

2. For each of these examples, courage and seeing opportunities, see *Inside-Out Wealth* (2010) and for more about systems, see *Systemic Coaching* (2012).

3. See *The Matrix Model* (2003).

Chapter 24

THE PARADOXICAL

CONVERSATION

"Promote those who deal best with paradox . . .
If the ability to deal with these paradoxes is the key to success,
then we should promote, at all levels,
those who show the greatest facility in doing so."
Tom Peters (1989)

"Beware of over-playing to your strengths.
That can get a person out of balance
creating negative results and consequences."
Graham Richardson (2002)

L ike the Integration Conversation (chapter 22) where there is internal
conflict which is experienced as stress, upsetness, distress, inability
to get one's act together, so this conversation also can be stressful and
confusing. Sometimes an issue, situation, or problem will seem like a
"contradiction to common sense." It will seem like there is an internal war
of two equal parts and yet upon examination we discover that this is not the
actual problem at all. This is especially so when the situation or context
goes completely contrary to expectation. In such situations, we say that the

structure or experience is self-contradictory or that it is a paradox.

One reliable and regular sign of paradox is that the problem does not, and will not, go away. Regardless of how sure you were about the solution, it keeps returning. Just when you think a situation is resolved, it returns and sometimes in full force. Another sign is that the problem seems to be resolved when actually it is only oscillating on and off, and then on again. It is this on and off nature which can then blind us to whether the situation is truly resolved or not.

Executive Paradoxes

Do paradoxical "problems" arise in Executive Coaching? You bet. What are the paradoxes that executives sometimes, often, or frequently experience that may come up in a coaching session? In Executive Coaching these paradoxical "problems" typically come up in *the either/or framework* when a senior manager or executive feels torn by the dilemma. Managing these ambiguities or dilemmas may take the form of many polarities:

*   Work or family
*   Individual or team
*   Planning or taking action
*   Cost or quality
*   Traditional or new
*   Centralized or decentralized
*   Autocratic or participatory, etc.
*   Integrity and authenticity or business ambition

Some executives find managing ambiguity very challenging and for them the process can derail them. Graham notes that the pursuit of integrity and authenticity as an example. An executive may believe that "honesty is the best policy" and yet find him or herself in situations which result in actually damaging relationships. So is "honesty the best policy"or does the expression of honesty also have to do with knowing when to have the right conversation, with the right person, at the right time and in the right way?

Paradox as the Confusion of Levels

What is a paradox and when and how does it show up in Executive Coaching? In Neuro-Semantics we use the Meta-States Model to define *a paradox as the confusion of levels.* That is, what is contradictory at one level, the primary level, makes perfect sense if you rise above that level and recognize the frame of meaning that establishes an understanding or classification about it at a higher level. What you feel and sense as the conflict of two equal conflicting parts is actually the failure to keep a class and a member of the class apart and distinctive.

Here is a famous, historical example. This paradox goes back as far as the first century. It was even quoted in the Bible by the apostle Paul.

> "One of themselves [Epimenides], a prophet of their own, said, 'The Cretians are always liars.'" (Titus 1:12)

Well, if Epimenides is a Cretan and he says that all Cretan are liars —"always liars"—then he must be lying because, after all, "all Cretans are liars." Yet if he is lying about that, then all Cretans are not liars because he is actually telling the truth. But if he is telling the truth, then "all Cretans (including himself) are liars," so he must be lying. But that must be the truth. So round and round we go—the statements seem contradictory. And so we have a problem:

> What's the truth? What's real and actual here?
> Where or what is the conflict?

If he's telling the truth, he is lying. If he is lying, then he is telling the truth, but that makes him lying. It's paradoxical. It's contradictory. Round and round we go. So let's stop and ask: *How* does this paradox work?

> The answer is: It works by confusing levels. It works by failing to sort out the levels. There are levels in these statements, but we do not see them. We do not hear them. It all seems to be about the same level. It seems an either-or conflict. He is *either* telling the truth *or* he is lying.

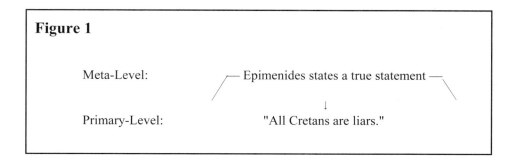

Figure 1

Meta-Level: ⎯ Epimenides states a true statement ⎯

Primary-Level: "All Cretans are liars."

At the first level, we have a statement, "All Cretans are liars." Now for the meta-state question: Does that statement refer to itself? *If* it includes itself, then we have the self-contradictory spiraling of statements that cannot be reconciled. But if it does *not* include itself, *if* the statement is not absolutely inclusive, then when we recognize that there are two levels here, there is no contradiction. The paradox is resolved.

Paradox is a confusion of levels. The statement about lying Cretans is a classification. The Cretans who lie are the members of the class. At one level is a statement that classifies the members of the class and this differs from the class. The class of elephants, for example, is not an elephant. It is a classification. The statement itself is not a member of the class. That's why we can make perfect sense *and* say such things as the following:

> "Never say never."
> "Never and always are two words one should always remember never to use."
> "I'm absolutely certain that nothing is absolutely certain."

Or we can write a book and title it, "This Book Needs No Title." (Raymond M. Smallya, 1980). Now the title of the book makes sense and we don't have to conclude that it is self-contradictory or that the book has no title. It does. It makes sense *because* we keep the levels separate and *to the extent* that we keep the levels separate. Confuse them and you create an unsolvable paradox and along with it—confusion and conflict. This explains that power of paradoxical interventions such as the "Be Spontaneous" paradox, or "Try really hard right now to have a panic attack," or "Since you have insomnia, try to stay up all night and don't try to go to sleep," etc. Such paradoxical interventions work because they establish new classifications and that changes the meaning frames.[1]

Paradox as Dichotomizing a Systems Continuum

There's another description of a paradox that describes these dynamics in a different way and which helps to understand the internal processes. In this description, a paradox arises from over-focusing on one side of a polarity so one fails to see the whole system—again failing to separate a class from members of a class. This kind of seeming contradiction, which arises from *either-or thinking and framing*, blinds us to the whole system so that we are incapable of seeing the oscillation of the system between opposing states.

Barry Johnson describes this in his book *Polarity Management* (1992) by postulating a continuum comprised of any pair of polar opposites: individual or team, planning or taking action, cost or quality, traditional or new, centralized or decentralized, autocratic or participatory, etc. To use his system to manage and to avoid paradoxes, take the opposites, put them on a continuum.

Figure 2

Individual (A) _____ Team (B)

Once you have a continuum, then identify the *upsides* of each. What are the values and benefits of each side (left and right)? What are the *downsides* of each? When you do this, you generate four quadrants (Figure 3).

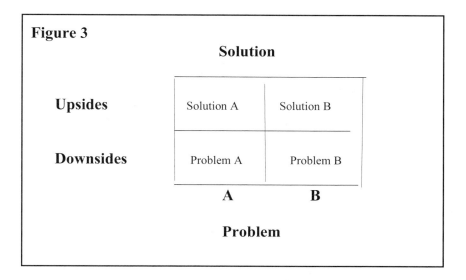

The problem-solution quadrants enables you so you can now see the whole. You can now see the relational parts—the felt "problem" and the assumed "solution" in context. Yet what we actually have here are interdependent opposites: individual—team. "I'll do it by myself—I'll cooperate with others." Johnson uses two questions to identify if we truly have a paradox structure:

> 1) Is the difficulty ongoing? (The problem does not go away.)
> 2) Are the two poles interdependent? (They are members of a class that is not identified.)

Typically when we have Problem A (the downsides of one side, see Figure

4) we go to Solution B (the upsides of the other side). Problem A comprise of all of the downsides of the left side of the continuum and Solution B are

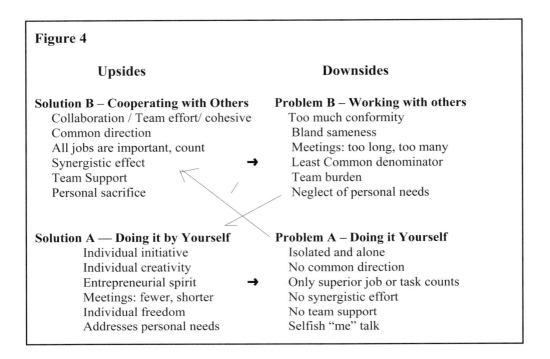

Figure 4

Upsides	Downsides
Solution B – Cooperating with Others	**Problem B – Working with others**
Collaboration / Team effort/ cohesive	Too much conformity
Common direction	Bland sameness
All jobs are important, count	Meetings: too long, too many
Synergistic effect	Least Common denominator
Team Support	Team burden
Personal sacrifice	Neglect of personal needs
Solution A — Doing it by Yourself	**Problem A – Doing it Yourself**
Individual initiative	Isolated and alone
Individual creativity	No common direction
Entrepreneurial spirit	Only superior job or task counts
Meetings: fewer, shorter	No synergistic effort
Individual freedom	No team support
Addresses personal needs	Selfish "me" talk

made up of all of the upsides of the right side of the continuum. So Problem A and Solution B are already over-exaggerated versions of the either–or continuum.

In the *system* of a polarity continuum, the Solution of one problem—when over-done—becomes the Problem that then needs a Solution. Yet *the kind of thinking* that created this problem (either-or thinking) is the kind of thinking that can't solve the problem, especially when the attempted solution also is *either-or thinking*. So we naturally go to the opposite side for what seems like a new solution. Of course, the either-or thinking will eventually exaggerate things and again we will go to the opposite solution. No wonder it goes round and round.

So what is the solution? It is to see, recognize, and value the hidden higher frame that can unite the paradox within the higher classification.
• But what is the hidden frame?

•   Where is it hiding and how do we bring it out into the open?

Structurally the continuum is actually inside a *both—and system.* Yet is being treated as an either—or polarity. That's the confusion that sets up the polarity. The either-or thinking keeps everything on the same level—just back and forth! That's why it oscillates. When the solution is over-done, we flip to the other side to a seemingly new attempted solution, but then that one is also over-done.

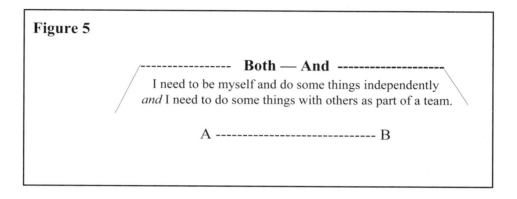

Figure 5

-------------- **Both — And** --------------------
I need to be myself and do some things independently
and I need to do some things with others as part of a team.

A ----------------------------- B

To escape the paradox we have to rise above the either-or polarity and classify it within the larger system of *both-and thinking.* Then we'll experience an insight which will resolve the paradox. Both solutions are valid responses within the same system— only at different times, for different purposes, and to different degrees.

This larger perspective solves the conflict. It does so by suggesting we maximize the upsides of each side of the continuum while minimizing the downsides. When one side resists the other side, see that resistance as actually communicating a potential resource. Structurally the pattern here involves opposites on a continuum yet because they are interdependent and make up a larger system, larger system that will oscillate back and forth. Like breathing the opposites of inhaling and exhaling makes up the whole— breathing.

    1) Do we have opposites?
    2) Are they related? Are they interdependent?

Holding the Paradoxical Conversation
As an Executive Coach, how do you conduct the Paradoxical Conversation?

First, differentiate the categories that are polar opposites.
Differentiation comes first. Differentiation is one of the first developmental stages as our brains grow and mature. As children we begin our cognitive development by asking, "What is it?" And our parents oblige us by pointing to things and classifying them with the labels that they use. We begin with binary thinking (either-or thinking) which is black-or-white: night/ day; mom/ dad, good/ bad, in/out, up/down, above/below, right/left, up/down, back/front, foreground/background, etc.

Binary thinking enables us to create the basic categories that we need in order to effectively navigate the challenges of life. So we polarize. We dichotomize to create the categorical opposites that helps us understand the basic structures of life. This would be no problem except when we leave it at that level, we end up living in a very rigid black-or-white world that doesn't adequately map reality when we grow up and enter the adult world.

Second, step back to get a systemic view.
The error that locks us into the polarized world is the error of *framing the polarities as mutually exclusive.* In reality they do not mutually exclude each other, they interpenetrate each other. Day merges into night and we have dusk and night merges into day and we have dawn. When we step back from the polarities of day and night, we have a higher classification or category: time. And when it comes to time we have many *degrees* as we can measure or scale it along degrees of light or dark. We need both.

Another error that can lock us into the stuckness of a polarized world is the reification of processes. To *reify* is to make a process real as if it were a thing. It is to *thing-ify* or linguistically to *nominalize.* That is, we take a process and turn it into an object, a noun ("a person, place, or thing") and by doing so we freeze frame our map of reality. So instead of seeing and reckoning with a living, moving, dynamic process (a verb), we freeze it and make it a thing. This results in a nominalization—a false noun. Then that false noun deceives us into assuming a world that is non-dynamic and non-systemic.

This is an inevitable aspect of language. In every culture and every language, parents not only point to things and give them names (chair, food, brother, ball, etc.),they also point to processes and give those dynamic activities names. In this way they nominalize (name) processes (good, bad, truth, relationship, motivation, etc.). They treat the activities as if they are "things."

By identifying these two errors, we now have some practical steps for moving beyond the polarization that creates the paradoxes.

    1) Scale the continuum of the polarities to see how the opposites interpenetrate each other in matters of degree. Scale the processes in terms of degree.

    2) Step back from the continuum and identify the larger frame or system within which it works. This enables you to thereby identify the classification within which the members of the class are held.

    3) Denominalize the nominalizations of the polar opposites to recover the processes. Once you do that you can then describe in sensory-based, empirical terms what's truly going on. This unfreezes the frozen map of the world so that it can move and breathe again.

    4) Welcome the tension as you hold the paradox open.

Let's look into these practical steps in more detail:

1) Scale the continuum of the polarities to see how the opposites interpenetrate each other in matters of degree.

As an Executive Coach begin by asking scaling questions and use the "fuzzy language" for degrees (e.g., never, rarely, sometimes, often, frequently, always).

    Are any of the words used to describe the problem *a relational term* so that it only makes complete sense when you have both sides? For example, if the word is "leadership" then *leading* (the verb hidden in the nominalization) is relational, depending, as it does, on *following*. What is the link between the two poles? How are they connected?

    To what extent is this X? To what degree? Percentage?

    How much is the X fully X? How much is it not?

    Where is the tipping point? At what point does a number of grains of sand become a heap?

2) Step back form the continuum and then identify the larger frame or system within which it works— the class.

This means to "go meta" and access an observation point for observing the system from outside the system (thinking outside the box that currently frames the opposites). Joe Cheal (2012) writes, "By seeing the whole as a continuum, it allows us to comment from a higher order of thinking (or higher logical level)." (p. 170). Now you can begin your questions:

When you step back and observe the polar opposites, what connects them? What are they both a part of?
What higher frame as a classification embraces or encompasses both of them?
When you rise above and transcend to a higher level while still including the polar opposites, what connects them?
If you named the continuum as a value continuum, what would you call it?
How can the two become one?

In the paradox of individual self and group the larger frame is "human nature." It is our nature to both individuate and to group (connect with others). While we are individual selves, we are also social beings.

3) Denominalize the nominalizations of the polar opposites to recover the processes. Then describe in sensory-based, empirical terms what's truly going on. This unfreezes the frozen map of the world so that it can move and breathe again.
As an Executive Coach this is where the Meta-Model of Language becomes the model of choice.[2] It enables you to facilitate a client to become more and more specific and precise.

Can you put X on the table? If not, could it be a pseudo-noun (nominalization)?
What is the hidden verb inside of the word you are using?
What is the action and processes that are operational in X?
When we unfreeze X so that we don't view it as a "thing" but as a process, what is going on?

4) Welcome the tension as you hold the paradox open.
"Holding a paradox open purposefully means focusing on the tension to generate a spark of creativity." When we do this, "tensions are held open to generate new ideas." (*Solving Impossible Problems*, 2012, p. 154)[3]

In this quotation, Joe Cheal recommends holding the paradox open in order to keep the tension going. When you are able to do that, then you can understand, and even predict, the circularity that occurs when someone oscillates between opposing poles. This, of course, requires embracing and living with uncertainty, ambiguity, and non-closure and as you do, you give yourself an opportunity to identify the hidden system. Then when you can identify the class— the paradox is resolved.

Your Executive Coaching Take Aways

Some so-called "problems" are not problems at all that need to be solved. They are paradoxes to be *resolved*. And they are resolved by sorting out the levels that have been confused.   That is, the seeming conflict and contradictions are actually involve confusing a higher level system of classification with the members of that class.

The Paradoxical Conversation is one that sorts out polarities that we or others have set up as opposites when, in truth, they are necessary facets (aspects) of the same system.

*   All problems are not actual problems, some are paradoxes. And whereas we solve problems, we resolve paradoxes.
*   The sign of a paradox is that the problem keeps returning. And because it doesn't stay solved, we often feel trapped in a box with no exit. What problems have you experienced that are like that?
*   How skilled are you for looking for the larger system and the hidden frames that lurk behind the either/or paradox?

End of Chapter Notes

1. Paradoxical interventions such as these have arisen from numerous models and fields. Viktor Frankl introduced many with his Logotherapy model, so also Milton Erickson in his medical hypnosis, so also Brief Psychotherapy by Steve de Shazer and Paul Watzlawick.

2. The Meta-Model is a communication model about how language works. It originally had 12 linguistic distinctions and was expanded in 1997 to 22 distinctions. Each distinction provides a place to ask questions that invites the speaker to go back to his or her experience and map their experience more specifically. This creates more precision and accuracy. See *The Structure of Magic* (1975, 1976) and *Communication Magic* (2000).

3. Joe Cheal's book, *Solving Impossible Problems* (2012) addresses many of the common dilemmas that torture business people and offers many creative insights for solutions.

PART III:

LAUNCHING YOUR

EXECUTIVE

COACHING

CAREER

Chapter 25

RUNNING AN

EXECUTIVE COACHING BUSINESS

How do you get started with Executive Coaching? Once you have readied yourself with the required knowledge, understanding, competency of skills, what is the process for beginning to engage in Executive Coaching?

Thoroughly Know What You are Doing
Do you have a thorough and comprehensive knowledge of Executive Coaching? If not, then you probably are not ready. So get yourself ready. This may involve reading in the area of Executive Coaching. It may mean reading in the area of leadership, presentation skills, shadowing and giving feedback, business, organizational development, etc. It may mean getting hands-on experiential training with a legitimate coach training program.[1]

Whatever you need to do in order to thoroughly know and understand Executive Coaching, if you're serious about this area, then invest your time and effort. Put your heart into it and do what it takes. How will you know that you have a sufficient understanding? See if you can answer the following questions:
•   What is the uniqueness of Executive Coaching? How is it unique?

- What distinguishes what an Executive Coach does and how does it differ from what a Life or Personal Coach, a Business Coach, an Organizational Coach, or a coach with a particular speciality such as presentation skills, media, conflict resolution, team building, etc.?
- What are the five to ten most basic and common issues that executives face and present when they ask for coaching?
- What are three to five of the unique challenges that executives face and that influence Executive Coaching?
- What are some of the commonalities among executives in terms of personality, whether male or female?

Once you have a thorough and comprehensive understanding, practice articulating these things. Practice so you can succinctly describe this unique coaching area. How well can you do that? Where do you get tongue-tied or stumble over your words when you attempt to describe what you do and the value that you offer? Your own clarity of this area will show up in your ability to be clear and expressive when asked what you do and how you do it. This will also enable you to have clearly in mind key distinctions when you coach.

Know Your Expertise and Focus
Even within a niche like Executive Coaching, there are many, many sub-niches for unique specialities. So even among Executive Coaches, they are not all the same. What is your speciality within this area? If you do not have a niche, what would be an area that you would love to develop expertise in?
- Visionary Leadership
- Managerial Leadership
- Presentation Skills
- Handling Media
- Conflict Resolution
- Avoiding Derailment
- Work/Life Balance
- Developing Teams
- Communication Excellence
- Negotiation
- Emotional Intelligence
- Career / Professional Development

What is your experience, studies, research, etc. that has enabled you to develop your expertise in a given niche? Why? Why is this area important to you? What do you love about it? How much is it your passion? As you answer these questions, are you able to succinctly and elegantly present what you do, why it is important, and how you go about doing it? To be able to launch out effectively, you will need to be able to do this.

The Art of Getting In

A question that every coach who is just beginning asks is, "How do you get in?" "What is the process by which a person can get into an organization or corporation as an Executive Coach?" With some organizations, all you have to do is call and ask about the company's procedures for getting onto the Provider List. The most progressive companies have set up assessment processes whereby coaches applying are invited to come in and coach a manager before an assessment committee.

Years ago (2001) when I asked Graham Richardson how he first began to get in, when he was a part of Stephenson Partnership, an Executive Coaching company in Sydney Australia. He described his process. It was (is) a process which involves a whole range of activities.

> "I read the paper to identify organizations having problems that I would like to solve. Then I study the organization to know if it is public or private, who the CEOs are, how they are doing, their strengths and weaknesses, etc. I will study with a long-term goal of getting in some three or six months later.
>
> Then to get in, I call the gatekeepers. But not to get in. I call them to establish a friendship with them, to become friends with them. My aim is to treat them well. I turn them into an internal coach for me to the executive. I enroll that person in my service by treating them with honor and making their day more enjoyable. I believe that most people mis-treat them and so I want to create an ally of them.
>
> I am careful to be polite, and to ask them, "When can I call you? I speak to them as *people* and ask them for permission, "May I call you? When would be convenient?"
>
> I find out about their birthdays, anniversaries, children, and so on. And I expect that one of the days when I call, they will be in a bad mood. That's when I can really help them."

Veronica Lim had a different story and a different strategy. When I first got acquainted with her, she was an Executive Coach in London, England and charging 500 pounds a coaching session (at the time the value of $750 USD). I asked her about how she got started. She said that after she took her NLP and Coach training and while she was still working as an accountant in the large bank, she contacted five of the senior managers there. They already knew her. She shared what she had been studying and her passion about going into coaching. Then she made each of them an offer.

> "I would love to give you six sessions of coaching to show you what I can do and to get feedback from you about what I did. The only thing I ask is that when we are done, if you like the coaching, you will write a testimony

for me and refer someone to me."

All five accepted her offer. She then went to work coaching them. After the six sessions with the five senior managers, everyone of them were so pleased and so convinced of the value she added, all five hired her as their Executive Coach. And everyone wrote testimonies for her as well as began making regular referrals to her.

Who do you already know in organizations or in managerial roles? Start there. Begin by asking those who you know, or have worked under for, honest feedback about being an Executive Coach. Do they think you are up to it in your knowledge, skills, and style? Any recommendations that they'd make to you? Would they make referrals?

Marketing and Selling Yourself as an Executive Coach
Consider the product and service that you are offering in coaching. What is the product? What is the service? How do you describe the value that you add to an executive or to an organization? The uniqueness of coaching is that ultimately your product and service is *you*. It is *the experience* that you give *through the conversation* that you facilitate. The essence of coaching is the *quality* of the conversation.

In Meta-Coaching we define Coaching as "a conversation like none other." It is "a conversation that gets to the heart of things—a person's unique *meanings* that defines and governs their sense of reality." Coaching is an inner game conversation that enriches a person's mental and conceptual understanding of self and others, that empowers one's abilities-to-respond, and that unleashes the known and unknown potentials awaiting to be identified and developed.

So what do we sell? The Coaching Conversations tell the story of what we sell and the value:
>Clarity of understanding so one knows what's important.
>Decisiveness and commitment to what's truly important.
>Strategic Planning that details *how* one will make the truly important real and actual in one's life and/or company.
>Resourced Experiences that enables one to access and mobilize the required internal and external resources.
>Generative Change for being able to take advantage of opportunities.
>Higher perspective awareness of effective and ineffective processes.
>Systemic understanding of how a person or a group operates within all of the systemic influences that are operating and the systemic leverage points of change.

Grand visions that excite and motivate a person or group for staying ahead of the competition and/or pioneering new visionary opportunities.

Problem-solving conversations that clearly defines the real problem, that exposes pseudo-problems (paradoxes) and that finds effective and sustainable solutions.

Preventive Feedback conversations that accelerates individual and/or collective learning.

Unleashing Potentials conversations that enable individuals and groups to actualize one's highest meanings and visions into one's best performances.

Effectively Contracting for the Executive Coaching

Every form of coaching involves consulting in order to contract for the coaching experience. This can be as simple as doing an "Introduction to Coaching" and offering a simple single page agreement that describes the coaching relationship. Or it can be much more complex, involving multiple meetings using various instruments for assessment, needs analysis, and explaining what a person is buying when purchasing coaching sessions.

In consulting as part of contracting for Executive Coaching, most coaches use *an exploring conversation* to discover if they want to coach a given client or if the client is ready. They use an exploration conversation primarily to assess the executive's needs for coaching. The purpose is to see if the executive's needs fit the coaching process or if the needs are more appropriate for consulting, training, or even therapy. The consultation is designed to qualify the client to make sure the person is coach-able, ready for the challenge of coaching, and able to handle the demands of coaching.

The purpose of the contracting is to enable people to be fully informed as to what coaching is and what it is not. Doing this lowers the likelihood of unrealistic expectations and disappointments. It also prepares a person for the stretching and challenging nature of coaching.

The Contracting Conversation

The process of contracting for a coaching contract is a Consulting Conversation. If you think of it as simply another "conversation," then you will probably more easily access your coaching skills and use them as in the process of contracting. Here you will want to present what Coaching is and how it differs from the other helping professions. You will want to present your style and focus. All this is designed to help both you and your potential client to make an informed decision as you qualify the person and as the client qualifies you.

In putting the contract together, you will want to make sure that the agreement will includes the following basics:

What?
- The goals and focus of the coaching.
- The kind of coaching (e.g., leadership development, groom for next level of functioning, shadowing and feedback, etc.)
- Your unique presentation— Consult/Coach, Trainer/Coach, Mentor/Coach, etc.

When?
- The length of time of sessions.
- The frequency of sessions.
- The overall length of the coaching program.

How?
- The methods to be used.
- The level of confidentiality desired.
- The use of assessments, when, which ones, etc.
- How and when it can be renewed or terminated.

How much?
- The cost and investment of the coaching program.
- The administrative process for invoicing.
- List of two or more packages, their costs, different opportunities within each.

Evidence?
- The evaluation of the coaching program, how to assess the ROI.
- The measurement process or tools (benchmarks) to be used.

When contracting for coaching, think of it as qualifying the person as a possible client rather than trying to "sell" your services. Think of it as qualifying both your prospective client, and yourself, with an eye on determining if there is a fit between you. Is there "chemistry" in how you interact with each other? Is the subject of the coaching program is something you are qualified to deal with? If you do this it will not feel that you are "selling." It will have a different feel. You are *qualifying a person* to check if he or she is ready for coaching.

The value of doing this is that it conveys the sense that you have nothing to sell or impose. Your conversation is simply one of discovery. You are simply discovering if coaching is the optimal methodology for the person. As you focus in qualifying the person, you will more likely be operating from the coaching attitude that you'll use when coaching.

When in the discovering mode and contracting for a coaching program, while you are not "coaching" properly, you will be using many of your basic coaching states and processes to gather information, assess the relationship, and test for ecology. If the contracting goes through and you take the person on as a coaching client, what you do in the contracting stage will set the pace for the coaching. It will establish frames and prime the person for both the coaching and for your style. Given this, it's important to be fully congruent in your coaching style so that the coach who later shows up will not be a completely different person.

Contracting is your time to set the frames and clarify the expectations so that the Executive Coaching isn't troubled by unrealistic expectations that would undermine its effectiveness. In contracting the frames that you'll want to make sure your client understands the following:

- *Coaching is not consulting.* You are not signing up to be the manager of the executive or a shadow consultant. You are a coach and you coach primarily by asking questions— questions designed to challenge and to get the client thinking outside the box.
- *The client is not a victim.* The client is totally responsible for his or her life. The coaching works to the extent the client assumes responsibility, accountability, and follow-through.
- *The coaching experience is direct, confrontational, and fierce.* The coach's job is to not let the client off the hook, but challenge (with compassion, respect, empathy of course) the executive with truth (the truth of the situation).

Getting Personal in the Contracting Conversation

To make your contract more personal, use the following statements in italics. Use these to co-create with your client a customized contract for many of the important aspects of the coaching.

- *What you can expect from me is ...*
    - Here you can share more specifically your style and way of doing coaching.
- *What I expect from you is ...*
    - Here, as you share your expectations, you get those out on the table and check to see how well they fit or do not fit with your client.
- *If either of us fail to come through on our promises and expectations, the consequence we are setting are the following.*
    - Establishing the consequences for a failure to follow through. This enables each person to be fully accountable to each other.
- *What help do we need from each other to honor our agreements?*

This question enables the conversation to flush out the good will and willingness in each party.
* *If we need to review and update this agreement, we will do this by...*
It's always best to make coaching agreements experimental and open to change rather than written in stone. In this way you can more easily update it and make more appropriate. Then the contract itself can be checked to see what's working and what is not working.

Familiarize Yourself with the Typical Goals of Executive Coaching
What do executives typically identify as their goals in the coaching? The following are among the things most often chosen:
* *Manage emotions and stress:* Improve tensions between organization, family, community, etc.
* *Professional development:* Improve one's ability to manage one's career and advance professionally.
* *Prevent derailment:* Identify blind spots and possible traps and/or interferences.
* *Increase capacity:* Increase capacity to manage an organization in terms of planning, organizing, staffing, etc.
* *Skill development and expansion*: Increase one's range, flexibility and effectiveness within one's behavioral repertoire of responses and skills.
* *Self-management:* Increase self-management ability in times of turbulence, crisis, and conflict.
* *Relational enrichment:* Improve one's psychological and social competencies in terms of social awareness, tolerance of ambiguity, flexibility in dealing with people, understanding and working with group dynamics, etc.
* *Learning acceleration:* Improve one's ability to learn and learning how to learn (meta-learning skills).
* *Lead teams:* Improve effectiveness of the organization by developing and leading self-managing teams.
* *Create a coaching culture:* Lead an organization to create the kind of culture that will support coaching.
* *Lead an organization:* Lead a company to become a self-actualizing company.

Coachability: Is the Executive Leader up for the Challenge?
As an Executive Coach, never jump into coaching an executive without assessing the person's ability to experience Executive Coaching. That is, check to make sure that the person who is to receive the coaching is *coachable.* Many executives are not. It's therefore simply a matter of

wisdom to qualify the person and see if the executive is coachable. People who are uncoachable typically are those who need serious psychotherapy. Indications that a person is not ready for coaching include:

___ Severe psychopathology: on psychoactive drugs, medication, diagnosed with a psychiatric disorder.

___ Severe interpersonal problems: Personality Disorders.[2]

___ Negative counter-transference

Determining Coachability

How will you know when someone is coachable? There are factors or variables that make up the quality that we call *coachable*.

___ Openness to becoming more self-aware

___ Forward looking

___ An embracer of change

___ Open to feedback, non-defensive

___ Ego-Strength to face reality

___ Emotionally intelligent and available

___ Responsible: Willing to be held accountable

___ Resilient: Competent to bounce back after a set-back

___ Motivated by dreams, values, and visions.

___ Patience / Persistence to stay with it

Coachability Factors: Yes/No To What Degree?

Yes/No — Degree

___ ___ Is this person open to change, learning, and personal development?

___ ___ Is this person hungry for making a change or transformation?

___ ___ Is this person open to receiving feedback?

___ ___ Does this person have sufficient ego-strength for facing reality?

___ ___ Can this person face challenges and cope with them?

___ ___ Is this person willing to be responsible for self and not a victim?

___ ___ Is this person committed and invested in his or her own development?

___ ___ Is this person willing to work and work in a disciplined way?

___ ___ Will this person follow through on assignments?

___ ___ Is this person ready and able to enter into a coaching relationship?

___ ___ Is this person ready and able to become vulnerable to a coach?

___ ___ Does this person have the patience to stay with the coaching process?

___ ___ Will this person take ownership of the process?

> *Do you have all "Yeses" to these questions?*

___ ___ Does the person have goals, hopes, and dreams?

___ ___ Does this person display extreme emotional states?

___ ___ Does the person have an *external check* as well as an internal check?

> *"Yeses" to these questions makes the person even more coachable, but these are not required.*

__   __ Do I (as the coach) have a good fit with this person?
__   __ Am I interested in supporting the person's goals in coaching?
__   __ Do I have the coaching expertise for coaching in this area?
         You need "yeses" to these which are about you as the coach.

__   __ Does this person show a high degree of defensiveness?
__   __ Is it likely that this person will miss or cancel sessions?
__   __ Will this person fall apart or go into fight/flight when facing challenges?
__   __ Is the person overly dependent, need "special" attention?
         *"Yeses" to these questions indicate that the person needs therapy
         or training rather than Coaching.*

Executive Preparation

In Executive Coaching, *you are leading the leader.* Because of this, you will need both "heart and backbone." Mary Beth O'Neill writes about this in her book, *Executive Coaching with Backbone and Heart* (2007). You will need backbone for the courage to speak, to command attention, and at times to take a back seat to let go and see what happens.

What if someone is almost ready, but not fully? If an executive is not fully ready, then sometimes you can set up coaching sessions to prepare the person to become fully ready. The aim would be to get your client to become emotionally ready to face challenges and develop the required stamina. It would be to become able to face the anxiety from the issues that might arise, to help build executive muscle. How? By coaching the person to develop ego-strength.[3] Then, Executive Coaching truly becomes a partnership—collegial and congenial.

Caveat Empor — Let the Buyer Beware

When working with businesses of any size, and perhaps especially with large corporations, every coach needs to especially be aware of invitations that are framed as working with someone who is "having problems." Whenever you hear those words, let them set off warning bells. Why? Fundamentally because that's not the design of coaching. Coaching is designed to work with people who are getting ready to step up to a whole new level of leadership and take on new challenges, not to fix "problem people."

Often an organization or a senior manager will bring in an external coach because the decision has already been made to terminate the person or make him redundant. In such cases the coach is either "a last ditch effort" to shape someone up and get them to reform. Or worse, it is a way to get evidence to justify the decision. Under such conditions, if you accept the coaching contract you become part of the conspiracy. And worse, it puts you into the position of an "Exit" Coach. Do that and you'll greatly curtail your ability to coach in that organization. Who then in the company would want to see you coming?

Sometimes this occurs because the senior manager or the CEO doesn't have the courage to do his or her job. In that case, work with that person to groom him or her for stepping up to leadership. Groom that person to be able to confront poor performance. If someone needs coaching in this situation—*it is the person bringing you in.* Focus on enabling that person to recognize his or her need for coaching.

For Executive Coaching to succeed *it must be seen and branded as a perk*— as a reward, as a sign that a person is highly valued and being groomed for the next level of responsibility and leadership. If indeed someone is not fit for a particular organization, meet with his or her manager and say so. Check with the person, check with the manager, and then consult to create a new contract. Perhaps the best choice might be to establish a coaching program for the person to find his or her best career choice and developing the inner resources for moving on. Perhaps it is to establish a coaching program to discover what beliefs or behaviors need to change so the person can stay.

Your Executive Take-Aways

Coaching is not only a skill-set, it is a business. Without the appropriate business skills, you could be a great coach and not only devoid of clients, but also unable to get clients. *Being* an effective coach is not the same as *running* an effective coaching practice. In the field of Coaching this is the greatest weakness of the majority of people in the field. While great with people, they are not so great in terms of their business skills and acumen.

If the business side of coaching is not your strength and you fully believe in the efficacy of coaching, then the obvious choice is to hire a Business Coach.

- What is your personal reason for Executive Coaching? What are your highest intentions?
- What aspect of Executive Coaching will you specialize in?
- What facets of Executive Coaching do you still need to develop or refine?
- Have you developed your contracting process? When will you sit down to do that?

End of the Chapter Notes

1. We designed the Meta-Coach System to be the most thorough, systematic and systemic coach training program. You can find a full description of Meta-Coaching, its modules and models on www.meta-coaching.org. See the Brochure as well as the many articles about Meta-Coaching.

2. See *The Structure of Personality: Ordering and Disordering Personality Using NLP and Neuro-Semantics* (2000).

3. We have a pattern, "Strengthening Ego-Strength" in the Meta-Coaching System. The pattern asks about what "strengths" or energies or resources a person needs for strengthening one's sense of self.

Appendix A

WHY EXECUTIVE COACHING IS NOT THERAPY

In many places, what is called "Coaching" is not actually coaching, it is therapy under the guise of coaching. How can a person tell? Ask about the psychology that the coach uses to inform his or her coaching. If it is one of the traditional forms of psychotherapy (psychoanalysis, emotional therapy, Gestalt, Rational-Emotive, etc.), then the "coaching" is probably a form of therapy with the design to heal, to get over the past, to become "okay" in one's identity, etc.

Therapy	Coaching
Time: Living entirely or mostly in the past.	Living in the present with an eye on the future.
State: Experiencing internal hurt, wounds, traumas.	Experiencing an anxiousness and restlessness for more, internal well-ness, and health.
Intention: Wanting safety, peace, equilibrium, quietness.	Wanting disequilibrium, challenge, to be stretched.
Self: Lacks ego-strength to face the world, to face a particular challenge	Has the ego-strength to face what *is* in one's world.
Lacks sense of value, worth and esteem for self.	Has unconditional self-value and worth, or some form of *conditional* self-esteem — medium to high.
Responsibility: Feels like a victim and has some or lots of victim *cause,* talk and mentality.	Feels high level responsibility and is *at* response-able and empowered. Little to no victim talk or thinking.
Power: Needs to be re-parented, easily experiences transference to the helper as if a new "parent."	Fully able to be an adult in thinking, feeling, accepting responsibility. Does not transfer past feelings of a parent to the coach.
Needs "fixing" — needs a remedy	Does not need "fixing" or any remedial

for problems of self.	solutions, wants generative change.
State: Resists change, fears to change, defends against it.	Embraces change, wants it, plans for it, gets excited about changing.
Reactive, defensive, fears to be open or vulnerable.	Proactive, open, disclosing, self-aware. Open vulnerability embraced as part of being a fallible human being.

Therapy:

The psychology of therapy is *a Remedial Psychology* that provides insights about how to nurture, support, listen, enable the expression of the person's story, to facilitate transference, to avoid counter-transference, and to re-parent and love the person back to health. It is a conversation that involves an independent–dependent relationship moving the client to more and more independence.

The therapist works to develop okayness in the client, to get him or her *up to okay*, to strengthen the person's ego-strength, to finish the so-called "unfinished" business of the past, and get the person *up to now*—in the present and ready for taking on life's challenges.

Coaching:

The psychology of coaching is *a Generative Psychology* that awakens, disturbs, challenges, and stretches to unleash more and more potential talents and possibilities. It is highly confrontative, direct, and explicit. It is a dialogue conversation between colleagues involving inter-dependent roles.

The Coach works to move the self-esteem to a totally *unconditional* status so the person does *not* have to prove anything to be fully and completely okay. This enables the person to now be ready for a new restlessness—a dis-equilibrium to take on life's challenges. To do more, feel more, be more, say more, do more, have more, and give more.

Appendix B

THE MIND-TO-MUSCLE PATTERN
Closing the Knowing-Doing Gap

Design: Turn highly informative, insightful, and valued principles into neurological patterns so that it becomes incorporated into muscle memory.

Distinctions: Your mind-body system naturally works to incorporate or embody ideas. You incorporate higher level ideas into your muscle memory as you learn, use repetition, and invite those learnings into your body. Take the principle and turn it into *procedural knowledge* so that it can easily be put into the neurology of your muscle-memory.

Elicitation Questions:
* What concept do you know intellectually but do not practice?
* What great principle do you know in your mind that would make a great difference if you could only get yourself to *act upon it* and do it?

The Pattern:
1) Principle: Identify a principle you want to incorporate into your neurology.
> What principle do you want to put into your neurology?
> What is your conceptual understanding of this idea?
> What do you know (understand or believe) about this that you want to set as a frame in your mind?
> How do you state it in the a way that's clear, succinct, and compelling?
> Use the sentence stem and fill it in — ***"I understand . . ."***

2) Belief: Describe the principle as a belief.
> Are you ready to believe this? State it as a belief.
> Do you believe it? Would you like to believe it?
> If you really, really believed that, would that make a big difference in your life?
> Use the sentence stem — ***"I believe . . ."***

3) Decision: State the belief as a decision.
> Would you like to live by that belief? [Yes.] You would? [Yes.] Really? [Yes.]
> Will you act on this and make it your program for acting?
> Use the sentence stem — ***"I will . . . I want . . . I choose to . . ."*** or ***"From this day forward I will ..."***

4) Emotion: State the Decision as a feeling or an experience.

As you state the belief decision, noticing what you feel, what do you feel?

What do you feel as you imagine living your life with this empowering belief and decision?

Be with those emotions . . . let them grow and extend.

Use the sentence stem— ***"I am feeling . . . I am experiencing ..."***

5) Action: Step forward and state as an action.

What one thing will you do tomorrow that will begin to manifest this in your life? And the day after that?

"The one thing that I will do today to make this real in my life is . . ."

6) Put the action with the spiral of your higher levels of mind.

As you fully imagine carrying out that one thing you will do today . . . seeing, hearing and feeling it you are doing this because you believe what? Because you've decided what? Because you feel what? And you will do what other thing? Because you understand what? Because you feel what? Because you've decided what? Because you believe what? And what other thing will you do?

Summary:

1) Principle or concept: "I understand ..." Or *"Theoretically, I realize..."*

2) *Belief: "I believe..."*

3) *Decision: "I will..."*

4) *Emotions: "I feel..."*

5) *Action: "The one thing I will do today to make this real in my life is..."*

Appendix C

LEADERS AND MANAGERS

Visionary Leadership Questions
Use the following questions to determine if your skills and interests support being a strategic, visionary leader:

First competency: *Vision and direction setting—dealing with and calling for change.*
1) What is the change that you see and are seeking to address?
2) What changes are needed? What are the details of the changes?
3) What vision are you awakening and inspiring people to?
4) What has to change in order for the vision to become a reality?
5) What direction have you set or are setting?
6) How are you setting that direction?
7) What does it mean to move in this direction, make these changes, and fulfil that vision?
8) How does that vision and those meanings add value to the people you are leading?
9) What other values do those meanings create for yourself and others?
10) What problems does the vision solve?

The second competency: *Aligning people—creating community and a social consciousness.*
1) How are you seeking to align people to the vision and change?
2) How aligned are the people who are following?
3) Who is helping you in the alignment? Who are your co-leaders?
4) What challenges and problems prevent the full alignment?
5) How are you demonstrating cooperation and collaboration?
6) How are you demonstrating alignment with your collaborators?

The third competency: *Solving problems—solving problems, resolving conflicts, innovating creative solutions.*
1) What obstacles are you (or will you) face in achieving the vision?
2) What are the biggest barriers to succeeding in your leading?
3) What leadership skills are you using in dealing with the obstacles?
4) How are you empowering people to handle the challenges?
5) What problem solving skills are you bringing to this
6) What conflicts in the culture need addressed?
7) What conflicts will arise in making this vision real?

Managerial Leadership Questions
Use the following questions to determine if your skills and interests support being a tactical leader, a managerial leader.

The first competency: *planning and budgeting.*
1) What plans have you created to actualize the company's vision?
2) How detailed are those plans?
3) What are the milestones and time-line of those plans?
4) To what degree have the craft people been involved in creating the plan?
5) How much will the plan cost in the next year, in the next five years?
6) How much product or service will have to be sold to make that commercially viable?
7) How will the plan be capitalized?

8) What will be the return on investment for stakeholders?

The second competency: *organizing and staffing.*
1) What is the organizational structure of the business?
2) How will that organization enable the plan to be carried out?
3) How efficient is that organization in terms of time, money, and energy?
4) What will be the specific skills that you will need at each stage?
5) What skills will you need for the next stage of development of the plan?
6) Do you have a profile that details the ideal skill set for each job?
7) Do you have a specific process for matching people with jobs?

The third competency: *controlling and problem solving.*
1) What processes have you set up for monitoring research and development, production, marketing and selling, and delivery?
2) How often will the monitoring occur?
3) Do you have a process for insuring quality all along the process?
4) Who specifically will be involved in the monitoring and feedback?
5) What processes have you established for performance review? How often?
6) What process will integrate new solutions so that they are incorporated into production?
7) What processes for handling motivation? Reception of feedback? Discipline?

•

BIBLIOGRAPHY

Arbinger Institute (2000). *Leadership and Self-Deception: Getting out of the box.* San Francisco: Berrett-Koehler Publishers, Inc.

Battley, Susan. (2006). *Coached to lead: How to achieve extraordinary results with an Executive Coach.* San Francisco: Jossey-Bass.

Belf, Teri-E. (2002). *Coaching with Spirit: Allowing success to emerge.* San Francisco, CA: Jossey-Bass/ Pfeiffer.

Bennis, Warren. (1989/ 2009). On Becoming a Leader: The Leadership Classic, Revised and Updated. NY: Basic Books.

Bennis, Warren (1989). *Why leaders can't lead: The unconscious conspiracy Continues.* San Francisco: Jossey-Bass, A Wiley Company.

Bossidy, Larry; Charan, Ram. (2004). *Confronting reality: Doing what matters to get things right.* New York: Random House.

Branson, Richard. (2012). *Like a Virgin: Secrets they won't teach you at Business School.* Random House Group: Virgin Books.

Bridoux, Denis C.; Merlevede, Patrick E. (2003). *Mastering Mentoring and Coaching with Emotional Intelligence: Increase your Job EQ.* UK: Crown House Publishing.

Buckingham, Marcus; Coffman, Curt. (1999). *First, break all the rules: What the World's greatest managers do differently.* NY: Simon & Schuster.

Charan, Ram; Drotter, Stephen Drotter; Noel James. (2001). *The Leadership Pipeline* . San Francisco: Jossey-Bass.
Chambers, Dave. (1997). *Coaching:*

Winning Strategies for every level of play. Buffalo, NY: Firefly Books.

Collins, Jim; Hansen Morten T. (2011). *Great by Choice: Uncertainty, chaos, and Luck— Why Some Thrive Despite them all.* New York: HarperCollins.

De Press, Max. (1989). *Leadership is an art.* New York: A Dell Trade Paperback, Bantam Doubleday Dell Publ.

De Vries, Manfred F.R. (2001). *The Leadership Mystique: An Owner's Manual.* London: Prentice Hall.

Dilts, Robert. (2003). *From Coach to Awakener.* Capitola, CA: Meta Publ.

Dotlich, David L.; Cario, Peter C. (1999). *Action coaching: How to leverage individual performance for company success.* San Francisco: Jossey-Bass: A Wiley Company.

Downs, Alan. (2000). *The Fearless Executive: Finding the courage to trust your talents and be the leader you are meant to be.* New York: AMACOM, American Management Association.

Downs, Alan. (2002). *Secrets of an Executive Coach: Proven Methods for Helping Leaders excel under Pressure.* New York: AMACOM: American Management Association.

Downey, Myles. (1999/ 2003). *Effective coaching: lessons from the coach's coach.* Australia: Thomson.

Drucker, Peter F. (1999). *Management Challenges for the 21st century.* New York: HarperBusiness.

Fournies, Ferdinard F. (1978/ 1987). *Coaching for improved work performance.* Blue Ridge Summit, PA: Liberty House.

Frisch, Michael; Lee, Robert, Metzger, Karen, Robinson, Jeremy; Rosemarin, Judy. (2012). *Becoming an Exceptional Executive Coach*. New York: AMACOM.

Gallwey, W. Timothy. (2000). *The inner game of Work: Focus, Learning, pleasure, and mobility in the workplace*. New York: Random House Trade Paperbacks.

Gardner, Howard. (1983). *Frames of mind: A theory of multiple intelligences*. New York: Basic Books.

Gardner, H. (1985). *The mind's new science: A history of the cognitive revolution*. New York: Basic Books.

Gardner, Howard. (1991). *The unschooled mind: How children think and how schools should teach*. New York: Basic Books.

Gardner, Howard. (1993). *Multiple intelligences: The theory in practice*. New York: BasicBooks.

Goleman, Daniel; Boyatzis, Richard; McKee, Annie. (2002) *Primal Leadership: Realizing the Power of Emotional Intelligence*. Boston, MA: Harvard business School Press.

Goleman, Daniel. (1995). *Emotional Intelligence*. New York: Bantam Books.

Goleman, Daniel. (1998). *Working with Emotional Intelligence*. New York: Bloomsbury.

Goleman, Daniel; Boyatzis, Richard; McKee, Annie. (2002). *The New Leaders: Transforming the art of leadership into the science of results*. London, UK: Timewarner paperback.

Grant, Antony; Greene, Jane. (2002). *Coach yourself: Make real changes in your life*. London: Pearson Education Unlimited.

Green, Jane; Anthony Grant. (2003).

Solution-Focused Coaching: Managing people in a complex world. *Pearson Education Limited*. Harlow Great Britain.

Hall, L. Michael. (2004– 2014). Series of Meta-Coaching Books: *Coaching Change, Coaching Conversations, Unleashed! Self-Actualization Psychology, Achieving Peak Performance, Unleashing Leadership, The Crucible and the Fires of Change, Benchmarking, Systemic Coaching, Group and Team Coaching*. Grand Junction, CO: Neuro-Semantic Publ.

Hecke, Madeleine (2007). *Blind Spots: Why Smart People Do Dumb Things*. Amherst, NY: Prometheus Books.

Heifetz, Ronald A. (1994). *Leadership without easy answers*. London, England: Belknap Press of Harvard University Press.

Hesselbein, Frances; Goldsmith, Marshall. (2006). *The leader of the future 2: Visions, strategies, and practices for the new era*. San Francisco: Jossey-Bass.

Hudson, Frederic M. (1999). *The Handbook of Coaching: A comprehensive resource guide for managers, executives, consultants, and human resource professionals*. San Francisco, CA: Jossey-Bass Publishers.

Jaques, Ellitott; Clement, Stephen D. (1991). *Executive Leadership: A Practice Guide to Managing Complexity*. Arlington, VA: Cason Hall & Co. Publ.

Kilburg, Richard R. (2000). *Executive Coaching: Developing managerial wisdom in a world of chaos*. Wash. D.C.: American Psychological Association.

Kotter, John P. (1985). *Power and Influence: Beyond formal authority*. New York: the Free Press.

Kouzes, James M.; Posner, Barry Z.

((2007). *The leadership challenge.* New York: John Wiley & Sons, Inc.

Krisco, Kim H. (1997). *Leadership and the Art of Conversation: Conversation as a Management Tool.* Rocklin, CA. Prima Publishing.

Lenhardt, Vincent. (2004). *Coaching for meaning: The culture and practice of coaching and team building.* London: Palgrave Macmillan.

Logan, Dave; King, John; Fischer-Wright, Halee. (2008). *Tribal Leadership: Leveraging Natural groups to build a thriving Organization.* New York: Harper Business.

Laborde, Genie. (1984). *Influencing with Integrity.* Palo Alto, CA: Syntony Publishing.

Maslow, Abraham. (1970). *Motivation and personality.* (2nd ed.). New York: Harper & Row.

Maslow, Abraham. (1968). *Toward a psychology of being.* New York: Van Nostrand.

Maslow, Abraham. (1953, 1971). *The farther reaches of human nature.* New York: Viking.

Maslow, Abraham H. (1998). *Maslow on management.* Originally, *Eupsychian management.* New York: John Wiley & Sons, Inc.

Maslow, Bertha G. (1972). *Abraham H. Maslow: A Memorial Volume.* Monterey, CA: Brooks/ Cole Publishing Company.

Maxwell, John C. (1995). *Developing the leader's around you.* Nashville, TN: Thomas Nelson Publishers.

McDermott, Ian; Jago, Wendy. (2001). *The NLP Coach: A comprehensive guide to personal well-being and professional success.* London: Platkus, Action Printing.

McLeod, Angus. (2004). *Performance Coaching: The handbook for managers, H.R. professionals and coaches.* Carmarthen, Wales: Crown House Publications.

Miller, Mark. (2013). *The Heart of Leadership: Becoming a Leader People Want to Follow.* San Francisco: Berrett-Koehler Publishers.

Mink, Oscar; Owen, Keith; Mink, Barbara. (1993). *Developing high-performance people: The art of Coaching.* New York: Addison-Wesley Publishing Com. Inc.

Mintzberg, H. (1994). *The Rise and Fall of Strategic Planning.* Prentice Hall: Hemel Hempstead.

Oakley, Ed; Krug, Doug. (1991). *Enlightened Leadership: Getting to the heart of change.* New York: Simon & Schuster.

O'Neill, Mary Beth. (2007). *Executive Coaching with backbone and heart:* A systems approach to engaging leaders with their challenges. New York: John Wiley & Sons, Inc.

O'Reilly, Charles A. III; Pfeffer, Jeffrey. (2000). *Hidden Value: How Great Comapnies Achieve Extraordinary Results with Ordinary People.* Boston, MA: Harvard Busienss School Press.

Patterson, Kerry; Grenny, Joseph; McMillan, Ron; Switzler, Al. (2005). *Crucial confrontations: Tools for resolving broken promises, violated expectations, and bad behaviors.* New York: McGraw-Hill.

Peters, Tom. (1987). *Thriving on Chaos: Handbook for a Management Revolution.* New York: Alfred A. Knopf.

Peters, Thomas J.; Waterman, Robert H. Jr. (1982). *In search of excellence: Lessons from America's Best-Run Companies.* New York: Warner Books.

Pfeffer, Jeffrey. (1994). *Competitive advantage through people: Unleashing the power of the work force.* Boston MA: Harvard Business School Press.

Rosinski, Philippe. (2003). *Coaching across cultures: New tools for leveraging national, corporate and professional differences.* London: Nicholas Brealey Publishing.

Schein, Edgar H. (1985). *Organizational Culture and Leadership.* San Francisco: CA. Jossey-Bass Publishers.

Scott, Susan. (2002). *Fierce Conversations: Achieving success at work and in life, one conversation at a time.* New York: Viking: Penguin Press.

Scott, Susan. (2009). *Fierce Leadership: A bold alternative to the worst "best" Practices of Business today.* New York: Broadway Business.

Shelton, Claudia. (2007). *Blind Spots: Achieve Success by Seeing What you Can't See.* New York: John Wiley & Sons. Inc.

Skiffington, Suzanne; Zeus, Perry. (2003). *Behavioral Coaching: How to build sustainable personal and organizational strength.* Sydney: The McGraw-Hill Companies.

Shula, Don; Blanchard, Ken. (1995). *Everyone's a coach: You can inspire anyone to be a winner.* New York: Harper Business.

Starr, Julie. (2003). *The Coaching Manual: The definitive guide to the process, principles, and skills of personal coaching.* London: Prentice Hall Business: Pearson Education.

Stephenson, Peter (2000). *Executive Coaching: Lead, develop, retain, motivated, talented People.* NSW: Australia: Stephenson Partnership Pty. Ltd.

Stowell, Steven J.; Starcevich, Matt. M.

(1987/ 1994). *The Coach: Creating partnerships for a competitive edge.* Salt Lake City: UT: Center for Management and Organization Effectiveness.

Ulrich, Dave; Zenger, Jack; Smallwood, norm. (1999). *Results-based leadership.* Boston, MA: Harvard Business School.

Ulrich, Dave; Smallwood, Norm (2003). *How Leaders Build Value: Using people, organization, and other intangibles to get Bottom-line Results.* New Jersey: John Wiley & Sons, Inc.

Ulrich, Dave; Zenger, Jack; Smallwood, norm. (2007). *Leadership Brand: Developing customer-focused leaders to drive performance and build lasting value.* Boston, MA: Harvard Business School Press.

Wheatley, Margaret. (1999). Leadership and the New Science: Discovering Order in a chaotic World. San Francisco: Berrett-Koehler Publishers.

Whitworth, Laura; Kimsey-House, Henry; Sandahl, Phil. (1998). *Co-Active Coaching: New skills for coaching people toward success in work and life.* Palo alto, CA: Davies-Black Publishing.

Whitmore, John. (1992/ 1998). *Coaching for Performance.* (Second edition). London: Nicholas Brealey Publ

Zeus, Perry; Skiffington, Suzanne. (2002). *The complete guide to Coaching at Work.* Sydney, Australia: The McGraw-Hill Companies, Inc.

Zoghlin, Gilbert G. (1991). *From executive to entrepreneur: Making the transition.* NY: AMACOM: American Management Association.

INDEX

L. Michael Hall, Ph.D.

L. Michael Hall is a visionary leader in the field of NLP and Neuro-Semantics, and a modeler of human excellence. Searching out areas of human excellence, he models the structure of that expertise and then turns that information into models, patterns, training manuals, and books. With his several businesses, Michael is also an entrepreneur and an international trainer.

His doctorate is in the Cognitive-Behavioral sciences from Union Institute University. For two decades he worked as a psychotherapist in Colorado. When he found NLP in 1986, he studied and then worked with Richard Bandler. Later when studying and modeling resilience, he developed the Meta-States Model (1994) that launched the field of Neuro-Semantics. He co-created the *International Society of Neuro-Semantics* (ISNS) with Dr. Bob Bodenhamer. Learning the structure of writing, he began writing and has written more than 40 books, many best sellers in the field of NLP.

Applying NLP to coaching, he created the Meta-Coach System, this was co-developed with Michelle Duval (2003-2007), he co-founded the Meta-Coach Foundation (2003), created the Self-Actualization Quadrants (2004) and launched the new Human Potential Movement (2005).

Contact Information:
> P.O. Box 8
> Clifton, Colorado 81520 USA
> (1-970) 523-7877

Websites:
> www.neurosemantics.com
> www.meta-coaching.org
> www.self-actualizing.org
> www.meta-coachfoundation.org

Graham Richardson, Master Coach

Recognized as a pioneering Executive Coach in Australia, Graham is renowned for his million dollar plus annual income from Coaching. Graham's career includes Managing Director, Board Member and Senior Executive positions in advertising and marketing. Working for three of the world' top advertising agencies, and servicing the world's top brands and services, he had intimate contact, at senior levels, with such business sectors as FMCG, Automotive, Financial Services, Personal Care, Food, Liquor, Government Agencies, Airline and Travel, and Tobacco.

His success has always been based on developing outstanding relationships with clients, where he has proved able to stabilize large, difficult situations and turn them to everyone's advantage. He has found that building team structures, with highly motivated, dedicated and enthusiastic members, constantly produces extraordinary results for clients and service organizations alike.

He has been coaching Senior Executives for over seven years, with over 12,000 hours of coaching in total. Graham is passionate about the human element in business and is dedicated to helping top management realize their personal and corporate goals in making a difference for themselves and others.

Graham is a Master Practitioner in Neuro-Linguistic Programming, an accredited International Neuro-Semantic Trainer, and Master Coach, and is a qualified Train The Trainer through AIM, a graduate High Performance Coach and a member of the International Coach Federation. Graham is also qualified in the practices of Frameworks for Change, Australian Values Inventory, Human Synergistics LSI, Team Management Systems TMP, Crucial Conversations and Active Learning "Play of Life." He is also accredited as an Executive Coach to a number of different global organizations.

Graham is committed to working in areas that effectively provide change management and workplace transformation, Management and Leadership Training, Executive Development, Team Facilitation and Conflict Resolution. Graham dedicates his life to learning how to learn for himself and others, and is actively engaged in his own professional development to this end.

Horizons Unlimited P/L — gr@horizonsunlimited.com.au
Phone: Sydney, Australia — 9388 7878

Books by L. Michael Hall, Ph.D.

NLP and Neuro-Semantics:
1) *Meta-States: Mastering the Higher Levels of Mind* (1995/ 2000).
2) *Dragon Slaying: Dragons to Princes* (1996 / 2000).
3) *The Spirit of NLP: The Process, Meaning and Criteria for Mastering NLP* (1996).
4) *Languaging: The Linguistics of Psychotherapy* (1996).
5) *Becoming More Ferocious as a Presenter* (1996).
6) *Patterns For Renewing the Mind* (with Bodenhamer, 1997 /2006).
7) *Time-Lining: Advance Time-Line Processes* (with Bodenhamer, 1997).
8) *NLP: Going Meta — Advance Modeling Using Meta-Levels* (1997/2001).
9) *Figuring Out People: Reading People Using Meta-Programs* (with Bodenhamer, 1997, 2005).
10) *SourceBook of Magic, Volume I* (with Barbara Belnap, 1997).

11) *Mind-Lines: Lines For Changing Minds* (with Bodenhamer, 1997/ 2005).
12) *Communication Magic* (2001). Originally, *The Secrets of Magic* (1998).
13) *Meta-State Magic: Meta-State Journal* (1997-1999).
14) *When Sub-Modalities Go Meta* (with Bodenhamer, 1999, 2005). Originally, *The Structure of Excellence.*
15) *Instant Relaxation* (with Lederer, 1999).
16) *User's Manual of the Brain: Volume I* (with Bodenhamer, 1999).
17) *The Structure of Personality:* Modeling Personality Using NLP and Neuro-Semantics (with Bodenhamer, Bolstad, and Harmblett, 2001).
18) *The Secrets of Personal Mastery* (2000).
19) *Winning the Inner Game* (2007), originally *Frame Games* (2000).
20) *Games Fit and Slim People Play* (2001).

21) *Games for Mastering Fear* (with Bodenhamer, 2001).
22) *Games Business Experts Play* (2001).
23) *The Matrix Model: Neuro-Semantics and the Construction of Meaning* (2003).
24) *User's Manual of the Brain: Master Practitioner Course, Volume II* (2002).
25) *MovieMind: Directing Your Mental Cinemas* (2002).
26) *The Bateson Report* (2002).
27) *Make it So! Closing the Knowing-Doing Gap* (2002).
28) *Source Book of Magic, Volume II, Neuro-Semantic Patterns* (2003).
29) *Propulsion Systems* (2003).
30) *Games Great Lovers Play* (2004).

31) *Coaching Conversation, Meta-Coaching, Volume II* (with Michelle Duval & Robert Dilts 2004, 2010).
32) *Coaching Change, Meta-Coaching, Volume I* (with Duval, 2004).
33) *Unleashed: How to Unleash Potentials for Peak Performances* (2007).
34) *Achieving Peak Performance* (2009).
35) *Self-Actualization Psychology* (2008).
36) *Unleashing Leadership: Self-Actualizing Leaders and Companies* (2009).
37) *The Crucible and the Fires of Change* (2010).

38) *Inside-Out Wealth* (2010).
39) *Benchmarking: The Art of Measuring the Unquantifiable* (2011).
40) *Innovations in NLP: Volume I* (Edited with Shelle Rose Charvet; 2011).
41) *Neuro-Semantics: Actualizing Meaning and Performance* (2011)
42) *Group and Team Coaching* (2013)
43) *Executive Coaching: Facilitating Excellence in the C-Suite* (2014)

Other books:
1) *Emotions: Sometimes I Have Them/ Sometimes They have Me* (1985)
2) *Motivation: How to be a Positive Influence in a Negative World* (1987)
3) *Speak Up, Speak Clear, Speak Kind* (1987)
4) *Millennial Madness* (1992), now *Apocalypse Then, Not Now* (1996).
5) *Over My Dead Body* (1996).

Order Books from: **NSP: Neuro-Semantic Publications**
                           P.O. Box 8
                           Clifton, CO. 81520—0008 USA
                           (970) 523-7877

Neuro-Semantics as an Association

In 1996 Hall and Bodenhamer registered "Neuro-Semantics" and founded *The International Society of Neuro-Semantics* (ISNS) as a new approach to teaching, training, and using NLP. The objective was to take NLP as a model and field to a higher level in terms of professional ethics and quality. Today Neuro-Semantics is one of the leading disciplines within NLP as it is pioneering many new developments and demonstrating a creativity that characterized NLP when it was new and fresh.

Dr. Hall is known as a prolific writer, having authored 41 books (2011) in the field of NLP and several others, many of them best sellers through *Crown House Publishes* (Wales, UK) and many of them translated into numerous languages: German, Dutch, Italian, Spanish, Russian, Japanese, Chinese, Arabic, Norwegian, Portuguese, etc.
www.neurosemantics.com
www.meta-coaching.org
www.metacoachingfoundation.org
www.self-actualizing.org

The Meta-Coaching System

As a complete and comprehensive coaching system, the *Meta-Coaching System* began in 2001 when L. Michael Hall, Ph.D. modeled four expert coaches. He then translated the Neuro-Linguistic Programming (NLP) and Neuro-Semantic models to fit with the burgeoning field of Coaching. As a systemic model, the Meta-Coaching System enables a professional Coach to answer the question: *How do you know what to do, when to do it, with whom to do it, how to do what you're doing, and why?*

When you can think strategically as a Coach, you will be able to recognize where you are with a client and what to do. Having a theoretical model that answers the *why are you doing that?* question saves your coaching from being a grab-bag of tricks or coaching-by-the-seat-of-your-pants.

To met this rigorous criteria, the Meta-Coaching System is based on eight models—models which are based in Cognitive-Behavioral, Developmental, and Self-Actualization psychologies. The design is to give Meta-Coaching a scientific basis. Then as a coach you will not fall back on what you "feel like" on a certain day, your "intuitions" (which may be your own unresolved issues), or some trick that you have picked up on a weekend training.

Today Meta-Coaching standards are the highest in the field of Coaching as it offers specific behavioral benchmarks for every one of the 50 coaching skills. It also has developed a Benchmarking Intangibles Model for how to generate rigorous benchmarks for any value or skill. The Meta-Coaching System also has an accountability structure to the ethics and standards which governs every licenced Meta-Coach.

With this book there are now 11 books that detail out the entire curriculum of Meta-Coaching, and several more in the works. The Meta-Coaching System is inclusive of other systems as Meta-Coaches around the world in 42 countries are often on the board of ICF and many other Coach training programs. Trainings in Meta-Coaching occur every year dozens of times in every continent. For more information, see www.meta-coaching.org and www.metacoachfoundation.org.